INTERNATIONAL APPLICATIONS OF PRODUCTIVITY AND EFFICIENCY ANALYSIS

A Special Issue of the Journal of Productivity Analysis

edited by

Thomas R. Gulledge, Jr.

C.A. Knox Lovell

Reprinted from the Journal of Productivity Analysis
Vol. 3, Nos. 1/2 (1992)

KLUWER ACADEMIC PUBLISHERS
BOSTON/DORDRECHT/LONDON

Distributors for North America:
Kluwer Academic Publishers
101 Philip Drive
Assinippi Park
Norwell, Massachusetts 02061 USA

Distributors for all other countries:
Kluwer Academic Publishers Group
Distribution Centre
Post Office Box 322
3300 AH Dordrecht, THE NETHERLANDS

Library of Congress Cataloging-in-Publication Data

Internatioanl applications of productivity and efficiency analysis /
edited by Thomas R. Gulledge, Jr. and C.A. Knox Lovell.
p. cm.
Includes bibliographical references.

1. Industrial productivity--Measurement--Congresses.
2. Efficiency, Industrial--Measurement--Congresses. I. Gulledge, Thomas R., 1947- II. Lovell, C.A. Knox.
HD56.25.I58 1992
658.5'036--dc20 92-11877
CIP

ISBN 978-90-481-5793-8

Printed on acid-free paper.

JOURNAL OF PRODUCTIVITY ANALYSIS
Vol. 3, Nos. 1/2 June 1992

INTERNATIONAL APPLICATIONS OF PRODUCTIVITY AND EFFICIENCY ANALYSIS

A Special Issue of the Journal of Productivity Analysis

The Journal of Productivity Analysis, 3, 5 (1992)

Editors' Introduction

The Joint National Meeting of The Operations Research Society of America and The Institute of Management Sciences held in Philadelphia in October 1990 had as its theme "Productivity and Global Competition." When we were invited to organize a cluster of sessions, we decided to follow the conference theme as closely as possible. Hence, we titled our cluster "Productivity and Efficiency Analysis," and we invited scholars from countries around the world in the fields of operations research/management science and economics to present articles that would provide empirical applications of modern productivity and efficiency measurement techniques. We ended up with a cluster of 20 articles authored by scholars from 10 countries on five continents. The best of these articles are augmented by two additional articles to form this issue. All articles have survived a rigorous refereeing process, and we want to thank the many referees for their efforts.

We do not wish to summarize each article in the issue, but we do wish to bring some features of the issue to the readers' attention. First, the range of techniques utilized in these articles is extremely broad; there is hardly a currently accepted approach to frontier analysis that is not employed here. Indeed, several of the articles provide new extensions of existing techniques or develop new techniques. Second, most of the articles use panel data, and the variety of approaches to the analysis of panel data is impressive. Third, the range of empirical applications is at least as broad as the range of techniques, and many of the applications are of considerable policy relevance.

Thomas R. Gulledge, George Mason University
C.A. Knox Lovell, University of North Carolina at Chapel Hill

The Journal of Productivity Analysis, 3, 7–23 (1992)

Efficiency and Ownership in Swedish Electricity Retail Distribution*

LENNART HJALMARSSON AND ANN VEIDERPASS
Department of Economics, University of Gothenburg, Sweden

Abstract

This article examines the efficiency of electricity retail distributors in Sweden in a multiple output multiple input framework. Productive efficiency measures are calculated by use of different versions of the non-parametric Data Envelopment Analysis (DEA) method. Comparisons are made between different types of ownership and between different types of service areas.

The study indicates a rather low level of technical efficiency, a high level of scale efficiency in urban service areas, but a fairly low level of scale efficiency in rural areas. The results show no significant differences in efficiency between different types of ownership or economic organization.

1. Introduction

The electricity industry has been a frequent candidate in the wave of public sector deregulation and privatization. This has spurred the interest in methods for efficiency analyses of the industry and the determinants behind efficiency variations. Due to the homogeneity of output and to ample data, electricity generation has been studied frequently in the past, while relatively less research effort has been spent on retail distribution.

This study concentrates on the analysis of productive efficiency in the local retail distribution of electricity in Sweden in 1985. In the study, different versions of the Data Envelopment Analysis (DEA) method are applied together with different specifications of output and input. The data are presented in Section 3.

DEA is a linear programming technique for the construction of a non-parametric, piecewise linear convex hull to the observed set of output and input data; see, for example, Charnes and Cooper [1985] for a discussion of the methodology. The DEA approach defines a non-parametric frontier which may serve as a benchmark for efficiency measures.

Electricity generation, and to some degree national grid transmission, is characterized by large indivisible investments, immobile capital and sunk costs. In electricity distribution, on the other hand, investments are undertaken more gradually, in smaller steps and the capital stock is fairly mobile. It is, at least in principle, possible to move transformers, poles and wires from one location to another. Although it may not be very important from an economic point of view, a second hand market for equipment, in particular for transformers, does exist. As a production process, generation is fairly similar to heavy industry production, while distribution is more similar to light industry. In generation, productivity

*Paper presented at ORSA/TIMS joint national meeting, Productivity and Global Competition, Philadelphia, October 29–31, 1990.

growth is extremely dependent on lumpy investments in capital equipment, while in distribution productivity growth is mostly dependent on the efficient use of labor, i.e., management. Therefore, dynamic efficiency is much less of a problem in retail distribution. *Productive and managerial efficiency* is the main concern.

A number of technical and organizational factors influence economies of scale in electricity distribution. Technical economies arise from distribution equipment leading to economies of density, economies in capacity expansion and economies in the provision of capacity to meet peak requirement. Organizational economies may arise due to staff specialization. In empirical studies, as well as in deregulation analyses, considerable attention has also been paid to the scale properties of electricity distribution and to the optimal size structure of the retail sector. Consequently, we are also interested in *scale efficiency.*

A retail distributor provides electricity services to different categories of customers. The customer categories may be divided as follows:

- low voltage vs. high voltage customers
- customers in densely vs. sparsely populated areas
- industry vs. commercial vs. residential customers, etc.

Since the service costs are a function of these and other characteristics of the service area, a multiple output framework seems appropriate. Consequently, we have used multiple output models and applied different specifications of DEA models.

The estimated non-parametric frontiers serve as the basis for measurements of productive efficiency. The measures applied are Farrell type ray measures; for a generalization of Farrell's measure into input saving, output increasing and scale efficiency, see Førsund and Hjalmarsson [1974, 1979]. Minimizing input use for a certain output level seems a more reasonable objective for an individual distributor than maximizing output for a given input level. In this study, the input saving measure is thus regarded as the most relevant measure of technical efficiency.

The main inputs are labor and different types of capital. Capital is represented by power lines and transformer stations.

Output may be modeled in several different ways. We employ low voltage energy and high voltage energy supplied, as well as the number of low voltage and high voltage customers. This is a traditional way to model output in the electricity distribution sector.

While much has been written on the efficiency of the electricity industry, most studies have focused on electricity generation; see, for example, Atkinson and Halvorsen [1986], Farber [1989], Färe, Grosskopf and Lovell [1985], Joskow and Schmalensee [1987], Melfi [1987], Nelson [1990], and Pescatrice and Trapani [1980]. However, there are a few related studies of efficiency in electricity retail distribution. Weiss [1975], Meyer [1975] and Neuberg [1977] apply a cost function approach when analyzing distribution returns to scale, and in the latter two cases also public/private cost differences for US distributors. Other US studies are Henderson [1985], Roberts [1986], and Nelson and Primeaux [1988].

Ministry of Energy, New Zealand [1989] studies performance indicators and economies of scale in retail distribution in New Zealand. The purpose is to provide input for the policy debate about the New Zealand electricity industry deregulation. Labroukos and Lioukas [1988] use a parametric deterministic Cobb-Douglas frontier approach in an efficiency study of electricity districts in Greece.

Salvanes and Tjotta [1990] analyze the degree of returns to scale and returns to network density on the basis of a translog cost function. Returns to density measures the economies of increasing the amount of electricity supplied when the network is held constant. Returns to scale measures the combined economies of increasing the amount of electricity supplied and the network. They find no evidence of economies of scale for a large output range including the mean sample distributor (approximately 20,000 customers served). For rather small distributors, however, the elasticity of scale exceeds one; e.g., distributors serving approximately 5000 customers the elasticity of scale is 1.04.

There are fewer studies applying a non-parametric approach. Thomas, Greffe and Grant [1985] use the DEA technique to measure the efficiency of electric co-operatives in Texas and Weyman-Jones [1991] applies DEA to analyze the comparative efficiency of twelve area electricity boards in England and Wales prior to their privatization in 1990.

The conclusions to be drawn from earlier studies are that we should apply both constant and variable returns to scale models and that our main model should contain both energy supplied and the number of customers supplied as outputs.

2. Efficiency measures and data envelopment analysis

The DEA method is closely related to Farrell's [1957] original approach and should be regarded as an extension of that approach initiated by Charnes et al. [1978] and related work by Färe et al. [1985]. Compared to Farrell's approach it offers a more operational framework for the estimation of efficiency; efficiency is calculated separately and directly for each production unit in turn, while at the same time the location of the corresponding linear facets is determined. Compared to a parametric frontier with analogous scale properties, it yields the more pessimistic convex best-practice frontier. (The non-convex "staircase" free disposable hull approach of Deprins et al. [1984] yields an even more pessimistic picture of the best-practice technology.)

In the DEA approach Farrell efficiency measures can be defined in the usual way; see Førsund and Hjalmarsson [1974, 1979]. Farrell provided a methodology by which technical efficiency could be measured against an efficiency frontier, assuming constant returns to scale. The production set obtained is represented by a convex set of facets, i.e., the production frontier obtained is the boundary of the free disposal convex hull of the data set.

Farrell's original approach, of computing the efficiency frontier as a convex hull in the input coefficient space, was reformulated by Charnes et al. [1978] into calculating the individual input saving efficiency measures by solving an LP-problem for each unit under the assumption of constant returns to scale.

In this approach the efficiency of a micro unit is measured relative to the efficiency of all the other micro units, subject to the restriction that all micro units are on or below the frontier.

As for the scale properties of the best-practice frontier, two different cases are distinguishable. With reference to Figure 1, where A, B, C and D are different micro units, the following convex hulls are identified:

- OBG with constant returns to scale (CRS)
- EABCF with variable retuns to scale (VRS)

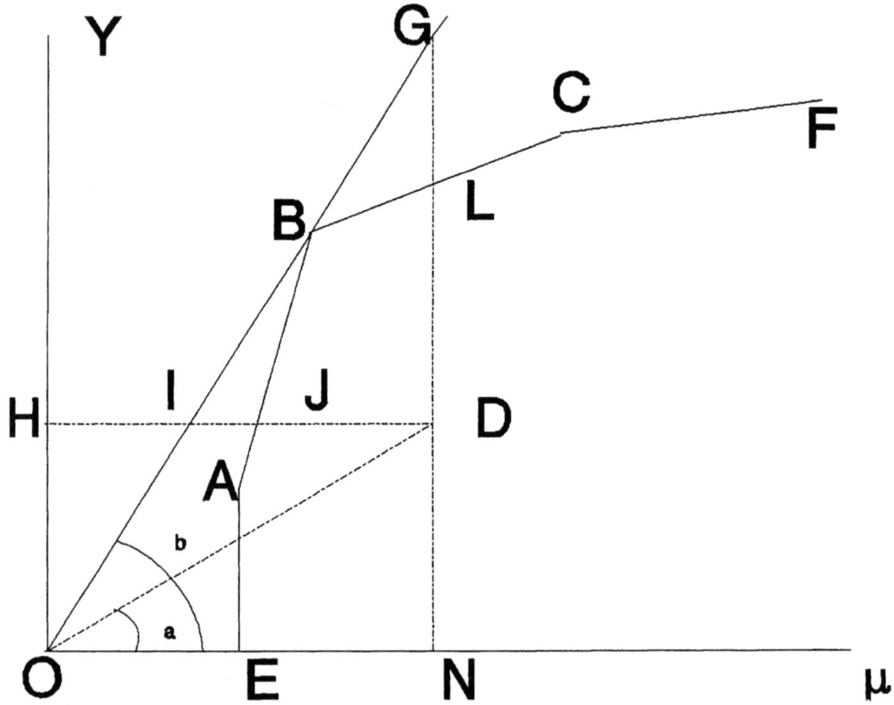

Figure 1. Illustration of DEA efficiency measures.

Based on this figure, the efficiency measures used here can now be defined. In the VRS case we define the input saving efficiency as

$$E_1 = HJ/HD,$$

i.e., the ratio between the potential use of input with frontier technology and the actual use of input when keeping output constant.

The output increasing efficiency is defined as

$$E_2 = ND/NL,$$

i.e., observed output relative to potential output had the observed amount of input been used with frontier technology.

Since input saving appears to be more reasonable as an objective for a distributor than output maximization, the E_2 measure is less relevant. Thus, we concentrate on input saving efficiency and scale efficiency, the latter being obtained as

$$E_3 = a/b = HI/HD,$$

i.e., the ratio between the input coefficients at optimal scale and the observed input coefficients.

In the CRS case, the input saving efficiency becomes

$$E_1 = HI/HD,$$

i.e., scale efficiency in the VRS case is equal to input saving efficiency in the case of constant returns to scale. Scale efficiency has, of course, no meaning in the case of constant returns to scale. (By definition, constant returns to scale imply that the elasticity of scale is equal to 1 everywhere in the input space, i.e., all output levels are technically optimal. Consequently, $E_3 = 1$ for all units.) Pure scale efficiency, denoted by E_4, i.e., the distance to optimal scale after moving the average unit to the frontier in the horizontal direction (see Førsund and Hjalmarsson [1979]) is

$$E_4 = E_3/E_1.$$

The interpretation of this measure is analogous to that of (gross) scale efficiency, E_3.

One way to determine whether a unit is in the increasing or in the decreasing output range is to compare the technical efficiency values (see Førsund and Hjalmarsson [1979, 1987]):

$$E_1 > E_2 => \text{increasing returns to scale}$$

$$E_1 < E_2 => \text{decreasing returns to scale.}$$

Summary measures of efficiency for the entire sector may be constructed in various ways. In this study, we use the constructed average unit for the industry (by taking the arithmetic average of each type of input and output, i.e., the total sector values, divided by the number of distributors) and calculate individual measures of efficiency, denoted by S_i, for this unit. We will also use the arithmetic average of individual efficiency measures, denoted by S_0, in some comparisons.

The adjacent LP-problem that must be solved for different micro units, e.g., unit d in point D with output y_d and input x_d, to obtain the input saving measure under variable returns to scale (where λ_d is a vector containing the non-negative weights, λ_{dj}, which determine the reference point) is

$$\min_{\lambda_d} E_{1d} \tag{1}$$

subject to the following restrictions:

$$y_{rd} \leq \sum_{j}^{N} \lambda_{dj} y_{rj}, \qquad r = 1, \ldots, m, \tag{1a}$$

$$E_{1d} x_{id} \geq \sum_{j}^{N} \lambda_{dj} x_{ij}, \qquad i = 1, \ldots, n, \tag{1b}$$

$$\sum_{j}^{N} \lambda_{dj} = 1, \tag{1c}$$

$$\lambda_{dj} \geq 0, \quad j = 1, \ldots, N, \tag{1d}$$

where m is the number of outputs, n is the number of inputs and N the number of units.

Restriction (1a) implies that the reference unit must produce at least as much as unit d, while restriction (1b) implies that the efficiency adjusted volume of input used by unit d must at least amount to the input volume used by the reference unit.

Restriction (1c) is the condition for VRS. If this restriction is omitted, CRS is implied. E_1 and E_2 then coincide, and both coincide with E_3 in the case of VRS.

When efficiency is measured along a ray from the origin, a micro unit may turn out as fully efficient, although it is not fully efficient in the sense that it is dominated by another unit (regardless of assumptions about scale property). In empirical applications, this can be controlled for by inspection of the slack variables.

3. Electricity distribution in Sweden

The Swedish electricity retail distribution sector consisted of 329 firms in 1985. While some of the distributors are partially or entirely vertically integrated, most of them have no significant production of their own. They generally purchase power from the Swedish State Power Board or from investor-owned utilities.

The ownership as well as the organizational structure vary considerably. Municipal companies or utilities supply the greatest number of customers, approximately 65 percent, while the State (mainly the State Power Board) supplies slightly more than 10 percent of the market for final consumption. The privately owned power companies supply approximately 20 percent of the total number of customers. Economic associations and mixed ownership companies supply the remaining 5 percent.

The data used in this study comprise information on 285 Swedish retail electricity distributors during 1985. Only distributors who supply more than 500 low voltage customers and employ more than five individuals are included. However, due to missing observations the number of firms in the analysis varies between 142 and 143 depending on the model specification. The fact that 95 percent of the market for final consumption is supplied by two thirds of the distributors (slightly more than 200 distributors), while the remaining third supplies only five percent of the customers, naturally affects the availability and quality of data on the smaller distributors. The construction of data is based on information received from the Association of Swedish Electric Utilities (SEF), Statistics Sweden (SCB), and different retail distributors.

Although some distributors are at least partially vertically integrated, data on distribution are both clearly identifiable and separable. The risk of vertical integration causing biased results is therefore negligible.

Henderson [1985] argues that utilities are vertically integrated firms that generate, transmit and distribute power and that decisions at one stage may affect decisions at a second stage, implying that it may not be possible to study transmission and/or distribution in isolation from generation. In spite of these statistical non-separability results, we will argue that there are no obvious reasons why electricity distribution could not be analyzed separately from generation and transmission. There are hardly any significant technical or transaction cost reasons for vertical integration in the electricity industry. The main reason for vertical integration is market power—not efficiency.

In the study, multiple output-multiple input models are employed. As for output, the following variables are included in the analysis:

Y_1 denotes low voltage electricity received by customers. Unit of measurement: MWh.
Y_2 denotes high voltage electricity received by customers. Unit of measurement: MWh.
Y_3 denotes the number of low voltage electricity customers.
Y_4 denotes the number of high voltage electricity customers.

With regard to input, different combinations of the following data are employed:

L denotes hours worked (by all employees). Unit of measurement: h.
K_1 denotes low voltage power lines. Unit of measurement: km.
K_2 denotes high voltage power lines. Unit of measurement: km.
K_3 denotes total transformer capacity. Unit of measurement: kVA.

Table 1 shows the combinations of outputs and inputs used in the models:

Table 1. A survey of the models applied in this study.

Model	1	2	3
Number: N	142	143	142
Outputs			
Y_1	X	X	
Y_2	X	X	
Y_3	X		X
Y_4	X		X
Inputs			
L	X	X	X
K_1	X	X	X
K_2	X	X	X
K_3	X	X	X

The first model, Model 1, is considered the main model, while Models 2 and 3 are included as a kind of sensitivity analysis and a way to separate the energy (density) and the customer (partial scale) dimensions of electricity distribution.

The data set is presented in Tables 2a and 2b. To keep the length of the article within reasonable proportions, the tables display the statistics of Model 1 only. The tables include summary statistics covering the main types of ownership/economic organization: municipal companies, municipal utilities, private companies and economic associations. Since the number of firms in other categories is very low, these are not displayed separately, although they are included in the complete data set.

Table 2a. Summary statistics on outputs (Model 1).

Output	Y_1	Y_2	Y_3	Y_4
ALL	N = 142			
Mean	267261	668685	23034	39
Stdv	533671	5674271	49231	95
Max	4465764	67395393	418094	824
Min	166	53	690	1
PRIVATE	N = 11			
Mean	379545	1119667	33007	98
Stdv	549573	1827657	37656	189
Max	1754422	4873771	112315	683
Min	166	3565	2043	2
MUN COM	N = 38			
Mean	209665	93123	16210	24
Stdv	171497	139891	13848	21
Max	727840	716864	61515	92
Min	35994	2513	2480	3
MUN UT	N = 68			
Mean	281449	144243	26984	36
Stdv	504601	318028	58983	53
Max	3544000	2005696	418094	288
Min	29426	1879	2059	1
EC ASC	N = 13			
Mean	53991	14151	3195	5
Stdv	55554	21869	2655	5
Max	182239	78474	10097	13
Min	9016	53	690	1

Table 2b. Summary statistics on inputs (Model 1).

Input	L	K_1	K_2	K_3
ALL	N = 142			
Mean	238362	1149	951	136464
Stdv	1427860	2696	4924	287005
Max	16824582	27221	57875	2408000
Min	142	4	4	3
PRIVATE	N = 11			
Mean	217571	2676	1865	233709
Stdv	297132	4083	2813	333862
Max	976194	11954	8499	957000
Min	142	4	4	3
MUN COM	N = 38			
Mean	87102	903	529	106955
Stdv	79287	860	512	90227
Max	374324	3938	2669	428700
Min	5211	99	61	17500
MUN UT	N = 68			
Mean	152299	862	390	128810
Stdv	364708	1103	668	260272
Max	2543837	5269	4609	2063300
Min	10422	88	20	17400
EC ASC	N = 13			
Mean	24318	313	201	30354
Stdv	19287	236	207	30934
Max	58190	751	799	101500
Min	2606	60	35	4300

In general, there is a large variation in firm size in all categories. Economic associations are, on average, much smaller than other organizations and municipally owned companies are substantially smaller than municipal utilities.

The regional dimension is also of interest. Table 3 provides information on the urban/rural dimension. All distributors that supply a community with more than 5000 inhabitants are classified as urban.

Table 3. The regional structure of Swedish electricity distribution.

Area	Urban %	Rural %
All	61	39
Private companies	32	68
Municipal companies	76	24
Municipal utilities	93	7
Economic associations	12	88

Private companies and economic associations are concentrated to rural areas, while municipal distributors, and municipal utilities in particular, dominate the urban electricity distribution.

4. Empirical results

There is no general agreement in the literature on the scale properties of electricity distribution. In principle, it is important to distinguish between returns to network density, i.e., the economies of increasing electricity supply when the network is held constant, and returns to scale, i.e., the economies of increasing both electricity supplied and the network. For independent distributors there is clear evidence of returns to density, but much less indicating returns to scale. Consequently, we regard both the CRS and the VRS case as significant.

From the DEA models we obtain a number of different efficiency and scale measures, shadow prices and slacks for each of the firms. As discussed above, we concentrate on the input saving measure of technical efficiency E_1 and with regard to structural efficiency measures, we will use the measures corresponding to E_1, i.e., structural input saving technical efficiency S_1, and E_3, i.e., structural scale efficiency S_3, structural pure scale efficiency S_4 ($= S_3/S_{1}$), but also the arithmetic mean of the E_1-measures, denoted S_0. The XXdifference between S_0 and S_1 reflects the size distribution of units. Recall that (the numerical values of) input saving technical efficiency in the CRS case coincides with scale efficiency in the VRS case. Pure scale efficiency is obtained as the ratio between scale efficiency and technical efficiency. Therefore, the presentation of CRS results serves the dual purpose of presenting results from a constant returns to scale model as well as scale efficiency results from a variable returns to scale model. All mean efficiency values (S_0), are calculated based on the frontier of the complete data set of each model.

4.1. Individual efficiency

Table 4 introduces the rank correlations between the different approaches. For all three models we compare the efficiency ranking of all units according to input saving efficiency.

Table 4. Summary statistics on efficiency measures. The Spearman rank correlation coefficient.

Model	VRS	CRS
1/2	.82	.84
1/3	.80	.81
2/3	.53	.53

A high correlation between Model 1 and the other two models might be expected, while the low correlation between Models 2 and 3 may seem somewhat surprising. However, one should not expect the same efficiency scores, since the two models represent two different output dimensions, density and scale.

Although the rank correlation between Models 2 and 3 was low, a closer inspection of individual figures reveals only a few units with substantially changed efficiency scores. The difference in efficiency scores exceeded 0.30 in 9 units only.

Table 5 compares variable returns to scale, VRS, with constant returns to scale, CRS, versions of the three models. The rank correlation coefficients are high. With regard to efficiency ranking, the scale properties thus seem to be of minor importance.

Table 5. Summary statistics on efficiency measures. The Spearman rank correlation coefficient, number of frontier units and structural efficiency.

Model	1	2	3
VRS/CRS Rank correlation	.83	.83	.82
VRS Number of frontier units	44	22	32
CRS Number of frontier units	25	13	19
VRS Structural efficiency S_1	.63	.62	.45
CRS Structural efficiency S_1	.62	.61	.45
VRS Pure scale efficiency S_2	1.00	.98	1.00
VRS Average efficiency S_0	.85	.77	.77
CRS Average efficiency S_0	.80	.72	.71
CRS S_0/VRS S_0	.94	.94	.92

The number of fully efficient, i.e., frontier units vary considerably (from 13 to 44) between the models. The four-output VRS model yields the largest numbers of fully efficient units, while the CRS case of Model 2 yields the lowest number. Naturally, fewer units are on the frontier in the CRS cases. The latter units are also fully scale efficient in the VRS cases.

The entire efficiency distribution for Model 1 in the VRS case is presented in Figure 2.

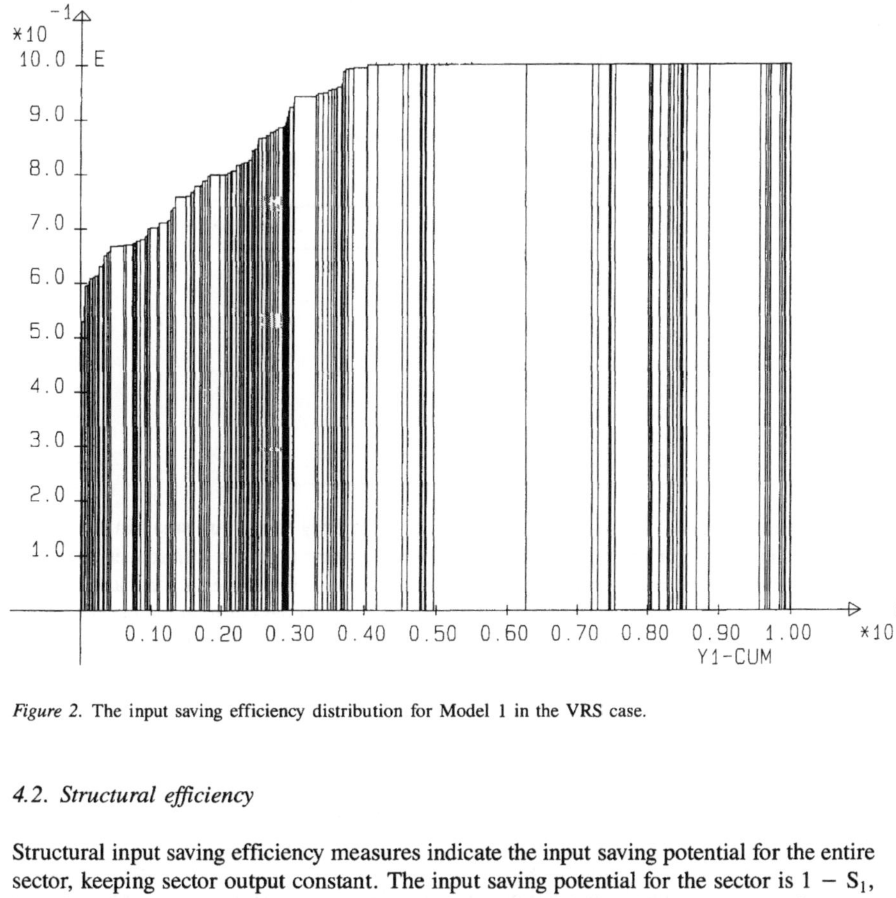

Figure 2. The input saving efficiency distribution for Model 1 in the VRS case.

4.2. Structural efficiency

Structural input saving efficiency measures indicate the input saving potential for the entire sector, keeping sector output constant. The input saving potential for the sector is $1 - S_1$, i.e., the structural measure in the VRS case of Model 1 is 0.63, which means that the input saving potential is 37 percent (see Table 5).

The S_1 values almost coincide in the VRS and the CRS cases of the respective models. If the underlying technology is variable returns to scale, this means that inefficiency, on the average, is not due to scale inefficiency, but to technical inefficiency. Pure scale efficiency, S_4, i.e., the distance to optimal scale after moving the average unit to the frontier in the horizontal direction is very close to one in all models.

In general, the input saving structural efficiency values must be regarded as rather low. This is particularly true in the case of Model 3, but also in the case of Models 1 and 2, the values are rather low. The arithmetic averages, S_0, are somewhat higher, but still fairly low. This may be an indication of a low competitive pressure in the sector. The fact that the S_0-values are higher than the corresponding S_1-values indicates that the largest units are less efficient than the smallest ones.

As for the variation in efficiency between different distributors, one should expect external background factors such as load density, number of farm households, the urban rural dimension, etc. to be of importance. Table 6 displays summary statistics on efficiency measures for urban and rural areas.

Table 6. Summary statistics on efficiency measures. Arithmetic average of individual efficiency measures. Urban—rural dimension.

Model	Urban S_0	Rural S_0
1 VRS	.86	.83
1 CRS	.83	.71
2 VRS	.77	.76
2 CRS	.74	.65
3 VRS	.79	.73
3 CRS	.76	.59
1 CRS S_0/VRS S_0	.97	.86
2 CRS S_0/VRS S_0	.96	.86
3 CRS S_0/VRS S_0	.96	.81

With regard to Model 1, the differences in mean efficiency values are small in the VRS case, and slightly larger in the CRS case. This indicates that (i) when differences in scale are accounted for, the mean efficiency level is more or less the same in rural and urban areas, but it also indicates that (ii) several small rural units are less efficient when constant returns to scale are imposed. As shown by the Model 3 results, rural efficiency is significantly lower than urban in terms of the number of customers supplied. The lower scale efficiency in rural areas is also illustrated by the ratios between the mean efficiency values of the constant and the variable returns to scale cases shown in the bottom rows of Table 6.

To further analyze possible causes of efficiency differences, the efficiency scores were regressed against the following background variables: average load/maximum load in terms of full capacity utilization hours per year, the number of low voltage and high voltage customers per km low voltage and high voltage power lines respectively, and the proportion of farming households. However, no significant parameter estimates were obtained, except in the case when full capacity utilization time entered as a single variable in the regression.

4.3. Ownership, organization, and efficiency

This section studies differences in efficiency between different types of ownership and economic organization. We distinguish between private companies, municipally owned companies, municipal utilities and economic associations (the latter a kind of co-operatives).

The number of state owned distributors in our data set is too small to be included in this comparison. In some US studies of the performance of public and private utilities, public utilities are found to be more efficient than investor-owned (see Atkinson and Halvorsen [1986], Neuberg [1977], and Pescatrice and Trapani [1980]. The regulatory structure, rate of return regulation of private firms, seems to be an important contributing factor to this result. Since the Swedish regulatory structure is quite different from (and almost the reverse of) that of the US, we should not expect the same relative differences in efficiency between public and private enterprises in Sweden. The summary statistics of mean efficiency, S_0, for all models are presented in Table 7.

When scale is accounted for, the differences in efficiency between the different types of ownership and organization are very small. The municipal utilities show the highest values and the economic associations show the lowest values. In the CRS cases the differences are larger. Still, the municipal utilities show the highest mean efficiency and the economic associations the lowest.

Table 7. Summary statistics on efficiency measures. Arithmetic average of individual efficiency measures. Ownership and organization.

Model	1		2		3	
Scale Properties	VRS	CRS	VRS	CRS	VRS	CRS
ALL	N = 142		N = 143		N = 142	
Mean	.85	.80	.77	.72	.77	.71
Stdv	.15	.16	.16	.15	.18	.19
Max	1.00	1.00	1.00	1.00	1.00	1.00
Min	.44	.31	.33	.31	.40	.21
PRIVATE COMP	N = 11		N = 11		N = 11	
Mean	.85	.77	.76	.70	.70	.60
Stdv	.15	.17	.17	.16	.22	.21
Max	1.00	1.00	1.00	1.00	1.00	1.00
Min	.61	.51	.51	.46	.43	.36
MUNICIPAL COMP	N = 38		N = 38		N = 38	
Mean	.82	.78	.74	.70	.74	.71
Stdv	.15	.14	.14	.13	.17	.17
Max	1.00	1.00	1.00	1.00	1.00	1.00
Min	.53	.50	.51	.50	.42	.39
MUNICIPAL UT	N = 68		N = 69		N = 68	
Mean	.89	.86	.80	.77	.82	.79
Stdv	.13	.13	.14	.14	.15	.16
Max	1.00	1.00	1.00	1.00	1.00	1.00
Min	.60	.58	.49	.47	.51	.49
ECONOMIC ASC	N = 13		N = 13		N = 13	
Mean	.79	.63	.77	.59	.72	.53
Stdv	.19	.18	.21	.15	.24	.16
Max	1.00	.99	1.00	.83	1.00	.87
Min	.44	.31	.44	.31	.40	.21

In terms of energy supplied (Model 2), the differences in mean efficiency in the VRS case are remarkably small. The differences are, however, larger in terms of customers supplied (Model 3). Municipal utilities are slightly more efficient in terms of number of customers supplied than in terms of energy supplied, while the opposite holds true for private companies and economic associations.

If the underlying technology is variable returns to scale, this indicates substantial differences in scale efficiency. Recall, however, that the comparison is based on arithmetic averages of individual efficiency scores and consequently, we cannot obtain pure structural efficiency, as defined in Section 2, by dividing the VRS by the CRS measures. We may, nevertheless, regard the ratio between these means as an indication, not an exact measure, of pure scale efficiency.

The pattern that emerges displays a high "average pure scale efficiency" in the case of municipal utilities (CRS S_0/VRS S_0 = 0.97) and companies (0.95), a relatively lower pure scale efficiency in the case of private companies (0.91) and a fairly low pure scale efficiency for economic associations (0.80). The latter ones are in general very small (see Table 2). In the process of structural rationalization in Sweden during the last decades, the number of economic associations has decreased substantially.

Since electricity distribution is more costly to perform in rural areas than in densely populated areas, one should expect a higher average efficiency for municipal utilities and municipal companies than for private companies and economic associations (although municipal companies often include a substantial amount of rural areas (see Table 3).

A slightly different picture is obtained when considering some partial measures of labor productivity derived from Table 2. Since overstaffing may be a problem in public undertakings, we have studied the partial labor input coefficients. Somewhat surprisingly perhaps, we find that, in terms of the number of working hours per low voltage MWh, municipal companies and economic associations obtain the lowest values, 0.41 and 0.45 respectively, while the coefficients for municipal utilities and private companies are 0.54 and 0.57. As for the number of working hours per low voltage customer, the figures are less surprising. Municipal companies and municipal utilities show the lowest values, 5.37 and 5.64 respectively, while the coefficients for private companies and economic associations are higher, 6.59 and 7.61. The approximate numbers of customers per km low voltage line are 10 for private companies and economic associations, 18 for municipal companies and 32 for municipal utilities. *A priori*, investments, maintenance and measurement are all labor intensive activities which should be more costly to perform in rural areas in a sparsely populated country like Sweden. However, since these figures are partial, one should be cautious about drawing conclusions concerning relative efficiency.

Interviews with managers of distribution companies confirm that due to the lack of cost pressure, overstaffing is a not unlikely feature in municipal electricity distribution. Several rural distributors are also considered to be of suboptimal size. Therefore, the general conclusion is that productive efficiency is the main problem in urban and scale efficiency the main problem in rural electricity distribution, particularly for the economic associations.

5. Concluding remarks

The following main conclusions may be drawn from the analysis:

1) the main efficiency problem in Swedish electricity retail distribution is to achieve a higher degree of technical efficiency. The present level of structural input saving efficiency is rather low.
2) Rural distribution is also characterized by a relatively low degree of scale efficiency.
3) Ownership, economic organization or service area do not seem to be related to efficiency in any significant way. Urban distribution is found to be slightly more efficient than rural distribution.

   (*A priori*, one would expect urban distribution to be more efficient than rural, although it would not be possible to predict the magnitude of the efficiency differences.)

The, on average, low efficiency level seems to indicate a lack of competition in the industry. A situation which is not easily overcome. The present system relies on yardstick competition (which primarily puts pressure on the rural distributors) and the renewal of concessions. What the system lacks, is an efficient pressure on the urban distributors. There is no strong direct price regulation of electricity distribution in Sweden. According to the municipality law, an undertaking performed by a municipality is not permitted to be profitable—only to break even. In addition, there is a price regulation board to which consumers may (although rarely do) complain about too high electricity prices, but this board plays a minor role as a price level regulator. It has proved more efficient to sue municipalities for overcharging. In our view, the municipality **"not for profit law"** is a fairly efficient instrument against attempts from the municipalities to use electricity pricing as an instrument of taxation. Since the municipalities in general have rather favorable geographical conditions for electricity distribution, they can attain relatively low electricity prices. Yardstick competition puts a pressure on the rural (mostly private) distributors to set a price level which does not deviate too much from that of the surrounding service areas. In addition, the National Energy Administration Board, which is responsible for the structural rationalization policy of the electricity distribution sector, supervises the productive efficiency and handles the renewal of the time constrained concessions. If a distributor is not regarded as efficient enough, it will not get its concession renewed and its service area is usually merged with an adjacent service area.

Due to different incentive structures, one might expect efficiency differences between municipal and private undertakings. The lack of competition and private benchmarks of urban (municipal) distribution costs indicate a fairly modest cost pressure. Furthermore, the boards of directors are generally politically appointed (but not directly elected) and represent political parties whose objectives may not be cost minimization. Municipal companies are probably less politicized than utilities. Due to the higher distribution costs, however, one should expect a high pressure on rural distribution to reach an efficiency level which makes it possible to obtain a price level that does not deviate too much from surrounding urban areas. This kind of yardstick competition seems to be fairly important in Sweden.

Acknowledgments

We thank Hans Bjurek, Finn Førsund, and three anonymous referees for helpful comments. Support from the following sources is gratefully acknowledged: Swedish State Power Board, Swedish Energy Administration Board, Jan Wallander's Research Foundation, and Gothenburg Business School Foundation.

References

Atkinson, S.E., and R. Halvorsen. (1986). "The Relative Efficiency of Public and Private Firms in a Regulated Environment: The Case of U.S. Electric Utilities." *Journal of Public Economics* 29, pp. 281–294.

Charnes, A. and W.W. Cooper. (1985). "Preface to Topics in Data Envelopment Analysis." *Annals of Operations Research* 2, pp. 59–94.

Charnes, A., W.W. Cooper, and E. Rhodes. (1978). "Measuring the Efficiency of Decision Making Units." *European Journal of Operational Research* 2 (6), pp. 429–444.

Deprins, D., L. Simar, and H. Tulkens. (1984). "Measuring Labor-Efficiency in Post Offices." In M. Marchand, P. Pestieau, and H. Tulkens (eds.), *The Performance of Public Enterprises: Concepts and Measurement.* Amsterdam: North Holland Publishing Co.

Farber, S.C. (1989). "The Dependence of Parametric Efficiency Tests on Measures of the Price of Capital and Capital Stock for Electric Utilities." *The Journal of Industrial Economics* 38 (2), pp. 199–213.

Farrell, M.J. (1957). "The measurement of productive efficiency." *Journal of Royal Statistical Society* A 120, pp. 253–290.

Färe, R., S. Grosskopf, and C.A.K. Lovell. (1985). *The Measurement of Efficiency of Production.* Boston, MA: Kluwer-Nijhoff Publishing.

Førsund, F.R. and L. Hjalmarsson. (1974). "On the Measurement of Productive Efficiency." *Swedish Journal of Economics* 76, pp. 141–154.

Førsund, F.R. and L. Hjalmarsson. (1979). "Generalized Farrell Measures of Efficiency: An Application to Milk Processing in Swedish Dairy Plants." *Economic Journal* 89, pp. 294–315.

Førsund, F.R. and L. Hjalmarsson. (1987). *Analyses of Industrial Structure: A Putty-Clay Approach. IUI* Stockholm: Almqvist & Wiksell International.

Henderson, J.S. (1985). "Cost Estimation for Vertically Integrated Firms: The Case of Electricity." In Michael Crew (ed.), *Analyzing the Impact of Regulatory Change in Public Utilities.* New York: Lexington Books.

Joskow, P.L. and R. Schmalensee. (1987). "The Performance of Coal-Burning Electric Generating Units in the United States: 1960–1980." *Journal of Applied Econometrics* 2, pp. 85–109.

Labroukos, N.S. and S. Kioukas. (1988). "Measuring Technical Efficiency: An Application to Electricity Districts." Unpublished.

Melfi, C.A.. (1987). "Technical and Allocative Efficiency in Electric Utilities." Unpublished.

Meyer, R. (1975). "Publicly Owned Versus Privately Owned Utilities: A Policy Choice." *Review of Economics and Statistics* 62 (4), pp. 391–399.

Ministry of Energy, Wellington, New Zealand (1989), "Performance Measures and Economies of Scale in the New Zealand Electricity Distribution System." In N.S. Wyatt, M.R. Brown, P.J. Caragata, A.J. Duncan, D.E.A. Giles (eds.).

Nelson, R.A. (1990). "The Effects of Competition on Publicly-Owned Firms. Evidence from the Municipal Electric Industry in the US." *International Journal of Industrial Organization* 8, pp. 37–51

Nelson, R.A. and W.J. Primeaux, Jr. (1988). "The Effects of Competition on Transmission and Distribution Costs in the Municipal Electric Industry." *Land Economics* 64 (4), pp. 338–346.

Neuberg, L.G.. (1977). "Two Issues in the Municipal Ownership of Electric Power Distribution Systems." *Bell Journal of Economics* 8 (1), pp. 303–323.

Pescatrice, D.R. and J.M. Trapani III. (1980). "The Performance and Objectives of Public and Private Utilities Operating in the United States." *Journal of Public Economics* 13 (2), pp. 259–276.

Roberts, M.J. (1986). "Economies of Density and Size in the Transmission and Distribution of Electric Power. *Land Economics* 62, pp. 337–346.

Salvanes, K.G. and S. Tjotta. (1990). "Cost Differences in Electricity Distribution: Economies of Scale and Economies of Density in the Norwegian Electricity Distribution Industry." working paper, Center for Applied Research, Oslo, Norway.

Thomas, D.L., R. Greffe, and K.C. Grant. (1985). "Application of Data Envelopment Analysis to Management Audits of Electric Distribution Utilities." *Public Utility Commission of Texas.* Austin, Texas, USA.

Weiss, L.W. (1975). "Antitrust in the Electric Power Industry." In A. Phillips (ed.), *Promoting Competition in Regulated Markets.* Washington D.C.: The Brookings Institute.

Weyman-Jones, T.G.. (1991). "Productive Efficiency in a Regulated Industry. The Area Electricity Boards of England and Wales." *Energy Economics* 13, pp. 116–122.

The Journal of Productivity Analysis, 3, 25–43 (1992)

A Comparison of Parametric and Non-Parametric Efficiency Measures: The Case of Norwegian Ferries[1]

FINN R. FØRSUND
Department of Economics, University of Oslo, and Centre for Research in Economics and Business Administration, SNF Oslo

Abstract

The trunk road system in Norway has to be supplemented by a number of ferries due to the long coastline with numerous islands and fjords. Most of the ferries are run by private companies, but at a loss. The deficits are covered by the Ministry of Transport. The subsidies have risen rapidly in the last years and have focussed attention on whether the ferries are really run as efficiently as possible. To change the incentives to economize, a lump-sum payment is considered. To implement such a system, an initial assessment of reasonable input requirements is needed. The aim of this article is to provide such a yardstick by establishing a best practice frontier. Both a non-parametric and a parametric approach to a deterministic frontier are tried and differences of results discussed. Peculiarities due to choice of methods are revealed. The efficiency distributions are quite similar for the two methods except for scale efficiency, where the parametric method indicates substantial unrealized scale economies, while the non-parametric approach shows the largest and some small ferries to be scale efficient. The results indicate a substantial rationalization potential of about 30 percent in total.

1. Introduction

Road transportation along the Norwegian coast is difficult and costly because of a sparse population and numerous islands and fjords. In spite of an increasing number of bridges, there are still about 150 ferry distances, serviced by about 250 ferries. In 1988, the cost of running these ferries amounted to about 40 percent of maintenance of public roads.

The institutional arrangements make ferry transport an interesting topic for study, from a research as well as from a financial point of view. Most of the ferries are run by private companies, but at a loss. The deficits are covered by Directorate for Road Transport (DRT for short). In 1988, this amounted to 500 million NOK (about $80 million). Although inspection of accounts may to a certain extent reveal loss incurring practices, it is obviously very difficult to disentangle difficult conditions, for example, heavy weather from sloppy practices.

It seems reasonable to assume that change of incentives could produce favorable results. One such arrangement under consideration is to award a lump-sum payment to specific tasks, such as providing transport over a specific distance. Any surplus should then be kept by the company, as should losses be borne. To launch such a system one would need an initial assessment of reasonable costs. The aim of the present project is to provide such a yardstick. Hence, we aim at estimating input requirement by an efficient producer.

Our way of approaching the problem is to seek out the most efficient of the observed ferries. It is worth noting that none may actually be efficient, in the blueprint sense

(Førsund and Hjalmarsson [1987]). Both a deterministic parametric and non-parametric frontier[2] will be calculated in order to bring out advantages and disadvantages of the methods (see e.g. Banker et al. [1986], Banker et al. [1988], Banker et al. [1990], Bjurek et al. [1990], and Ferrier and Lovell [1990] for comparative studies of non-parametric and parametric frontiers).

2. Methodology

In order to measure efficiency of micro units one needs a benchmark and operational definitions of efficiency measures. We shall try both a parametric and a non-parametric frontier as benchmark, and use Farrell [1957] based definitions of technical efficiency.

2.1. Comparative studies

When choosing between the parametric and non-parametric approach, any additional information about the type of activity under study must be drawn upon. It cannot be decided a priori what is the best approach. Any information about scale and substitution properties is best handled within a parametric approach. However, the popular choice of translog form is due to lack of any specific information. The functional forms used are at best approximations to underlying production functions. As remarked by Afriat [1972] the properties of the functions "are not deliberate empirical hypotheses, but are accidental to technical convenience of the functions." The non-parametric approach, pioneered by Farrell and developed and greatly improved as to computability by Charnes et al. [1978] and termed DEA (Data Envelopment Analysis), consisting of fitting linear facets seems more appropriate when our knowledge of underlying technologies is weak. The approach can quite straightforwardly handle multiple outputs. Given its flexibility, it yields the most pessimistic best practice frontier while keeping the property of convex output and input sets.[3]

When comparing the abilities of the parametric and non-parametric approaches to shed light on the nature of efficiency and the structure of technology, following up the preferred "methodology cross-checking principle" of Charnes et al. [1988] it is difficult to structure unambiguously comparable models.

The most recent comparison of the two approaches on a common body of data is Bjurek et al. [1990] and Ferrier and Lovell [1990]. Banker et al. [1988] and Banker et al. [1990] are based on generating artificial data from prespecified parametric technologies. Banker et al. [1986] compares results based on DEA with an econometrically estimated cost function of a COLS (Corrected Ordinary Least Squares) type, i.e., the cost function is an average function except for the intercept term, which is adjusted so that all costs are higher or equal to best practice.

In Bjurek et al. [1990] two parametric specifications, Cobb-Douglas (CD) and a flexible quadratic function (QD), both within a deterministic framework, are tried on a time series of cross-section data sets for about 400 social insurance offices, specifying four outputs and one input. The non-parametric variable returns to scale specification envelops the data most closely, resulting in a significantly higher number of fully efficient units. The CD and QD results are quite close, and the general impression is that measures of structural efficiency are surprisingly similar for all approaches for all years.

Ferrier and Lovell [1990] estimate a stochastic cost frontier of the translog form on a body of bank data with five outputs and three inputs for the 575 units. The non-parametric approach is deterministic and efficiency scores are calculated relative to the production frontier. They found a lack of close harmony as regards efficiency score distributions, but more similar results as regards returns to scale properties. In spite of the non-parametric specification being deterministic and thus treating noise, if any, as inefficiency, this specification yields the highest efficiency scores. The differences between the approaches are tentatively explained by the fact that a stochastic specification is compared with a deterministic one, and by comparing efficiency scores based on a cost frontier to scores based on a production frontier. The inherent problem of an econometric parametric approach imposing structure both on the technology and the distribution of inefficiency is also pointed out.

In view of the experiences of the research quoted above, it seems most appropriate to proceed with either a deterministic or a stochastic frontier for both methods. Since stochastic non-parametric models are difficult to implement (see Sengupta [1987] for a development of chance constraints, and Petersen and Olesen [1989] for another approach based on time series of panel data), a deterministic framework is chosen in the sequel. As a parametric form a flexible function would have been most appropriate. However, the popular translog form did not perform satisfactorily on the data set at hand, so a more restrictive homothetic form with a Cobb-Douglas kernel is used. The results of Ferrier and Lovell [1990] indicate that this additional restriction is not that crucial when comparing with non-parametric frontiers. Following the previous comparative studies the comparisons will focus on similarities or dissimilarities of the distributions of the efficiency scores, and scale properties.

2.2. *Efficiency measures*

The efficiency measures adopted in the sequel are the Farrell efficiency measures as generalized to variable returns to scale technologies in Førsund and Hjalmarsson [1974, 1979b, 1987]. The system of efficiency measures introduced there is adapted in this article and set out below and illustrated by using observation K in figure 1.

E_1 = input saving technical efficiency = HJ/HK
E_2 = output increasing technical efficiency = NK/NL
E_3 = gross scale efficiency = HI/HK = NK/NM
E_4 = pure scale efficiency (input corrected) = E_3/E_1 = HI/HJ
E_5 = pure scale efficiency (output corrected) = E_3/E_2 = NL/NM.

Note that the input saving measure for CRS technology coincides with the gross scale efficiency measure for VRS technology.

The interpretation of the scale measures is different from the technical efficiency measures. The measure E_3 is the ratio of the minimal input coefficients (or maximal productivities) at the frontier and the observed input coefficients of a unit. The pure measure E_4 has similar interpretation and the pure measure E_5, also. Thus, the scale measures do not directly show input saving or output increasing as E_1 and E_2 do. To realize the frontier minimal input coefficients both output and input in general have to change.

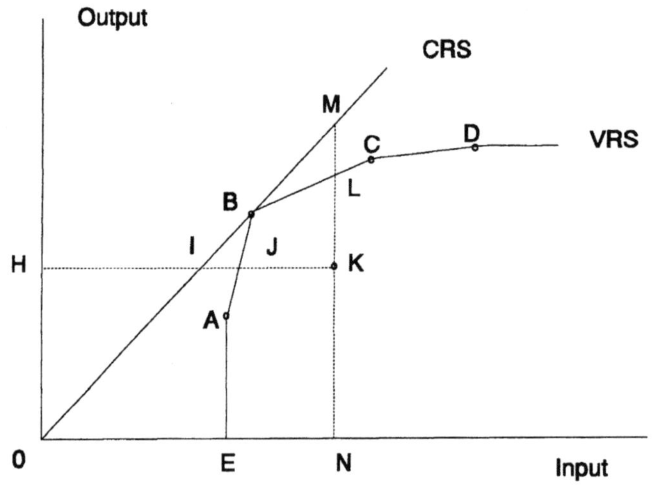

Figure 1. Non-parametric frontier and efficiency measures

2.3. The DEA approach

We will choose the non-parametric Farrell frontier allowing variable returns to scale as the benchmark. The DEA technique developed by Charnes and Cooper and associates consists of calculating the efficiency measure for each unit in turn at the same time as determining the location of the corresponding linear facets.

The Farrell input saving measure is found by solving the following linear program for each unit, k:

$$\underset{\lambda_{kj}}{Min}\ E_{1k} \tag{1}$$

subject to

$$y_{rk} \leq \sum_{j=1}^{n} \lambda_{kj} y_{rj},\ r = 1, \ldots, s, \tag{1a}$$

$$E_{1k} x_{ik} \geq \sum_{j=1}^{n} \lambda_{kj} x_{ij},\ i = 1, \ldots, m, \tag{1b}$$

$$\sum_{j=1}^{n} \lambda_{kj} = 1, \tag{1c}$$

$$\lambda_{kj} \geq 0, j = 1, \ldots, n, \tag{1d}$$

y_{rk} = output of type r for unit k,
x_{ik} = input of type i for unit k,
λ_{kj} = weight for unit j's outputs, inputs defining unit k's reference point.

Constraint (1a) says that the reference unit must produce as much output as unit k. Constraint (1b) states that the efficiency corrected use of inputs of unit k must at least equal the amounts employed by the reference unit. Since the correction number is the same for all types of input, we have a proportional reduction of observed inputs.

Constraint (1c) restricts the best practice technology to permit variable returns to scale because the frontier is a convex envelopment of the data set.

The positive weights λ_{kj} in the solution of (1) show which units span the frontier technology for the facets in question. It is well known that the maximal number of units spanning the frontier for each unit is equal to the sum of outputs and inputs in problem (1) (minus one for the efficiency variable plus one for the constraint (1c)).

The output increasing efficiency measure is then calculated by solving the following linear program:

$$\underset{\lambda_{kj}}{Max}\ 1/E_{2k} \tag{2}$$

subject to

$$(1/E_{2k})\, y_{rk} \leq \sum_{j=1}^{n} \lambda_{kj} y_{rj},\ r = 1, \ldots, s, \tag{2a}$$

$$x_{ik} \geq \sum_{j=1}^{n} \lambda_{kj} x_{ij},\ i = 1, \ldots, m, \tag{2b}$$

$$\sum_{j=1}^{n} \lambda_{kj} = 1, \tag{2c}$$

$$\lambda_{kj} \geq 0, j = 1, \ldots, n. \tag{2d}$$

Observed outputs of unit k are now efficiency-adjusted upwards to be less or equal to outputs at the frontier reference point. The correction factor is the same for all outputs implying a proportional change of observed outputs.

Calculation of scale efficiency measures are, of course, only relevant when specifying a VRS technology. Referring to figure 1, we have in general that the input saving efficiency measure E_1 with CRS as reference technology, HI/HK, is equal to the gross scale efficiency measure, E_3, with VRS as reference technology. The pure measures of scale efficiency can then easily be calculated according to the definitions above.

Any scale inefficiency is due to either decreasing or increasing returns to scale. To determine what is the case one can, for unique solutions, most conveniently inspect the sum of weights $\Sigma_j \lambda_{kj}$ for the E_1-calculations with CRS technology. If the sum of weights is less than one, we have increasing returns at the adjusted point J on the VRS frontier. A sum less than one means that the best practice points determining the CRS frontier technology are scaled downwards when defining the reference points on the CRS frontier. The units located on the CRS frontier must, of course, also be on the VRS technology.

Consider the data points A–D, K illustrated in figure 1. Unit B is the only one with positive weight when solving problem (1) without constraint (1c) for unit K. In order to scale point B down to the reference point I the optimal weight must be $OI/OB < 1$.

If the sum of weights is greater than one this implies that we have decreasing returns at the adjusted points. The reference points are in general found by scaling up from observed points defining the CRS technology.[4]

By the nature of placing the benchmark technology as a linear faceted convex lid over the observations increasing returns can only be experienced from the start[5] of the output ranges. When specifying VRS there must be at least one unit on the frontier that has constant returns. Very efficient large units could lead to most of the reference technology exhibiting constant returns, while efficient units of medium size divide the set in smaller units having increasing returns and larger units having decreasing returns. Note that the concept of large and small when we have multiple outputs is not quite clear cut. Scale properties are usually evaluated along rays with fixed proportions between the outputs. When changing output proportions scale properties may well change even if the units keep their size.

A general feature of the DEA approach when specifying VRS is that units at both ends of the size distribution may be identified as efficient simply for lack of other comparable units. In figure 1 both units *A* and *D* will be efficient. It is a general identification problem whether scale inefficiency of technically efficient units is real or due to the VRS specification and the method of enveloping the data. A special technical feature of the DEA method should also be mentioned. Units located at the horizontal and vertical extensions of Farrell's original unit isoquant will get efficiency values of one. For instance, a unit located on the line EA in figure 1 will get the technical efficiency score of one even though unit *A* uses the same amounts of inputs, but produces more output. Thus, units placed on vertical or horizontal edges of the frontier technology are not efficient in the Pareto sense. Problems of this nature may be revealed when the solution of problem (1) or (3) for units with technical efficiency scores of one we also find slacks in the input or output constraints. (See, e.g., Ali [1989] for a discussion and a method, adapted in our study, of finding the Pareto dominated efficient units.)

2.4. *The parametric frontier*

The main idea of the deterministic parametric frontier function is that all observations are restricted to be below or on the function when calculating the parameters. We will here employ a homothetic form with a Cobb-Douglas kernel function allowing in a simple way variable returns to scale:

$$y^{\alpha} e^{\beta y} = A \prod_{j=1}^{4} x_j^{a_j}. \tag{3}$$

In logarithmic form, this function is linear in the parameters. The philosophy of fitting best practice frontiers is that the function should show the observed units as efficient as possible (see Farrell [1957] and Afriat [1972]). Following the tradition of Aigner and Chu [1968], this is achieved by minimizing the (simple) sum of deviations from the frontier. The frontier function (3) can be established by solving the following linear programming problem (see Førsund and Hjalmarsson [1979a, 1987]):

$$Min \sum_{i=1}^{n} [lnA + \sum_{j=1}^{4} a_j lnx_{ij} - \alpha lny_i - \beta y_i] \tag{4}$$

subject to

$$lnA + \sum_{j=1}^{4} a_j lnx_{ij} - \alpha lny_i - \beta y_i \geq 0, \; i = 1, \ldots, n, \tag{4a}$$

$$\sum_{j=1}^{4} a_j = 1 \tag{4b}$$

(linear homogeneity of the kernel function),

$$\alpha, \beta, a_j \geq 0. \tag{4c}$$

Optimal scale is of special interest. The scale elasticity function is:

$$\epsilon(y) = \frac{1}{\alpha + \beta y}. \tag{5}$$

3. Data

3.1. *Data sources*

For the analysis reported in this article, we have used two main sources of data. The most important is yearly accounts over the years 1984–1988 of costs associated with the running of each ferry. Covered by the data are all ferries which make up a part of the main road system of Norway, which is the responsibility of the Government. These data are reported by ferry companies to the authorities (DRT), as a basis for the support given to the companies. As noted in the introduction, most of the ferry transport runs at a loss, which is covered by central authorities.

The accounting data cover all expenses related to the running of ferries: wages and social costs, fuel, maintenance and insurance. Capital costs are generally reported insofar as it consists of interest on debt. Return on owners' capital is hardly reported. In addition to data in value terms, there is also information on the time in service and the total number of kms run per year for each ferry.

The other important data source is the register of ferries held by DRT, containing information on the type, size, vintage, price, speed, etc. of ferries. We linked the two data sets, obtaining times series data for each ferry for the period 1984–88. In the present study, we will only utilize the data set for 1988 due to the construction of the maintenance variable as explained below.

3.2. *Output*

Given the data available at this stage, we have chosen as product, termed PK, the total length run in 1988 multiplied with the capacity, PB, of the ferry in (standardized) cars.

Other aspects of ferry service output are the number of ports to call on and the length of the crossing. If long distances are easier to service (per km) than short distances, due to the latter requiring a lot of maneuvering, unit fuel consumption will differ, as it will due to systematic different exposure to rough weather. Our data does not as yet allow identification of which distances the ferries have sailed, only the total number of kms.

3.3. *Input*

Input of fuel constitutes around 15 percent of total cost, excluding capital costs. Companies report cost of fuel per ferry and the unit price of fuel paid. This price varies a lot across companies, and we have used the reported company price to convert the value of fuel into volume per year per ferry, termed FU. This procedure rests on the assumption that the reported price from a company applies to all ferries run by this company (there are 23 ferry companies and about 250 ferries).

In principle, data should allow input of labor to be measured in two ways. First, total wages, WG, are reported. However, heterogeneity of labor will create problems. Even in the presence of cost minimization (which we assert is far from certain given the incentive structure) and identical production functions for all units, total labor cost will vary across units if prices of different types of labor vary across units (ferries), i.e., due to variations in local labor markets.

Second, one could use reported crew-size and number of shifts. Unfortunately, the latter piece of information is missing for many ferries. In addition, overtime is not included. Furthermore, there is no information on composition of crew.

As a way to check the link between the two measures, we ran a regression of total regular wages, excluding overtime and social cost, on crew size multiplied by number of shifts (man-shifts) where this is available for about 100 of the ferries. We also ran wages on man-shifts multiplied by the number of days the ferry had been in service in 1988, divided by 360 (fraction of year in service). The regressions indicate that wages have a strong linear relation with the direct measures of crew size, and we have used total wages as an indicator of labor input.[6]

Capital input can be measured in physical or value terms. In value terms, we have experimented with estimating market value from the insurance premium. However, we found the capacity of the ferry, in number of (standardized) cars, PB, as the most reliable capital measure (see Førsund and Hernaes [1990]).[7]

Maintenance and repair may vary a lot from year to year, since major replacements are required at fixed intervals, i.e., every four years. Furthermore, repairs may occur lagged in relation to distance sailed. Therefore, for each ferry, we calculated average cost per km over a five year period and multiplied by kms in 1988. The predicted cost incurred in 1988 was termed MN.

At this stage, it was important to check out the methods, and explore the basic production of transport services with ferries in normal traffic. Therefore, we have excluded ferries with incomplete information about any of the variables and those in service less than five years, since they had not yet had any chance to go through a full maintenance cycle. Excluded were also ferries without positive inputs of all types. This leaves us with 138 out of the original 236 ferries in service in 1988. The ferries included in our data set represent 65 percent of the total cost in 1988, excluding capital cost. An overview of the variables we used is given in table 1.

Table 1. Production of transport services.

	Total	Across ferries			
		Average	Stand.d.	Max.	Min.
PK Total transport (1000 unit-kms)	306616	2222	1872	9261	6
WG Wage sum (1000 NOK)	438194	3175	1357	7141	1
FU Fuel (1000 litres)	73100	529	346	1810	6
MN Maintenance (1000 NOK)	111987	811	392	2215	10
PB Capital (Capacity)	5307	39	22	140	12

4. Empirical results

4.1. Non-parametric frontier

The figures 2a–2c should be read in the following way: Each histogram represents one unit. The size of ferries measured by output is shown by the width of the histogram. The efficiency scores calculated as the solutions to the programs (1) and (2) are measured on the ordinate axis. The units are ordered according to increasing value of the efficiency score.

The input saving efficiency measure E_1 is shown in figure 2a for variable returns to scale as the best practice technology. Let us start by looking at the right-hand tail of efficient units. There are in fact 12 units that are efficient representing about 10 percent of total output. Moving to the left, efficiency falls off rather evenly down to the value of about 0.70 corresponding to a cumulated output share of 0.15 (units having efficiency scores of less than 0.70 have 15 percent of output), and then there is a rapid fall down to 0.45 for units in this interval representing about 15 percent of total output. The figure 0.45 means that this least efficient ferry could produce the observed output with only 45 percent of observed inputs. As regards the connection between size and efficiency we see that we have both large and small ferries as efficient, but with a clear tendency of the smallest ferries being concentrated at the tail of the distribution with least efficient units.

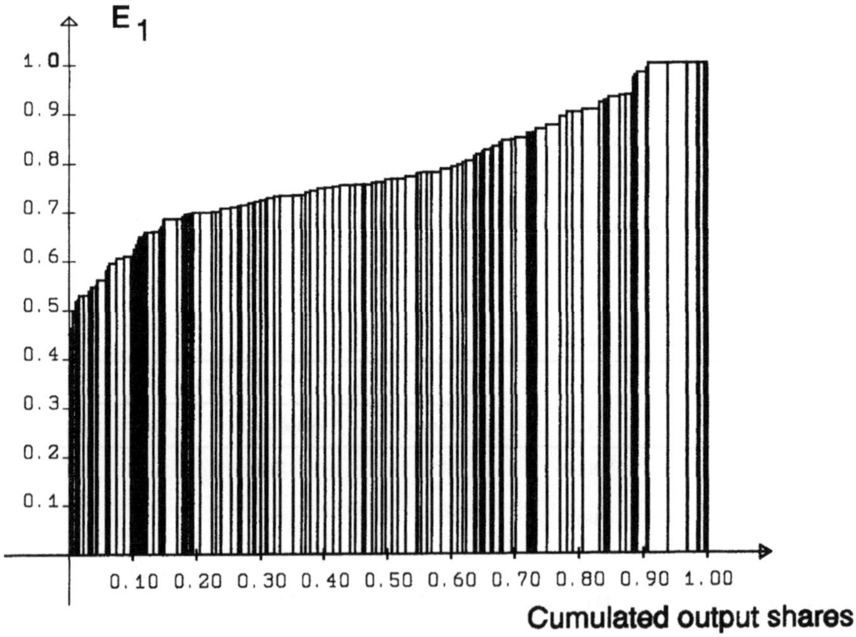

Figure 2a. Input-saving efficiency non-parametric frontier.

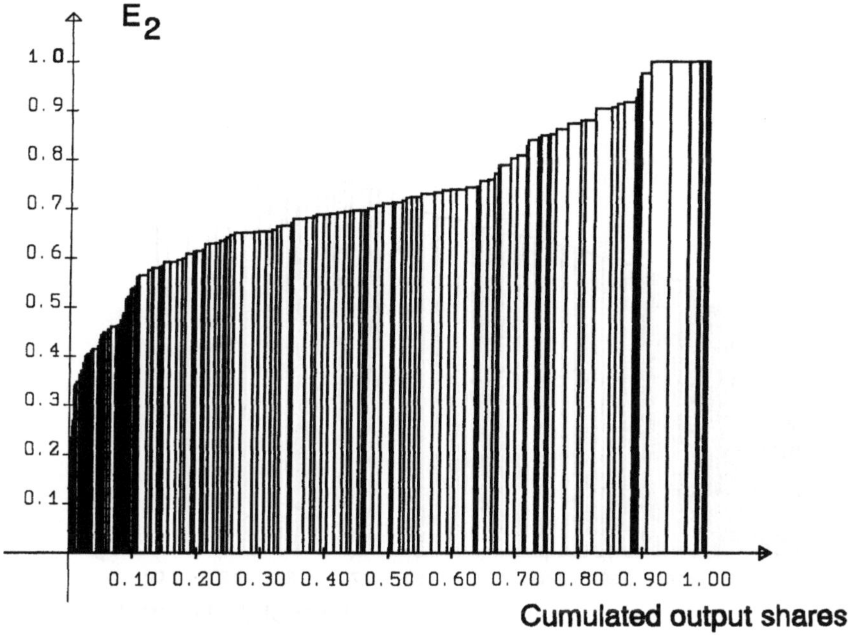

Figure 2b. Output-increasing efficiency non-parametric frontier.

Inspecting the distribution of output increasing efficiency, E_2, in figure 2b the positive correlation between size and efficiency is even more pronounced. The shape of the distribution is otherwise very similar to the distribution for E_1. The interpretation of a number is now the ratio of observed output to potential output at the frontier employing the observed amounts of inputs. There is also here a rapid deterioration in efficiency for the tail of least efficient ferries representing about 10 percent of total output from 0.55 to 0.23. The least efficient tail encompasses the lion's share of the small ferries.

The distribution for gross scale efficiency is shown in figure 2c. We have a group of five scale efficient units with about 8 percent of total output. Note that both large (the two largest) and small units (disappearing as vertical lines) are scale efficient. Even with only one output the faceted surface of the frontier implies that optimal scale, i.e., scale elasticity of one, is not unique with respect to output. The smallest ferries are now among the least efficient and almost all belong to the least efficient tail of about 20 percent of total output, with the range between 0.19 and 0.55. Size is obviously positively correlated with efficiency.

As pointed out in Section 2 the scale efficiency measure, E_3, for the VRS technology can be interpreted as the input saving efficiency measure for the CRS technology. Recalling figure 1, we have that units such as unit A being efficient under VRS become quite inefficient when assuming CRS. The importance of the choice of technology is clearly demonstrated for such units.

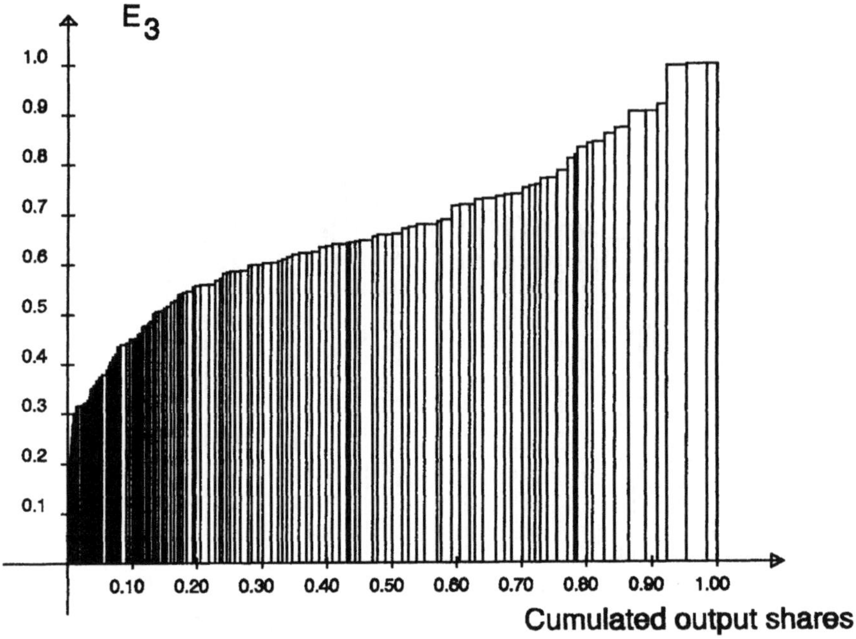

Figure 2c. Gross scale efficiency non-parametric frontier.

4.2. Parametric frontier

The parameter values obtained from solving the LP-problem (4) are shown in table 2. We have a corner solution of zero for the labor kernel parameter, and a rather high value for the capital kernel parameter.[8] A zero value for a parameter does not, of course, mean that we could do without labor in the production of ferry services. The data set does not allow us to recover the real impact of labor, because one or more units are efficient in more than one dimension at the same time. However, we still claim that measuring efficiency relative to our calculated frontier is meaningful. The labor dimensions of efficiency is lost or (at best) covered by another input. Since we use physical capacity for capital input there is by regulation a high correlation with minimum labor requirement.

Table 2. Parameters of the production function.

$$y^{\alpha} e^{\beta y} = A \sum_{j=1}^{4} x_j^{a_j}$$

Constant	Kernel parameters a_j				Scale parameters	
lnA	Labor	Fuel	Maint.	Capital	α	β
−1.37	0	0.19	0.18	0.62	0.51	0.037

The scale parameters yield an optimal scale significantly larger than the biggest ferry in the sample:

$$y_{\epsilon=1} = \frac{1-\alpha}{\beta} = 13.08. \tag{6}$$

The average output size is 2.22, and the largest ferry has 9.26 car kilometers per year (in millions). The graph of the frontier function over the observed output range is shown in figure 3 expanding the inputs proportionally from average observed values. Increasing returns is clearly exhibited.

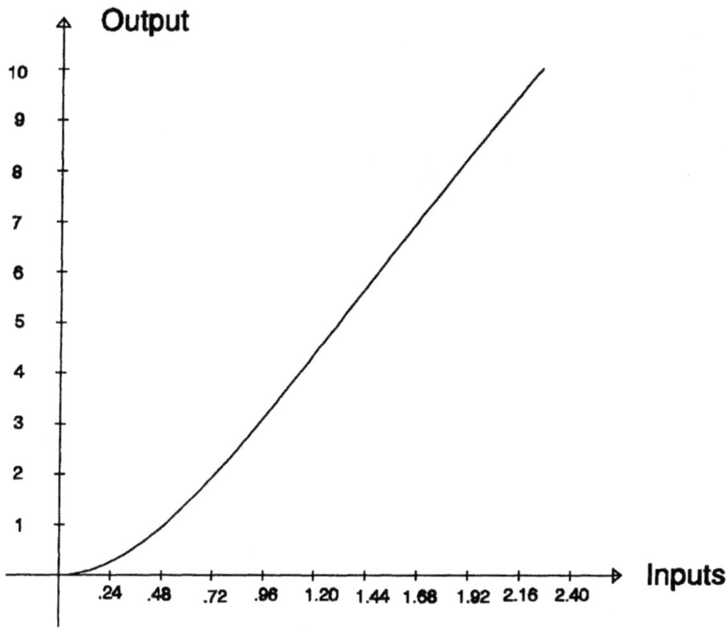

Figure 3. Frontier production function graph.

The efficiency distributions are shown in figures 4a–4c. Starting with input-saving efficiency, the group of most efficient units comprising about 10 percent of output is split into two with units representing about half of the output share having efficiency scores of 0.95. The tail of least efficient units represents about 10 percent of output with scores starting in the range of 0.65 falling rapidly down to 0.35. The main bulk of units representing 80 percent of output has a fairly even distribution in the range from 0.90 to 0.68. Except for the two tails, there is no clear cut picture of efficiency and size. At the best practice tail,

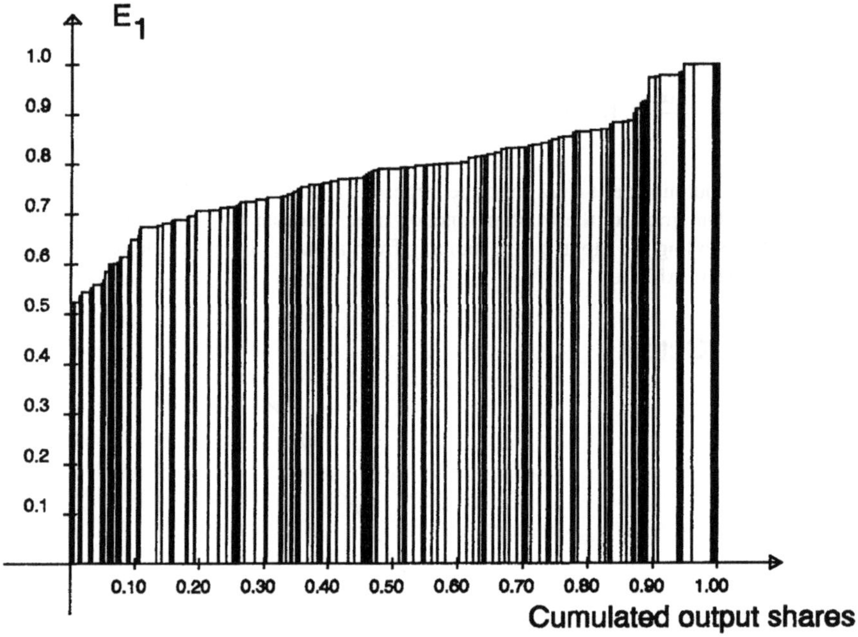

Figure 4a. Input-saving efficiency parametric frontier.

the two largest ferries are among the most efficient and at the worst practice tail, small units are overrepresented.

The general picture remains the same for the distribution of output-increasing efficiency scores. The skewness is somewhat more pronounced with the range of the main share of units starting at the level of 0.85 and ending at 0.60, and the share of the worst practice tail increasing to 15 percent of output over the range 0.60 to 0.25. The correlation of size and efficiency scores is the same as for the input-saving measure.

The scale efficiency distribution in fig. 4c reveals a strong correlation between size and efficiency score, the correlation coefficient being, in fact, 0.87.[9] The worst-practice tail starting at a value of 0.40 and falling rapidly to 0.10 covers about 15 percent of output. There are only two units, the two largest, that obtain scale efficiencies above 0.90, the bulk of units being distributed over the range of 0.75 to 0.40. In our specification of a homothetic parametric frontier, the scale elasticity is a unique function of the (single) output level (eq. (5)) and optimal scale is outside observed size. The distributions of pure scale efficiency measures must then be perfectly correlated with size, but for the gross scale measure individual technical inefficiencies create variation.

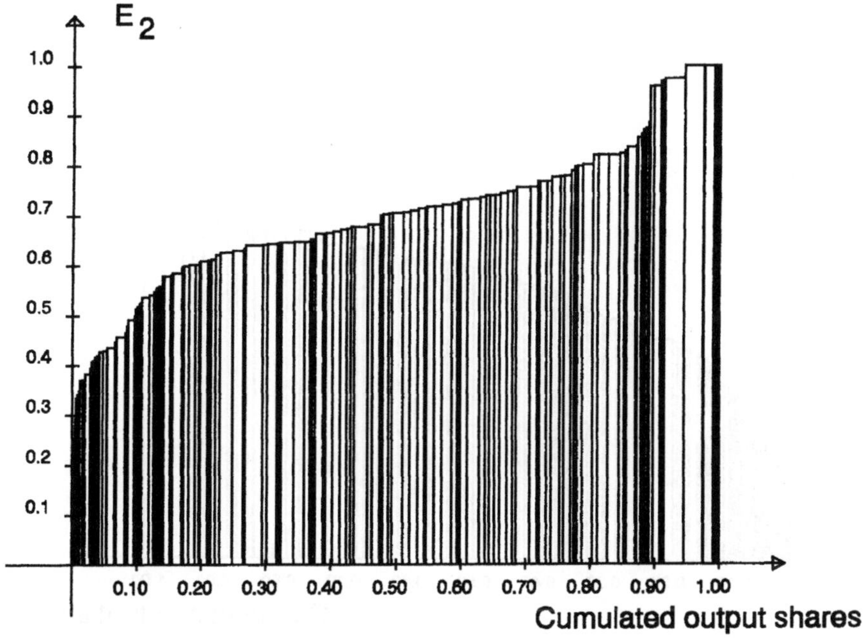

Figure 4b. Output-saving efficiency parametric frontier.

4.3. Comparing non-parametric and parametric frontier

Comparing the distributions for the input-saving and output-increasing efficiency measures with the ones based on the non-parametric frontier we see that they are remarkably similar in shape. As to the best-practice tail, we now have fewer units being on the frontier, down from 12 to 5. But units not being 100 percent efficient belonging to this tail are very nearly so. The biggest difference is the stronger correlation between size and efficiency in the non-parametric case. This is especially pronounced for output-increasing efficiency.

The figures also give information about efficiency structure for the whole sector. If a horizontal line at level one is introduced in figures 2a–b and 4a–b, the proportion of areas between the line of one and the top of the histograms and the total areas can be used directly for structural measures. The sum of relative input saving, 1-E_1, weighed with observed output share, and the sum of output increase relative to potential output, 1-E_2, weighed with observed output share, can be read off as such area ratios.[10] The total input-saving potential is for both specifications of the frontier about 30 percent. If possible output increase compared with observed output is wanted, the area between the line of one and the top of the histograms should be compared with the area of the histograms. The latter calculation yields very similar figures of about 40 percent possible (weighed) output increases.

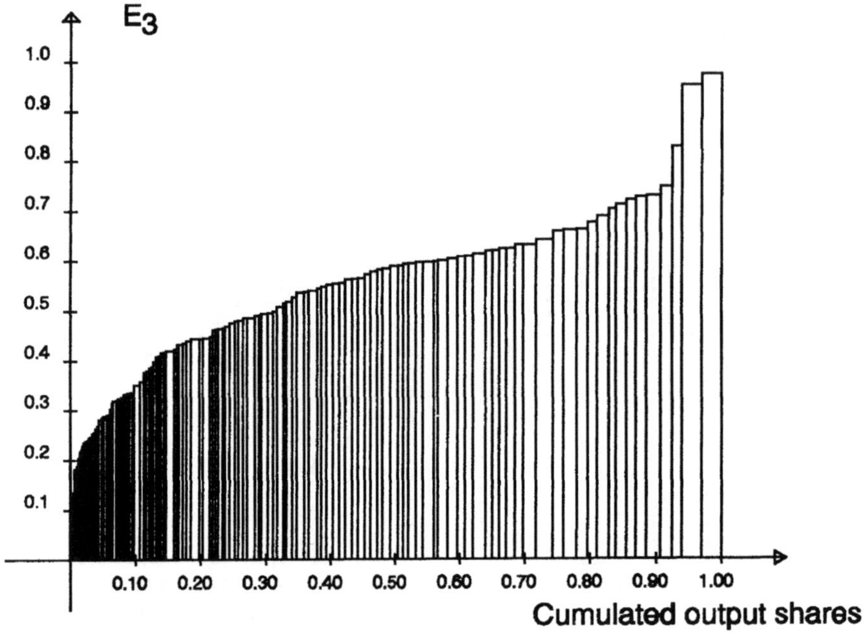

Figure 4c. Gross scale efficiency parametric frontier.

The distributions for gross scale efficiency are quite similar as to correlation size and efficiency scores, but the range of efficiency values is shifted downwards in the parametric case. In the non-parametric case, five units are actually 100 percent scale efficient, the two largest, a medium-sized one and two very small ones. Since output is one-dimensional, it is rather surprising that two so small units are scale efficient, but it is a consequence of special input combinations. This cannot happen in the parametric case due to the functional form we have imposed, therefore this aspect is not pursued further.[11]

The correlations between the efficiency scores of the parametric and non-parametric frontiers are set out in table 3. They are all significant and rather high. The rank correlations are higher than the simple correlation. The rank correlation is highest for the gross scale measure. The scores based on the parametric frontier are perfectly correlated with size, and the high value of 0.79 shows that scores based on the non-parametric frontier also are highly correlated with size.

In order to bring out differences of results between the two approaches due to choice of method itself, the most efficient units are analyzed in table 4. The efficiency scores for the three efficiency measures for both methods are set out in increasing size of the units. In accordance with figure 1, we have some very small units that are technically efficient relative to the non-parametric frontier, while they have low efficiency scores according to the parametric frontier. This is due to the fact that the parametric frontier starts

Table 3. Correlations between DEA and parametric frontier efficiency scores.

Efficiency measures	Pearson	Spearman
E_1	.60	.69
E_2	.70	.73
E_3	.74	.79

Table 4. Size distribution of efficient units.

		Input saving E_1		Output increasing E_2		Gross Scale E_3	
Unit	Output	DEA	Par. frontier	DEA	Par. frontier	DEA	frontier
50	.01	1	.25	1	.07	.67	.01
72	.06	1	.45	1	.22	.36	.05
74	.06	1	.61	1	.38	.50	.07
49	.08	1	.65	1	.43	1	.09
1	.08	1	.62	1	.40	1	.08
76	.22	1	1	1	1	1	.22
47	.56	1	.94	1	.89	.77	.32
71	.96	.97	.98	.93	.97	.51	.43
66	1.13	.98	.98	.94	.97	.36	.47
42	1.23	.86	1	.85	1	.82	.49
18	1.37	1	1	1	1	.64	.52
70	2.06	.92	.98	.88	.96	.68	.60
20	2.55	1	.88	1	.82	.84	.59
78	3.14	.94	.97	.91	.96	.77	.70
73	4.66	1	1	1	1	1	.83
114	9.26	1.00	.98	1.00	.97	1.00	.95
111	9.26	1	1	1	1	1	.97

at the origin while the non-parametric frontier starts at these observations. Increasing the size above the levels where difference in methods dictate the results, we see that the two methods yield very similar results for the efficient units. However, for gross scale efficiency the differences are more pronounced especially for small output values.

5. Concluding remarks

From an efficiency analysis point of view, the results so far indicate a substantial variation in efficiency across ferries with a potential for input saving in total in the range of 30 percent and output increase in the range of 40 percent. These results are independent of whether the frontier is parametric or non-parametric. Also, for individual efficiency scores the methods yield very similar results. The differences are mainly to be found at the extreme ends of the size distributions. Since the non-parametric method envelops some of the smallest units by construction these will appear as efficient, while this will not be the case for the parametric frontier starting at the origin. However, the parametric frontier could also be specified to start outside the origin. The scale properties are different for the two approaches. Due to the method of a convex envelope, real economies of scale at large units will be difficult to detect, as is evident from looking at figure 1. In the parametric case, we found considerable economies to scale even at the output level of the largest observed units. Since we placed more restrictions on the scale properties than strictly necessary (due to computational considerations), this difference should not be stressed unduly, but it reflects an inherent difference between non-parametric and parametric approaches. Our results differ from the findings in Ferrier and Lovell [1990] of similarity as regards scale properties, but not efficiency distributions, and are more in accordance with the overall impression in Bjurek et al. [1990] of the same structure being revealed by the method. The early contribution of Banker et al. [1986] found different scale properties and only similarities between efficiency distributions if the constant returns property of the econometrically estimated cost function was imposed on the DEA calculations. It seems safe to conclude that no general pattern has emerged yet as to the outcome of the two methods, so we can only appeal to further investigations for some general insights to appear.

Notes

1. I am indebted to three referees for forcing me to improve significantly the quality of the study. Any remaining shortcomings are, of course, my responsibility.
2. The non-parametric case is studied in more detail in Førsund and Hernaes [1990].
3. The staircase approach of Henry Tulkens, (see Deprins et al., [1984]) gives an even more pessimistic picture of the best practice, but the production sets are not convex. See, however, Bøs [1988] for arguments against convex production sets.
4. If both E_1 and E_2 are calculated for VRS technology the average scale property for inefficient units, i.e., the average scale elasticity over the frontier from J to L in Fig. 1, can also be determined using the rule in Førsund and Hjalmarsson [1979b, 1987]:

   $E_1 > E_2 \Rightarrow$ increasing average returns to scale.

   $E_1 < E_2 \Rightarrow$ decreasing average returns to scale.
5. The meaning of start is not necessarily small output levels. A starting facet may extend to high output values.
6. The linear regressions gave standard errors of less than two percent of predicted mean wage levels (see Førsund and Hernaes [1990] for further details).
7. The spread in the values for the ferries seemed unreasonably high compared with the difference in physical capacity, and the efficiency scores varied between the same units for the different value definitions.
8. Such corner solutions are a possible feature of the LP-formulation and comparable to getting wrong signs when estimating stochastic frontiers. In Albriktsen and Førsund [1990], applying the same model to building industry, the same type of problem is encountered with the capital parameter obtaining zero value.
9. The correlation between the input-corrected pure scale measure, E_4, and size is one since all units are below optimal scale. The decrease to the value 0.87 is due to technical inefficiency being part of the gross scale measure.
10. The possible slacks in input and output constraints in the non-parametric model are disregarded in this interpretation.
11. As pointed out in Section 2 a more general specification like the translog is logically a better choice when comparing scale properties. However, within our deterministic LP-formulation the translog specification did not perform so satisfactorily with respect to general economic implications.

References

Afriat, S.N. (1972). "Efficiency estimation of production functions." *International Economic Review* 13, pp. 568–598.

Aigner, D.J. and S.F. Chu. (1968). "On estimating the industry production function." *American Economic Review* 58, pp. 226–239.

Albriktsen, R.O. and F.R. Førsund. (1990). "A productivity study of the Norwegian building industry." *The Journal of Productivity Analysis* 2, pp. 53–66.

Ali, A.I.. (1989). "Computational aspects of data envelopment analysis." Paper presented at a conference on *New Uses of DEA in Management*, Austin Texas.

Banker, R.D., R.F. Conrad, and R.P. Strauss. (1986). "A comparative application of data envelopment analysis and translog methods: An illustrative study of hospital production." *Management Science* 32, pp. 30–44.

Banker, R.D., A. Charnes, W.W. Cooper, and A. Maindiratta. (1988). "A comparison of DEA and translog estimates of production frontiers using simulated observations from a known technology." In A. Dogramaci and R. Färe (eds.), *Applications of modern production theory: Efficiency and Productivity.* Boston: Kluwer Academic Publishers.

Banker, R.D., V.M. Gadh, and W.L. Gorr. (1990). "A Monte Carlo comparison of two production frontier estimation methods: Corrected ordinary least squares and Data Envelopment Analysis." Paper presented at a conference of New Uses of DEA in Management, Austin, Texas.

Bjurek, H., L. Hjalmarsson, and F.R. Førsund. (1990). "Deterministic parametric and non parametric estimation of efficiency in service production. A comparison." *Journal of Econometrics* 46, pp. 213–227.

Bös, D. (1988). "Recent theories on public enterprise economics." *European Economic Review* 32, pp. 409–414.

Charnes, A., W.W. Cooper, and E. Rhodes. (1978). "Measuring the Efficiency of Decision Making Units." *European Journal of Operational Research* 2 (6), pp. 429–444.

Charnes, A., W.W. Cooper, and T. Sueyoshi. (1988). "A goal programming/constrained regression review of the Bell System breakup." *Management Science* 34, pp. 1–26.

Deprins, D., L. Simar, and H. Tulkens. (1984). "Measuring Labor-Efficiency in Post Offices." In M. Marchand, P. Pestieau, and H. Tulkens (eds.), *The Performance of Public Enterprises: Concept and Measurement.* Amsterdam: North Holland Publishing Co.

Farrell, M.J. (1957). "The measurement of productive efficiency." *Journal of Royal Statistical Society, Series A*, 120 (III), pp. 253–281.

Ferrier, G.D. and C.A.K. Lovell. (1990). "Measuring cost efficiency in banking: Econometric and linear programming evidence." *Journal of Econometrics* 46, pp. 229–245.

Førsund, F.R. and E. Hernaes. (1990). "Ferry transport in Norway: An application of DEA analysis." *Working Paper No. 45,* Centre for Applied Research, Department of Economics, University of Oslo.

Førsund, F.R. and L. Hjalmarsson. (1974). "On the measurement of productive efficiency." *Swedish Journal of Economics* 76, pp. 141–154.

Førsund, F.R. and L. Hjalmarsson. (1979a). "Frontier production functions and technical progress: A study of general milk processing in Swedish dairy plants." *Econometrica* 47, pp. 883–900.

Førsund, F.R. and L. Hjalmarsson. (1979b). "Generalized Farrell measures of efficiency: An application to milk processing in Swedish dairy plants." *Economic Journal* 89, pp. 294–315.

Førsund, F.R. and L. Hjalmarsson. (1987). "Analyses of Industrial Structure: A putty-clay approach." *The Industrial Institute for Economic and Social Research.* Stockholm: Almqvist & Wiksell International.

Petersen, N.C. and O. Olesen. (1989). "Chance constrained efficiency evaluation." *Publications from Department of Management*, No. 9, Odense University.

Sengupta, J.K. (1987). "Data envelopment analysis for efficiency measurement in the stochastic case." *Computers and Operations Research* 14, pp. 117–129.

The Journal of Productivity Analysis, 3, 45–65 (1992)

Allowing for Inefficiency in Parametric Estimation of Production Functions for Urban Transit Firms

BERNARD THIRY
Université de Liège and CIRIEC, Liège

HENRY TULKENS
CORE, Université Catholique de Louvain and Facultés Universitaires Saint-Louis, Bruxelles

Abstract

Efficient versus inefficient observations are first identified and evaluated numerically by the nonparametric free disposal hull (FDH) method. Next, parametric production frontiers are obtained by means of estimating translog production functions through OLS applied to the subset of efficient observations only. Technical progress is included at both stages. Monthly data from three urban transit firms in Belgium, to which this two-stage technique is applied, show widely varying degrees of efficiency over time and across firms, and much less technical progress than standard (i.e., non frontier) econometric estimates suggest.

1. Motivation, methodology and antecedents

In this article, we wish to experiment with, and further develop, a method designed to account for the possibility of technically inefficient behavior, in the process of estimating the parameters of production functions with technical progress.

Our motivation comes from both institutional and historical characteristics of three urban transit firms in Belgium that we have encountered in the course of a wider study of these firms' economic performance (Thiry and Tulkens [1988]). The three companies under review are public enterprises run by autonomous local management under the supervision of the Ministry of Communications. For many years, this supervision has been rather loose and substantially increasing deficits were incurred, covered by the overall State budget without much public discussion. Towards the end of 1982, however, the Belgian government drastically changed its policy, imposing severe financial constraints on these firms and reorganizing their top management.

These facts suggest that for these firms, at least until the imposed changes, the usual assumption that they operated on their production function, that is, on the boundary of their production set, can be questioned. However, prevailing methods of estimating production functions do rest on this assumption. Hence, the parameter estimates they yield are bound to be biased. Moreover, if one is willing to hypothesize that the 1982 changes may have had an impact on the degree of efficiency on the firms' operations, the production function estimation procedure should allow for possible changes over time in this respect.

Considerations of this nature are clearly at the origin of the literature on production frontiers.[1] This literature proposes several parametric estimation methods allowing for inefficiency that differ not only in their statistical properties, but more fundamentally, in the postulates on the basis of which they construct a frontier from observed data. These postulates essentially bear on properties of the boundary of the production set underlying the production function to be estimated.

Farrell [1957], for instance, postulates that the frontier be the boundary of the *free-disposal convex hull* of the data set, thereby implying that the production set of the firm be a convex polyhedron (containing the origin) in the input-output space. On the other hand, Aigner and Chu [1968] and others using so-called parametric methods, postulate that the frontier be a continuous function, the value of whose parameters are estimated so as to approximate the data set in some (appropriately defined) closest way. Here, the underlying postulate is that the production set of the firm be a *set whose boundary is smooth and representable by a parametric function*.[2]

As the production set of a firm is essentially an unknown for the outside observer of its inputs and outputs, one may feel that both of these approaches operate on the basis of rather strong assumptions on the structure and shape of this set. Weaker assumptions have been sought, and in Deprins, Simar and Tulkens [1984], it was proposed that a firm's production frontier be assumed to be simply the boundary of what can be called the *free-disposal hull*[3] (FDH) of the data set (including the origin).

Formally, let $Y_o \subset R_+^{p+q}$ denote the data set, whose typical element—called an observation—is (x^k, u^k), $x^k \in R^q$, $u^k \in R^p$, $k = 1, \ldots, n$, with x^k a vector of inputs, u^k a vector of outputs, and n the number of observations. The free-disposal hull of Y_o is the set defined as

$$Y_{FDH} = \left\{ \begin{bmatrix} u \\ x \end{bmatrix} \in R_+^{p+q} \,\middle|\, \begin{bmatrix} u \\ x \end{bmatrix} = \begin{bmatrix} u^k \\ x^k \end{bmatrix} + \sum_{j=1}^{q} \mu_j \begin{bmatrix} 0^p \\ e_j^q \end{bmatrix} - \sum_{i=1}^{p} \nu_i \begin{bmatrix} e_i^p \\ 0^q \end{bmatrix}, \right.$$

$$\left. (x^k, u^k) \in Y_o \cup \left\{ \begin{bmatrix} 0^p \\ 0^q \end{bmatrix} \right\}; \ \mu_j \geq 0, \ \nu_i \geq 0, \ j = 1, \ldots, p, \ i = 1, \ldots, p \right\},$$

where e_i^h is the ith column of the p-dimensional identity matrix, e_j^h the jth column of the q-dimensional identity matrix, and 0^p and 0^q are, respectively, the p and q-dimensional null vectors. This set is generated as the union of all orthants, positive in x and negative in u, whose origin is an observation (i.e., an element of Y_o).

Here, no convexity assumption is made, nor is it assumed that the boundary be representable by a continuous parametric function. Instead, we only assume, in the terms of Shephard [1970], free disposability of the inputs and outputs.[4] Hence the "free disposal hull" terminology used here to designate the constructed set.

Each of the three approaches (Farrell's, parametric, and free-disposal hull) yields a partitioning of the data set Y_o into two subsets: one containing the efficient observations only, the other containing the inefficient ones. The essence of the methodology on which this article rests is to estimate production functions and technical progress *from the efficient observations only.* This is what we do in sections 3 and 4.

For a given data set, the partitioning into subsets of efficient versus inefficient observations is dependent upon the assumptions made regarding the shape of the production set. A choice has thus to be made in this respect, for which the postulates just expounded provide a criterion.

As we have no reason to postulate convexity for the production sets of our transit firms, we shall not use the Farrell approach. On the other hand, we shall also refrain from using any of the parametric methods,[5] and this essentially because the specification itself of the functional form more often than not happens to be the unique reason for declaring an observation inefficient—typically when this observation becomes efficient under an alternative specification.[6] In other words, with parametric methods the efficiency criterion is inextricably mixed up with the selection of the appropriate functional form. With the two-step procedure advocated in this article, this confusion is avoided: one instrument is used for efficiency measurement and another one for parameter estimation.

While the point just made applies to both stochastic and deterministic parametric methods, there is a further drawback concerning deterministic methods, namely the intrinsic property of a priori restricting the number of observations that can be declared efficient, as pointed out in Førsund, Lovell, and Schmidt [1980].

Finally, and more fundamentally, we think that the free disposal criterion is closest to the concept of inefficiency itself: an observation which is dominated by another one in the free disposal sense (i.e., by one that uses less input to produce more output) is declared inefficient on the sole basis of the amounts of resources involved, irrespective of formal considerations such as convexity or functional form. We shall therefore postulate free disposal hull (FDH) production sets for the three companies to be analyzed, and henceforth call the procedure by which efficient versus inefficient data are sorted out in the data sets, the FDH method.[7]

In section 3, the data sets restricted to the efficient observations will be used to estimate a-temporal (or intertemporal) production functions. In section 4, they will be used to estimate temporal production functions, after having presented an extension of the FDH approach to allow for the possibility of technical progress.

The idea of estimating a production function from efficient observations only was already used by Kurz and Manne [1963]. However, the particular way in which they did it was subjected to detailed criticism by Johansen [1972], not so much for reasons of principle but rather because he showed that the procedure used by Kurz and Manne for selecting the efficient observations is valid only if the labor input is equal to unity in *all* the observations, a feature that is peculiar to the data set they were using. Johansen then makes the constructive suggestion of using, for the general case, ratios of input amounts *per unit of output*. While this is indeed an improvement towards more generality, it remains nevertheless restrictive in two other respects: first, only single output processes allow for constructing such ratios (with several outputs, aggregation would be necessary, entailing other biases in its own right); second, only under constant returns to scale does the dominance criterion, when applied to these ratios, correctly identify inefficiency.

Put in its proper historical perspective, this article's contribution to this methodology is thus threefold: (1) It frees the identification of efficient behavior from limitations on the number of outputs and/or inputs, as well as from assumptions as to returns to scale;[8] (2) it extends the FDH method to the combined identification of efficiency *and* of technical progress; (3) it proposes a two-stage method for estimating production characteristics from efficient observations only.

2. The data

Our data are monthly observations on quantities of output produced and quantities of inputs used by three urban transit firms in Belgium: the Société de Transports Intercommunaux de Bruxelles (STIB), the Société de Transports Intercommunaux de Liège (STIL), and the Société de Transport Intercommunaux de Charleroi (STIC). All three companies operate buses; STIB also operates tramways and a subway. The observation periods cover nine years (from January 1977 to December 1985) for STIB and seven years (from January 1979 to December 1985) for STIL and STIC. We thus have 108 observations for STIB and 84 for STIL and STIC.

Output, denoted by Y, is measured by the number of seats-kms monthly supplied (i.e., the number of seats available on all vehicles used multiplied by the number of kilometers travelled by all vehicles). This is a fairly standard measure of the output of mass transit firms. Thus, we do not take passengers-kms (these were unfortunately not available to us on a monthly basis), our efficiency and production function measures are to be seen as bearing on the production of transportation *capacity* rather than of actual transportation of passengers. Our choice is also justified by the observation that the relation between capacity supplied and passengers transported is an issue of adequacy between supply and demand—i.e., of *effectiveness*, rather than one of efficiency in the precise sense considered in production theory.

The output is assumed to be produced by means of three inputs: labor, H, measured by the total number of hours worked per month; energy, E, measured by the monthly number of kwhs (or equivalent) used; vehicles, PV, measured by the total number of seats-vehicles in the company's fleet, i.e., the number of seats available on all vehicles multiplied by the number of vehicles available.

Data on output and inputs are plotted on the three charts of figure 1. STIB is the largest company, STIL is middle-sized, and STIC is the smallest. Overall, quantities of output, labor and energy are quite variable. One may easily identify seasonal variations. Strikes explain the exceptionally small quantities observed during a few months. Seats-vehicles is the least variable input. Each company has known quite a different evolution of its fleet size: a slight decrease for STIC, a slight increase for STIL, and for STIB an increase from 1977 to 1981 followed by a decrease from 1983 to 1985.

3. A-temporal production functions

3.1. OLS on the full data sets

We first estimate a production function $Y = f(H, E, PV)$ for each one of the three companies using ordinary least squares. These should serve as benchmarks for our subsequent estimations. Choosing the translog specification,[9] namely

$$\log Y = \alpha_o + \sum_{i=1}^{3} \alpha_i \log X_i + \sum_{i=1}^{3} \alpha_{ii}(\log X_i)^2 + \sum_{i=1}^{3} \sum_{j>i} \alpha_{ij} \log X_i \log X_j$$

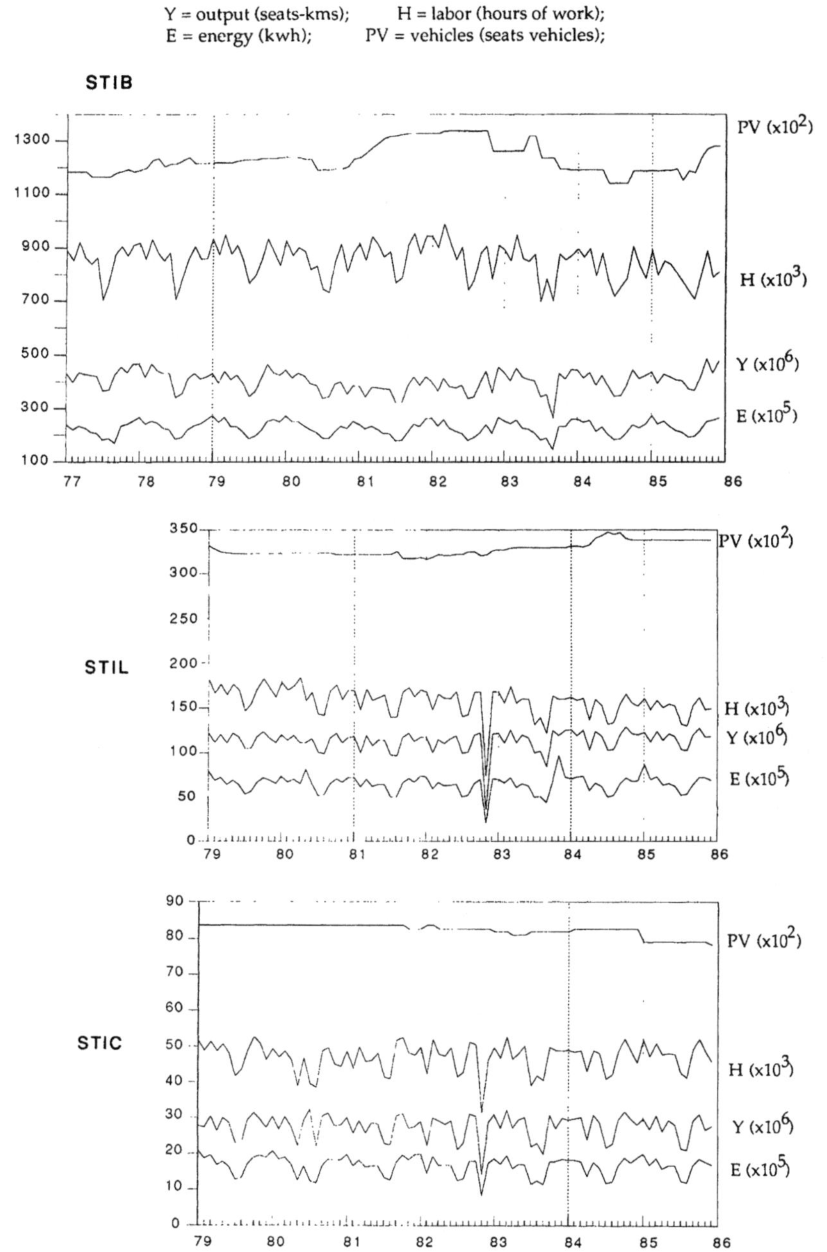

Figure 1. Output and input data for the three companies. January 1977 (or 1979)–December 1986.

with $X_1 = H$, $X_2 = E$, and $X_3 = PV$, OLS yields for the parameter estimates appearing in the columns labeled (1) in Table 1 below. We note that:

1. Judging by the value of the R^2 coefficients, the estimations provide a fairly good fit of the data.
2. The skewness coefficient of the distribution of the residuals[10] is significantly different from zero for the estimates pertaining to two of the three companies (STIL and STIC). This suggests an asymmetry due to a stronger weight of the negative residuals (i.e., those corresponding to observations that lie inside the production set determined by the estimated function).
3. In two cases (STIB and STIC), a negative value is obtained for the estimate (at the mean values of the inputs) of the partial elasticity of output with respect to the input *PV* (seats-vehicles). This contradicts production theory.[11] Note however that one cannot reject the hypothesis that this partial elasticity of output is constantly zero in the case of STIC.
4. The values (similarly computed at the mean values of the inputs) of the elasticity of output with respect to *H* (labor) differ noticeably across the three companies (.330 for STIB, .582 for STIL, .704 for STIC). This fact is not easily reconciled with casual observation, at least for the STIL and STIC companies, because these two do not differ much, neither in the types of vehicles used, nor in their labor practices; moreover, the two cities have a fairly comparable topographic structure.
5. The evaluations (at the mean values of the inputs) of the scale elasticity vary widely across the three companies: .228 for STIB (the largest company), 2.251 for STIL (middle-sized), and .332 for STIC (the smallest).

3.2. *Filtering the inefficient observations out of the data sets*

For the reasons explained in section 1, we now introduce the FDH method for eliminating from the data set of each company those observations that can be declared inefficient according to the criterion of free-disposal dominance. We briefly sketch out here how the method operates.[12]

For expositional ease, consider the case where $p = q = 1$. Then, for any observed vector (x^k, u^k), define the following subset of Y_o:

$$D(x^k, u^k) = \left\{ \begin{bmatrix} u^k \\ x^k \end{bmatrix} \right\} \cup \left\{ \begin{bmatrix} u \\ x \end{bmatrix} \in Y_o \,\middle|\, \begin{bmatrix} u \\ x \end{bmatrix} = \begin{bmatrix} u^k \\ x^k \end{bmatrix} - \mu \begin{bmatrix} 0 \\ 1 \end{bmatrix} + \nu \begin{bmatrix} 1 \\ 0 \end{bmatrix}, \mu > 0, \nu > 0 \right\},$$

i.e., the set of observations consisting of the union of the *k*th observation itself and of the observations that strictly dominate it, both in input and output.

Table 1. Parameters of production functions without trend.

Independent Variables	Param-eters	STIB		STIL		STIC	
		(1)	(2)	(1)	(2)	(1)	(2)
Intercept	α_0	87.470	795.574	−2,093.946	−1,761.264	−1,998.745	−1,347.008
		(0.24)	(1.26)	(−1.98)*	(−1.64)	(−1.66)	(−1.13)
Log H	α_1	95.788	−51.058	314.715	248.050	−111.980	−134.024
		(3.10)***	(−0.93)	(2.95)***	(2.32)**	(−1.41)	(−1.81)
Log E	α_2	−24.201	32.124	−179.213	−142.307	77.382	78.161
		(−1.20)	(1.04)	(−2.79)***	(−2.20)**	(1.97)*	(2.16)**
Log PV	α_3	−89.829	−122.135	310.567	267.512	455.692	335.525
		(−1.47)	(−1.40)	(1.76)*	(1.49)	(1.75)*	(1.34)
Log^2 H	α_{11}	3.896	5.163	−7.070	−6.475	4.359	1.979
		(2.86)***	(3.17)***	(−3.07)***	(−2.75)***	(1.46)	(0.67)
Log^2 E	α_{22}	−0.024	−0.236	−2.177	−2.192	−0.583	−0.884
		(−0.06)	(−0.63)	(−2.87)***	(−2.30)**	(−0.71)	(−1.13)
Log^2 PV	α_{33}	7.206	4.587	−11.798	−10.545	−25.617	−20.627
		(2.54)**	(1.30)	(−1.59)	(−1.40)	(−1.78)*	(−1.53)
Log H Log PV	α_{13}	−12.875	−1.996	−25.239	−19.709	5.771	10.680
		(−5.22)***	(−0.51)	(−2.81)***	(−2.17)**	(0.75)	(1.63)
Log E Log PV	α_{23}	5.678	2.493	15.197	12.063	−3.943	−5.483
		(3.86)***	(1.22)	(2.80)***	(2.16)**	(−1.02)	(−1.67)*
Log H Log E	α_{12}	−3.008	−3.886	7.495	7.175	−2.313	−0.287
		(−2.75)***	(−3.10)***	(2.89)***	(2.49)**	(−0.78)	(−0.10)
$e_H^{(3)}$		0.330	0.602	0.582	0.684	0.704	0.626
		[12.06]***	[15.14]***	[13.99]***	[17.03]***	[10.69]***	[9.56]***
$e_E^{(3)}$		0.467	0.341	0.234	0.240	0.284	0.411
		[24.27]***	[20.54]***	[5.43]***	[5.56]***	[9.18]***	[12.32]***
$e_{PV}^{(3)}$		−0.569	0.149	1.435	1.532	−0.656	0.084
		[13.29]***	[1.51]	[20.97]***	[20.02]***	[1.14]	[3.59]**
E.S.$^{(4)}$		0.228	1.092	2.251	2.456	0.332	1.121
R^2		0.784	0.928	0.974	0.987	0.932	0.971
Adj R^2		0.764	0.909	0.971	0.985	0.924	0.966
Numb. obs.		108	44	84	61	84	56
D.F.		98	34	74	51	74	46
$\sqrt{b_1}^{(5)}$		−0.280	−0.256	−0.489**	−0.408	−0.613**	−0.351
$F^{(6)}$		6.679***	8.203***	23.960***	20.446***	5.199***	3.597***

Figures in parentheses are t-statistics *denotes significance at a 10% level
**denotes significance at a 5% level
***denotes significance at a 1% level

Figures between brackets are F-statistics designed to test the significance of partial output elasticities.

(1) Regressions run over all the observations
(2) Regressions run over efficient observations only
(3) Partial output elasticities evaluated at the mean values of inputs
(4) Elasticity of scale evaluated at the mean values of inputs
(5) Skewness coefficients
(6) F-statistics designed to test the Cobb-Douglas function as a constrained version of the translog functions

If this set is a singleton, in which case it necessarily consists of observation k only, then the latter is free-disposal undominated, and hence is declared *efficient*.[13]

On the contrary, if the set $D(x^k, u^k)$ comprises more elements than just the kth observation, the latter is free-disposal dominated, and hence is declared *inefficient*. An example is given in figure 2, where the set $D(x^k, u^k)$ consists of the elements a, b, c and (x^k, u^k).

A measure of the degree of (in)efficiency of an observation is naturally provided by the distance between the observation and the boundary of the FDH production set constructed on the basis of all efficient observations. However, as the figure suggests, there are many ways to compute this distance: in units of output, in units of input, or by some combination of both. Whatever choice is made in this respect, the distance can be converted into an expression that we denote $E_d(x^k, u^k)$, taking values on the (0, 100] scale, with $E_d = 100$ for an efficient observation, and $E_d < 100$ for an inefficient one.[14]

Results of these FDH efficiency computations, done for each of the companies separately, are exhibited graphically on the three charts of Figure 3. We note that:

1. In the case of STIB, 64 out of the 108 monthly observations are declared inefficient (for both measures in output and in input; only the output measure appears on this and the other diagrams). They are concentrated in the middle of the observation period, which suggests that the boundary of the production set is jointly determined by the early and late observations.

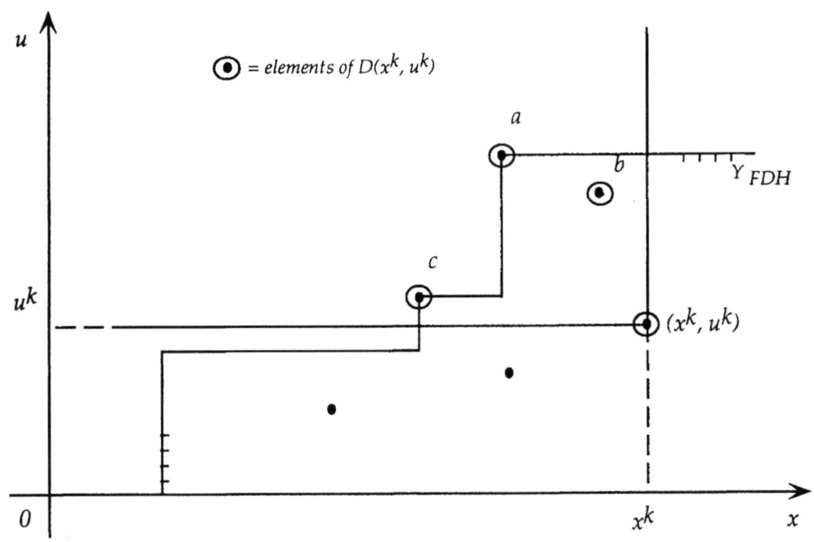

Figure 2. Observation (x^k, u^k) and its associated set $D(x^k, u^k)$.

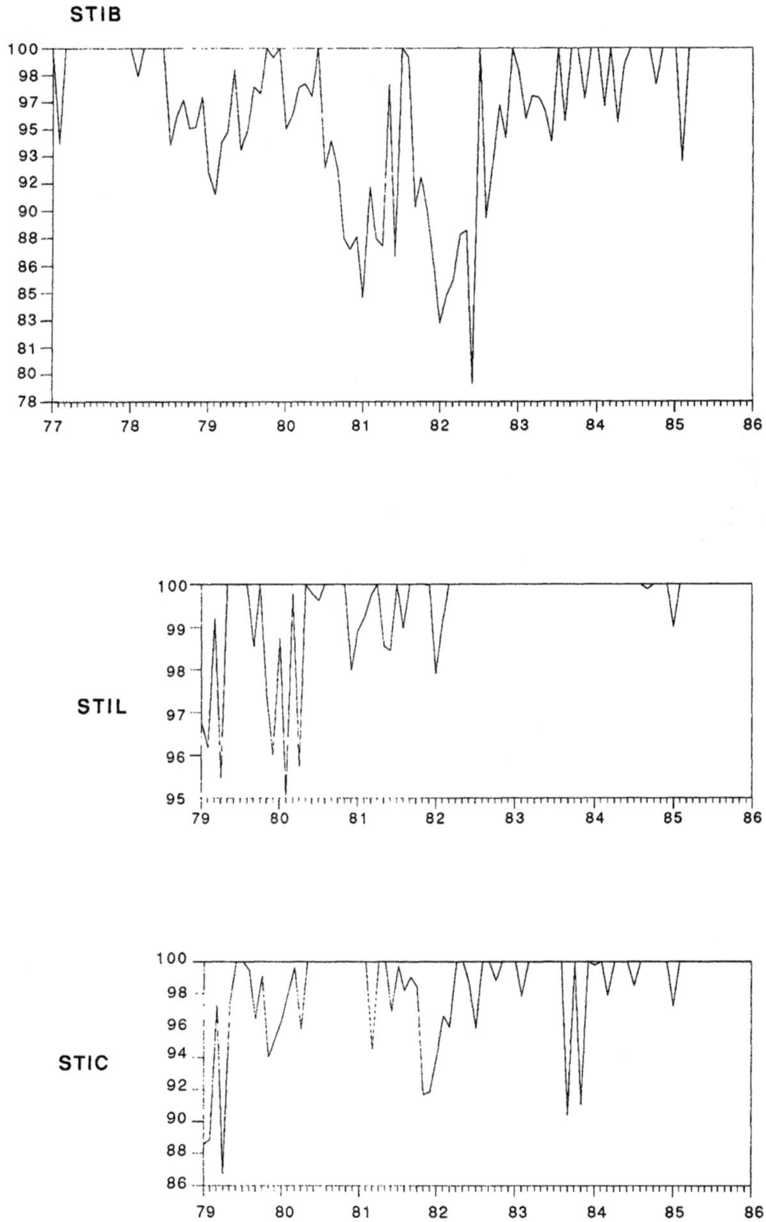

Figure 3. Intertemporal FDH efficiency measures (in output) for the three companies. January 1977 (or 1979)–December 1986.

2. In the case of STIL, only 25 out of the 84 observations made are (output-) inefficient (23 are inefficient both in output and in inputs). The inefficiencies are concentrated in the first half of the observation period, and many such observations are dominated by posterior ones. This indicates that the boundary of the production set is determined by the operation of the firm during the second half of the period.
3. In the case of STIC, 36 out of the 84 observations are (output-) inefficient (but only 28 are output- and inputwise). Here, the inefficiencies are spread across the entire period.

Overall, the efficiency performances of the three firms are quite different. STIL performs best, in terms of having both the lowest number of inefficient situations and the minimum degree of (in)efficiency, which is 95 in February 1980. STIC comes next in both respects, with a minimum efficiency degree of 87 in April 1979, and STIB is last with the worst situation in June 1982 for which the efficiency degree is only 79. Notice that the efficiency degree can be interpreted as the output level that a firm achieves as a percentage of the output of the (most) dominating situation, where by construction less of all the inputs was used. Thus, for example, a 79 means an output that is 21 percent below the output that the firm has actually achieved at some other time *with less of all the inputs*.

To proceed now to the re-estimation of production functions to describe the production frontiers in parametric terms, let us call the free-disposal undominated (FDU) data set the subset of Y_o that consists only of the observations declared efficient. This set is thus the result of our filtering of the original data sets from their inefficient observations, by means of the free-disposal criterion.

3.3. OLS on the FDU data sets

From the FDU data set just identified, we now re-estimate translog specifications[15] of the function $Y = f(H, E, PV)$ for each of the three companies separately, using OLS. We obtain for the parameters the results reported in columns labelled (2) in Table 1.

Referring to the five comments we made on the previous estimates, we now note that:

1. The R^2 and adjusted R^2 coefficients have increased in all cases, and most notably so for the STIB company, for which it was the lowest with the previous estimate. The quality of the adjustments, in terms of the explanatory power, is now very good but we cannot really compare with the R^2 obtained with full data sets because, by dropping inefficient points, we reduced the variation to be explained.
2. The two cases (STIL and STIC) of significantly negative skewness for the distribution of the residuals have now disappeared, the new coefficients being now insignificant. This suggests that the bias in the previous estimate was due to the now deleted inefficient observations.
3. The two cases (STIB and STIC) of negative (mean) values for the partial elasticity of output with respect to the seats-vehicles input (PV) have now disappeared. This reconciles our estimations with the predictions from theory.

4. The (mean) values of the elasticity of output with respect to *H* (labor), which were much different between the companies, are now quite close to each other, ranging between .602 (STIB) and .684 (STIL). As to the elasticity of output with respect to *PV* (seats-vehicles), substantial differences remain, but this may partly be explained by the fact that output does not react in the same way to a change in the average number of seats per vehicle and a change in the number of vehicles.[16]
5. All companies now exhibit increasing returns to scale, only slightly so for STIB and STIC, and even more strongly than before for STIL.

It also appears, finally, that the new estimates are closest to the previous ones in the case of STIL. This is explained, in part, by the fact that only 23 inefficient observations have been deleted here (out of 84), whereas in the case of STIB for instance, 64 such observations (out of 108) were filtered out. More generally, one may note that the number of deleted observations does not prevent re-estimating translog functions. If this number were large, the number of degrees of freedom might decrease excessively and even become negative. Such a situation is however least likely to occur with the FDH criterion, compared to all other nonparametric techniques for evaluating efficiency (as surveyed in Seiford and Thrall [1990], because these techniques always yield much less efficient observations, as reported in Tulkens [1991].

To conclude, we feel that the filtering of the data set by the free disposal criterion improves the economic quality of the estimations, in the sense that estimated production characteristics are more consistent with the predictions of economic theory. As the filtering rests on considerations that pertain to an essential characteristic of the production function (i.e., the fact of being the boundary of a set), we think it can be recommended as a complementary technique in the estimation of parametric production functions. It may also be seen as an alternative to the prevailing technique used for estimating stochastic production frontiers—namely the one proposed by Aigner, Lovell, and Schmidt [1977]—since account is taken of both inefficiency and classical noise (i.e., random components) in the data.

4. Temporal production functions with technical progress

4.1. Recognizing the time dimension

It was made clear in the previous section that free-disposal assumptions are sufficient to construct a production set, including its boundary, from observed data on inputs and outputs. When the data set extends over time—as is the case in our current application—it is natural to wonder, however, whether shifts of this boundary do not occur during the observation period, and in particular outward shifts, which are often taken to represent technical progress.

In this section, we extend our enquiry in this direction: on one hand, we want to identify shifts of the boundary of our assumed FDH production sets; on the other, we wish to estimate, on this basis, the parameters of efficient production functions that are allowed to shift over time.

4.2. Identifying shifts over time of the boundary of the FDH production set

Let the index $t = 1, \ldots, n$ denote the successive moments of time at which observations (x^k, u^k) of a given firm are made. Since only one observation of the firm is made at each t, the superscript k used so far can be given identical values as the time index.

When the time dimension is so recognized and the data set treated as a time series,[17] the issue of determining the firm's production set from observed data may be dealt with *sequentially*, that is, at each instant t, on the sole basis of the observations made up until that time (and not after); thus, from only the observations (x^k, u^k) such that $k \leq t$. The data set, denoted Y_o so far, is then to be considered sequentially too, i.e., by defining at each point in time t the subset of observations

$$Y_o^t = \{(x^k, u^k) \in Y_o \,|\, k \leq t\},$$

and thereby generating n successive observations sets Y_o^t, $t = 1, \ldots, n$, with the earlier ones being nested in the more recent ones.

For each one of these sets $Y^{t,o}$, $t = 1, \ldots, n$, the last observation (i.e., (x^k, u^k) where k equals t) is free-disposal undominated, and thus declared *sequentially efficient*, if the subset of $Y^{t,o}$ defined as

$$D^S(x^t, u^t) = \left\{\begin{bmatrix} u^t \\ x^t \end{bmatrix}\right\} \cup \left\{\begin{bmatrix} u \\ x \end{bmatrix} \in Y_o^t \,\middle|\, \begin{bmatrix} u \\ x \end{bmatrix} = \begin{bmatrix} u^t \\ x^t \end{bmatrix} - \mu \begin{bmatrix} 0 \\ 1 \end{bmatrix} + \nu \begin{bmatrix} 1 \\ 0 \end{bmatrix}, \mu > 0, \nu > 0\right\}$$

contains no other element than this observation itself. Otherwise, the observation is called *sequentially inefficient*. Indeed, the set just defined reveals that there is at least one earlier observation which dominates the last one under consideration. Except for the temporal dimension, this is a straightforward application of the notions developed in the previous section.

However—and this is a second and more novel aspect of this temporal extension—another form of dominance may also be identified. Consider a sequentially efficient observation at some time t. Among the (earlier) observations it dominates, there may exist some which were declared efficient, because of being undominated *at the time they were made* (see, for instance, observation $t = 8$ on figure 4, which dominates observations $t = 3$ and 6).

When an observation has the double property of being sequentially efficient *and* of dominating observations previously declared efficient, one must logically conclude that the boundary of the production set has locally shifted outwards, in other words, that local *technical progress* has occurred. This is illustrated by the cross-hatched area on figure 4.

The condition for an observation (x^t, u^t) to exhibit technical progress in this sense—let us call it *FDH technical progress*—may be expressed formally, in term which are somewhat symmetric to those used for determining FDH efficiency. Indeed, this condition is that the set

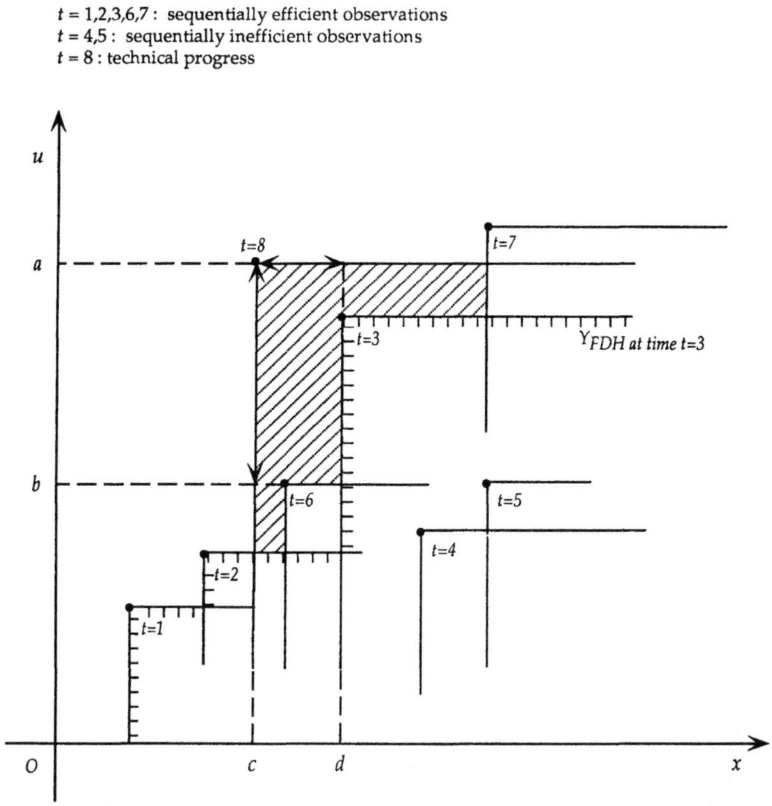

Figure 4. Sequential FDH production sets and technical progress.

$$P(x^t, u^t) = \left\{\begin{bmatrix} u^t \\ x^t \end{bmatrix}\right\} \cup \left\{\begin{bmatrix} u \\ x \end{bmatrix} \in Y_o^t \,\middle|\, \begin{bmatrix} u \\ x \end{bmatrix} = \begin{bmatrix} u^t \\ x^t \end{bmatrix} + \mu \begin{bmatrix} 0 \\ 1 \end{bmatrix} - \nu \begin{bmatrix} 1 \\ 0 \end{bmatrix}, \right.$$

$$\left. \mu > 0,\ \nu > 0, \text{ and } D^S(x, u) = \left\{\begin{bmatrix} u \\ x \end{bmatrix}\right\}\right\}$$

contains at least one more element than the observation (x^t, u^t) itself. If this set is a singleton, the unique element being then necessarily $\{(x^t, u^t)\}$, there is no technical progress at time t even if (x^t, u^t) is efficient; see e.g., the case of $t = 7$ on figure 4. For $t = 8$ on the contrary, there is technical progress, because the set $P(x^8, u^8)$ consists of the observations $t = 8$, 3, and 6.

Moreover, a measure of the degree of FDH technical progress can be associated with an observation t. This measure is formulated in output terms as the ratio of the output u^t to the output u^l achieved by the observation (x^l, u^l) in $P(x^t, u^t)$ with the lowest input;[18] see the vertical distance indicated below observation $t = 8$ (measured as ab along the u axis), the observation l being the one made at time $t = 6$. In input terms, the degree of technical progress is similarly computed as the ratio of the input x^t to the input x^m reported in the observation (x^m, u^m) in $P(x^t, u^t)$ with the highest output;[19] see the horizontal distance to the right of $t = 8$ (measured as cd along the x axis).[20]

Results from such computations performed on the data of our three companies are exhibited graphically on the charts of figure 5. We note here that:

1. In general, the sequential method implies by construction that at least the first observation is always efficient, and the few following ones have a high probability of being so too, because of the paucity of the observation set in the early periods. A similar argument can be made also as to (FDH) technical progress when it is observed at early times: it may in fact be only that improvements in efficiency occurred.
2. For STIB, 60 observations are sequentially (output-)inefficient, 45 are efficient, and 4 exhibit technical progress. The inefficiencies occur again in the middle of the observation period, and they reach the same bottom level of 79 in June 1982. On the other hand, three out of the four cases of technical progress occur towards the end (the early case is negligible in view of the argument made in (1) above); the maximum level of these cases is 103.1.
3. In the case of STIL, the picture reveals only 6 cases of (output-)inefficiency—in sharp contrast with the 25 cases alleged previously—with a worst case of 98.4 in July 1985. There are 9 cases of technical progress, most of which occur (in rather low amounts during the first half of the entire period. Virtually no progress occurs after the middle of 1982. The overall picture is one of steady efficiency, but little progress.
4. In the case of STIC, the picture is rather mixed: 13 cases of inefficiency (with a worst level of 90.4 in September 1983), but also 18 cases of technical progress—the largest such number over the three companies—many of which occurring in the later months, and with levels reaching 104.4 both in May 1981 and in July 1983.

The overall behavior of the firms again appears to be quite different. But the evaluation of those behaviors from the efficiency point of view is to be modified, in comparison with our conclusions in the previous section, with a much more favorable judgment on the smallest two firms. On the other hand, the unfavorable judgment on STIB is confirmed, and actually reinforced since the sequential approach is less demanding than the intertemporal one used before.

As to technical progress, it is not completely absent, but is only really perceptible in the case of STIC, at least when measured with this method.

By eliminating from the data sets all observations declared sequentially inefficient, we get *sequentially FDU* data sets, on which production functions with technical change can be estimated free from inefficiency in the observations.

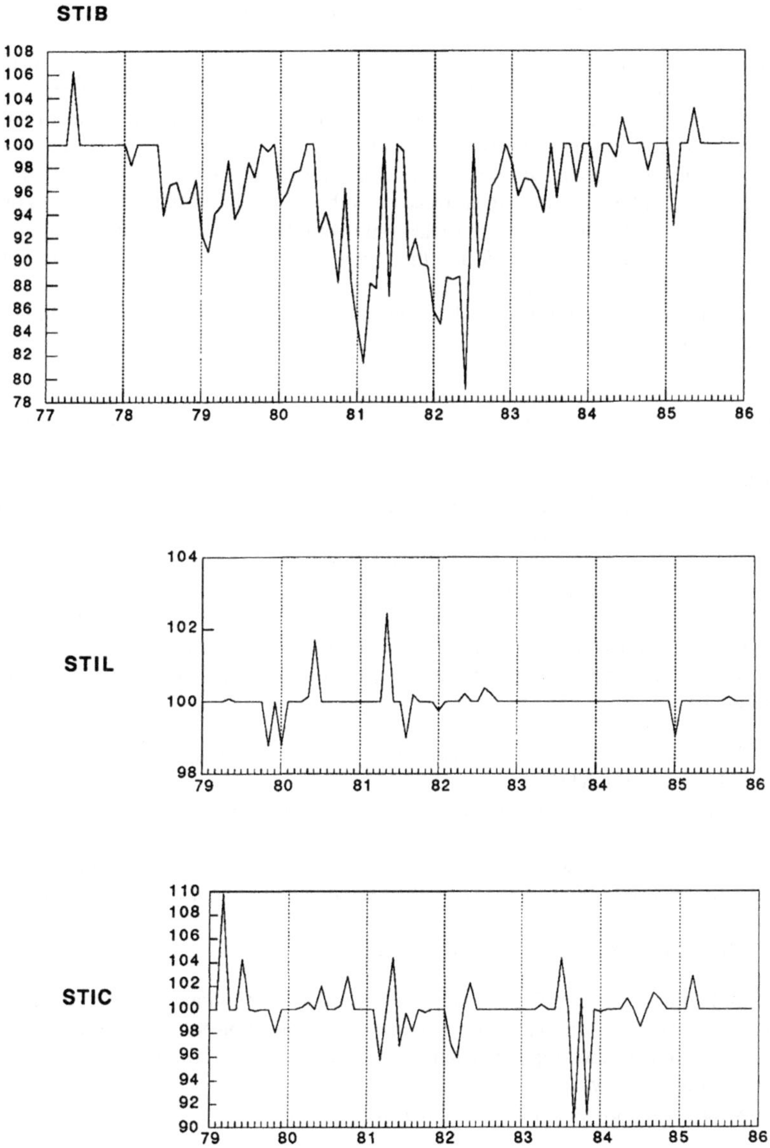

Figure 5. Sequential FDH efficiency and technical progress measures (in output). January 1977 (or 1979)–December 1986.

4.3. OLS with a trend, on the full and on the sequentially FDU data sets

Usually, estimates of production functions from time series include a trend for measuring technical progress. Proceeding in this way with translog specifications for the three companies, OLS yields the results reported in column (1) of table 2. Deleting the sequentially inefficient observations yields the results in column (2).

Before analyzing these results, we must point out that for each company we have estimated functions including either a simple linear trend or both linear and quadratic trends. In one case (STIB), trend coefficients were significant only with the latter specification, although in both of the other cases (STIL and STIC) the reverse was observed. Table 2 shows only the (in this sense) best specification for each company.

Considering the estimates on the full data sets and comparing them with those without trend (see table 1), we note that:

1. Trend coefficients are significant only in two cases (STIB and STIL): for STIL we observe a positive trend; for STIB we estimate a negative relationship between output and time from January 1977 until April 1981, and then a positive relationship. For the third company (STIC) we observe a positive, but not significant, trend coefficient.
2. The R^2 and adjusted R^2 coefficients have increased notably in the cases of STIB and STIL. This is completely consistent with the significance level of the trend coefficients.
3. In two cases (STIB and STIC), significantly negative skewness coefficients are obtained.
4. For STIB and STIC, the (mean) values of the elasticity e_{PV} of output with respect to the input *PV* have increased, although the elasticity is still negative in the case of STIB. This may be explained by collinearity between *PV* and the trend.[21]
5. Values of scale elasticity (at the mean of the data) are much higher for two companies (STIB and STIL).

Overall, the standard parametric method identifies some technical progress, over the whole period for STIL, and for STIB, over the recent years.

Moving to the results in column (2) of table 2, that is, when we restrict data sets to sequentially FDH efficient observations, and comparing these with the results of column (1), OLS estimates obtained for STIL and STIC appear to be almost unaffected. The fact that both sets of estimates are very close may be due to the very small number of observations deleted: 4 for STIL and 3 for STIC.

On the other hand, estimates for STIB are improved:

1. The R^2 and adjusted R^2 coefficients increase (as observed previously, this is due to the fact that the change in the data set has reduced the variation to be explained).
2. If the (mean) value of the output elasticity with respect to *PV* is still negative, it notably decreases in absolute value.
3. The skewness coefficient is no longer significantly negative.

We also observe that:

4. The (mean) value of the scale elasticity is not very close to one.
5. The relationship between output and time is still decreasing during the first half of the period and then increasing, but that both trend coefficients are now insignificant.

Table 2. Parameters of production functions with trend.

Independent Variables	Param-eters	STIB (1)	STIB (2)	STIL (1)	STIL (2)	STIC (1)	STIC (2)
Intercept	α_0	−272.636	664.591	−1,477.224	−1,387.744	−867.445	−1,500.192
		(0.78)	(1.07)	(−1.88)*	(−1.70)*	(−0.62)	(−1.07)
Log H	α_1	80.959	8.591	183.150	168.077	−93.702	−92.157
		(2.86)***	(0.17)	(2.26)**	(1.98)*	(−1.18)	(−1.18)
Log E	α_2	−23.594	−10.530	−95.000	−80.315	68.152	66.746
		(−1.28)	(−0.37)	(−1.95)*	(−1.53)	(1.73)*	(1.73)*
Log PV	α_3	−12.403	−107.435	216.797	194.811	196.629	337.633
		(−0.21)	(−1.22)	(1.65)	(1.42)	(0.64)	(1.10)
Log^2 H	α_{11}	1.985	4.381	−3.422	−2.863	3.878	3.359
		(1.54)	(2.58)**	(−1.93)*	(−1.47)	(1.31)	(1.15)
Log^2 E	α_{22}	−0.443	−0.448	−0.847	−0.377	−0.611	−0.817
		(−1.18)	(−1.14)	(−1.44)	(−0.45)	(−0.75)	(−1.01)
Log^2 PV	α_{33}	3.016	5.514	−8.242	−6.978	−10.870	−18.772
		(1.11)	(1.52)	(−1.49)	(−1.20)	(−0.64)	(−1.10)
Log H Log PV	α_{13}	−9.948	−7.615	−14.338	−12.562	4.313	4.363
		(−4.19)***	(−2.18)**	(−2.10)**	(−1.72)*	(0.56)	(0.58)
Log E Log PV	α_{23}	4.570	4.860	8.106	6.473	−3.262	−3.212
		(3.33)***	(2.48)**	(1.96)*	(1.40)	(−0.85)	(−0.85)
Log H Log E	α_{12}	−1.069	−2.262	3.114	2.075	−1.949	−1.310
		(−1.00)	(−1.86)*	(1.55)	(0.84)	(−0.66)	(−0.45)
t (coeff. multiplied by 10^2)	α_t	−0.356	−0.138	0.136	0.136	0.056	0.053
		(−4.69)***	(−1.56)	(7.83)***	(7.67)***	(1.59)	(1.50)
t^2 (coeff. multiplied by 10^4)	α_{tt}	0.338	0.130	—	—	—	—
		(4.92)***	(1.60)				
$e_H^{(3)}$		0.455	0.649	0.988	0.993	0.708	0.679
		[9.41]***	[8.16]***	[39.95]***	[35.33]***	[10.61]***	[10.87]***
$e_E^{(3)}$		0.378	0.344	0.004	0.010	0.295	0.310
		[14.90]***	[15.26]***	[1.05]	[1.04]	[9.07]***	[9.30]***
$e_{PV}^{(3)}$		−0.157	−0.015	0.891	0.848	0.312	0.038
		[4.81]***	[2.27]*	[10.11]***	[9.06]***	[1.35]	[1.61]
E.S.$^{(4)}$		0.676	0.993	1.883	1.851	1.315	1.027
R^2		0.827	0.911	0.986	0.986	0.934	0.938
Adj R^2		0.808	0.884	0.984	0.984	0.925	0.929
Numb. obs.		108	49	84	80	84	81
D.F.		96	37	73	69	73	70
$\sqrt{b_1}$ $^{(5)}$		−0.374**	−0.327	0.036	−0.040	−0.565***	−0.496***
$F^{(6)}$		3.737***	5.999***	28.492***	20.491***	4.512***	3.528***

Figures in parentheses are t-statistics *denotes significance at a 10% level
**denotes significance at a 5% level
***denotes significance at a 1% level
Figures between brackets are F-statistics designed to test the significance of partial output elasticities.
(1) Regressions run over all the observations
(2) Regressions run over efficient observations only
(3) Partial output elasticities evaluated at the mean values of inputs
(4) Elasticity of scale evaluated at the mean values of inputs
(5) Skewness coefficients
(6) F-statistics designed to test the Cobb–Douglas function as a constrained version of the translog functions

Of course, the stronger effect of filtering in the case of STIB is clearly due to the large number of observations deleted: 58.

On the issue of technical progress, its estimation based on trend coefficients in parametric functions do however clearly incorporate the evolutions of efficiency, as it appears from a comparison with the profiles of intertemporal FDH-efficiency measures of figure 3. The increases in efficiency for STIL and STIC transpire in their respective positive trend coefficients. In the case of STIB, the efficiency decrease in a first period, followed by an increase later on, concur with the quadratic convex form of the alleged technical progress there. This casts doubts on what is actually measured as technical progress in the parametric production functions estimates.

Let us point out finally that one may question the type of FDH filtering one should use: sequential or intertemporal? In favor of intertemporal filtering one may argue that trend coefficients are estimated by taking into account all the observations simultaneously and not sequentially. On the other hand, intertemporal filtering typically deletes more observations than sequential filtering because one observation may be first declared efficient with respect to past observations (that is, sequentially efficient), and be declared inefficient afterwards with respect to subsequent observations (and thus intertemporally inefficient). If one deletes such an intertemporally inefficient observation, it no longer plays a role in the production function estimation, and this is questionable. Note also that intertemporal filtering typically deletes more observations at the beginning of the period, and this may substantially affect the estimates of trend coefficients. In particular we observe such an impact for STIL and STIC: after deleting intertemporally inefficient observations, the trend coefficient estimate is insignificant for STIC and is reduced by half for STIL.

5. Conclusions

In this article, we estimate parametric production functions without assuming technically efficient behavior. To this effect, we used the method of filtering out from the data the observations that could be declared inefficient according to a criterion of free disposal dominance, and subsequently estimating the production functions by usual methods on the remaining efficient data. This procedure, already used in the literature for a-temporal production functions, was extended here to production functions with a trend, and based on an appropriate concept of sequential dominance.

Applying this to three urban transit companies in Belgium over the period 1977 (or 1979)–1985, we noticed first that technically inefficient behavior did indeed occur in these firms, sometimes to a large extent, and for periods of varying length. The three firms differ from one another substantially, though, in this respect. Most typically for the worst of them, the end of the year 1982 also appeared to be a time of drastic improvement.

Next, our estimates of parametric production functions on filtered out data sets did yield better results than usual methods in the sense that they are more consistent with the predictions of economic theory. They therefore seem to offer improved representations of the production frontier of the analyzed firms.

Finally, efficiency measures revealed that the usual parametric estimates of technical progress do reflect in this case both the temporal evolution of inefficiency and actual technical progress.

Acknowledgments

The authors express their thanks to Alexis Palm, Charles Nollet, Marie-Astrid Jamar and Philippe Vanden Eeckaut for their collaboration at various stages of this work. They are grateful to Léopold Simar, C. Knox Lovell, and especially the referees of this journal for their comments. The paper was presented at the European Meeting of the Econometric Society, Bologna, August, 1988, and at the 30th TIMS/ORSA Joint National Meeting, Philadelphia, October, 1990, as well as in seminars at Queen's University, Université de Montréal, Facultés Universitaires de Namur, CEPREMAP, Paris, and CORE, Louvain-la-Neuve. This research is part of two projects supported by the Belgian Ministry of Scientific Policy (Programmes d'actions concertées no. 84-89/61 with Université de Liége and no. 87-92/106 with CORE). Partial support from the Fonds de la Recherche Fondamentale Collective (convention no. 2.4528.88) is also acknowledged.

Notes

1. Excellent surveys of this literature are offered in Førsund, Lovell, and Schmidt [1980], Bauer [1990], and Seiford and Thrall [1990].
2. As mentioned in the survey paper by Førsund, Lovell, and Schmidt [1980] quoted above, the parametric methods further branch out into a deterministic approach (see, e.g., Deprins and Simar [1989] for a recent extension), and a stochastic one (originated by Aigner, Lovell, and Schmidt [1977]). The difference between these approaches lies in the assumption made not on the production frontier itself, but rather on the nature of the residuals generated by the estimation. Our development below may be seen as an alternative version of the stochastic parametric approach.
3. According to a terminology proposed by McFadden [1978] (p. 8) and used more recently in a quite different context by Bonnisseau and Cornet [1990].
4. Strictly speaking, strong disposability for the outputs and free disposability for the inputs. The disposability assumption is also made in both the Farrell and the parametric methods.
5. Here at least, among other reasons, because our attempts in Tulkens, Thiry, and Palm [1988], and Nollet, Thiry, and Tulkens [1988] were not very conclusive.
6. There may be other bad reasons to declare an observation inefficient, such as measurement errors and the presence of outliers.
7. Other applications of the FDH method are reported in Tulkens [1992].
8. Actually, this was achieved already in Deprins, Simar, and Tulkens [1984] for cross-sectional data, and in Tulkens [1986] for panel data; here we do it for time series of single firms.
9. On the basis of F-statistics, the Cobb–Douglas specification as an alternative for the translog (actually a constrained version of it) is rejected in all three cases. This supports the specification chosen.
10. Schmidt and Lin [1984] proposed using skewness in this context (denoted below as $\sqrt{b_1}$).
11. A referee argues that negative output elasticities may be due to the fact that some of the inputs are endogenous. In this instance however, we think that it is more likely that the source of this problem is due to the severe inefficiencies in the data (which our analysis precisely reveals!), rather than to endogeneity of the inputs.
12. See Deprins, Simar, and Tulkens [1984] and Tulkens [1986] for more detailed presentations and Tulkens [1992] for a recent discussion and extensions.
13. Indeed, it belongs to the free-disposal hull of Y_o, hence to the boundary of the postulated production set Y_{FDH}.
14. For the computational details, we again refer to the two references cited above. Let us point out, however, that in the multiple inputs case, the measure in inputs is taken to be a radial one.
15. F-statistics again reject the Cobb–Douglas function as an alternative specification, the choice of the translog being again thus supported.

16. In order to show that, let us first point out that the output variable can be expressed as the product of the number of seats-vehicles (*PV*) by the average number of kilometers travelled by all vehicles (*km*). Therefore, the output elasticity with respect to seats-vehicles is equal to one plus the elasticity of the average number of kilometers with respect to seats-vehicles $(\partial km/km)/(\partial PV/PV)$.

    The output elasticity will have values greater than one if the elasticity of *km* with respect to *PV* is positive. That may be the case if, holding constant labor and energy, an increase in *PV* goes along with a decrease in the number of vehicles, or if a decrease in *PV* goes along with an increase in the number of vehicles. For STIL we observe this first phenomenon. This may explain why we obtain evaluations of e_{PV} greater than one for this company.

    On the other hand, the output elasticity will have values lower than one if the elasticity of *km* with respect to *PV* is negative. This is expected when an increase in *PV* goes along with an increase in the number of vehicles or when a decrease in *PV* goes along with a decrease in the number of vehicles. Both phenomena are observed for STIB (increases in the beginning of the period; decreases in the recent years) and for STIC (the average number of seats by vehicles is roughly constant over the whole period). These evolutions may explain the very low estimates of e_{PV} for both companies.
17. If there were several firms, all observed at the same time t, the superscript k should then be kept as distinct from t and refer to the firms, the data set being then a time series of cross sections. This is the panel data case dealt with in Tulkens [1986].
18. If there are several observations with the same level of minimum input, the one with the highest output should be retained.
19. If there are several observations with the same level of maximum output, the one with the lowest input should be retained.
20. These simple formulations are valid for the single output and single input cases, respectively. With several outputs and/or inputs, these measures must be expressed in a radial way.
21. There is a negative correlation between *PV* and the trend in the case of STIC. For STIB we observe a concave second degree relationship between them. We owe this point to a member of the audience at our Bologna presentation.

References

Aigner, D. and S.F. Chu. (1968). "On estimating the industry production function." *American Economic Review* 58 (4), pp. 826–839.

Aigner, D., C.A.K. Lovell, and P. Schmidt. (1977). "Formulation and estimation of stochastic frontier production function models." *Journal of Econometrics* 6, pp. 21–37.

Bauer, P.W. (1990). "Recent developments in the econometric estimation of frontiers." *Journal of Econometrics* 46 (1-2)), pp. 39–56.

Bonnisseau, J.M. and B. Cornet. (1990). "Existence of marginal cost pricing equilibria: the non smooth case." *International Economic Review* 31, pp. 685–708.

Deprins, D. and L. Simar. (1989). "Estimation de frontières déterministes avec facteurs exogènes d'inefficacité." *Annales d'Economie et de Statistique* 14, pp. 117–150.

Deprins, D., L. Simar, and H. Tulkens. (1984). "Measuring labor efficiency in post offices." In M. Marchand, P. Pestieau, and H. Tulkens (eds.), *The performance of public enterprises: concepts and measurement.* Amsterdam: North Holland Publishing Co.

Farrell, M.J. (1957). "The measurement of productive efficiency." *Journal of The Royal Statistical Society, Series A*, 120, pp. 253–281.

Førsund, F., C.A.K. Lovell, and P. Schmidt. (1980) "A survey of frontier production functions and of their relationship to efficiency measurement." *Journal of Econometrics* 13, pp. 5–25.

Johansen, L. (1972). *Production functions: an integration of micro and macro, short run and long run aspects.* Amsterdam: North Holland.

Kurz, M. and A.S. Manne. (1963). "Engineering estimates of capital-labor substitution in metal machining." *American Economic Review* LIII (3), pp. 662–681.

McFadden, D. (1978). "Cost, revenue and profit functions." In M. Fuss and D. McFadden (eds.), *Production economics: A dual approach to theory and applications.* vol. 1: The theory of production. Amsterdam: North-Holland.

Nollet, Ch., B. Thiry, and H. Tulkens. (1988). "Mesure de l'efficacité productive: applications à la société de transports intercommunaux de Bruxelles." Chapter 3 in Thiry and Tulkens [1988].

Schmidt, P. and T. Lin. (1984). "Simple tests of alternative specifications in stochastic frontier models." *Journal of Econometrics* 24, pp. 349–361.

Seiford, L.M. and R.M. Thrall. (1990). "Recent developments in DEA: The mathematical approach to frontier analysis." *Journal of Econometrics* 46 (1–2), pp. 7–38.

Shephard, R.W. (1970). *Theory of cost and production functions.* Princeton N.J.: Princeton University Press.

Thiry, B. and H. Tulkens (eds.). (1988). *La performance économique des sociétés belges de transports urbains.* Liège, C.I.R.I.E.C.

Tulkens, H. (1986). "La performance productive d'un service public: Définitions, méthodes de mesure, et application à la Régie des Postes de Belgique." *L'Actualité Economique, Revue d'Analyse Economique.* (Montréal), 62 (2), pp. 306–335.

Tulkens, H. (1992). "On FDH efficiency analysis: some methodological issues and applications to retail banking, courts and urban transit." Revised version of CORE Discussion Paper no. 9050, Center for Operations Research and Econometrics, Université Catholique de Louvain, Louvain-la-Neuve; forthcoming in the *Journal of Productivity Analysis.*

Tulkens, H., B. Thiry, and A. Palm. (1988). "Mesure de l'efficacité productive: méthodologies et applications aux société de transports intercommunaux de Liège, Charleroi et Verviers." Chapter 2 in Thiry and Tulkens [1988].

The Journal of Productivity Analysis, 3, 67-84 (1992)

The Relative Efficiency of Public versus Private Municipal Bus Firms: An Application of Data Envelopment Analysis

KUO-PING CHANG AND PEI-HUA KAO
Department of Economics, National Tsing Hua University, Kuang Fu Rd., Hsinchu 300, Taiwan, R.O.C.

Abstract

This article has employed the data envelopment analysis method to evaluate the efficiency of the five bus firms in Taipei city. When vehicle kilometers (revenue or the measure combining vehicle kilometers, revenue and the number of traffic trips on routes) was used as the output measure, it concluded that the publicly owned Taipei Municipal Bus had increased (not increased) its technical efficiency after the government liberalized the urban bus market. This article also found that in both the one output (vehicle kilometers) and three outputs cases, Taipei Municipal Bus had, on an average, lower efficiency scores than the private firms, and that while each firm usually employed a linear production technology for several, consecutive years the private firms were more flexible in adopting different technologies.

1. Introduction

The issue of the relative efficiency of public and private firms has been extensively discussed by economists. The property rights literature, most commonly associated with the names of Alchian, Becker, and Demetz, suggests that because public ownership attenuates property rights, public enterprises perform less efficiently than private enterprises. However, "the existing empirical evidence actually provides weak support for this hypothesis" (Boardman and Vining [1989], p. 1).[1] In our opinion, whether public firms are less efficient or not is an empirical question. The literature of property rights has pointed out the costs of public ownership: Ownership is diffused among all members of society, and no member has the right to sell his share; hence, there is little economic incentive for any owner to monitor the behavior of the firm's management. But if the public firms have good incentive schemes (pecuniary or non-pecuniary), owners' monitoring will not be so important, and there is no reason to believe that these firms must perform poorly.[2]

In this article, the case study of the Taipei bus system addresses this issue: There are five intra city bus firms competing in Taipei city.[3] The Taipei Municipal Bus (TB) is publicly owned, while Hsin-Hsin (HH), Ta-Yao (TY), Ta-Nan (TN) and Kuang-Hua (KH) are privately owned. Until 1969, TB enjoyed a monopoly position in Taipei city. The four private firms became competitors in 1969 only when the government liberalized the market.[4] The time series data of 1956–1988 of TB and the time series data of 1970–1988 of TB and the four private firms are employed to answer the following two questions. First, has the publicly owned TB increased its efficiency after the government liberalized the market? Second, are the four private firms more efficient than TB? A "nonparametric," linear programming approach (the data envelopment analysis: DEA) was used to measure the firms' technical efficiency. When vehicle kilometers (revenue or the measure combining vehicle kilometers, revenue and the number of traffic trips on routes) is used as the output measure, it concludes that TB has increased (not increased) its technical efficiency after the government liberalized the urban bus market. This paper also finds that in both the one output (vehicle kilometers) and three output cases, TB had, on an average, lower efficiency scores than the private firms, and that while each firm usually employed a (linear) production technology for several, consecutive years, the private firms were more flexible in adopting different technologies.

The remainder of this article is organized into three sections. Section 2 shows that the DEA method, which linearly aggregates inputs and outputs, assumes linear production functions. Data and empirical results are discussed in Section 3. Concluding remarks appear in Section 4.

2. The Data Envelopment Analysis (DEA)

Charnes, Cooper, and Rhodes [1978] proposed the DEA method for measuring productivity (see also Färe, Grosskopf, and Lovell [1985]). The DEA method can be stated as follows. Let y_{rj} and x_{ij} be known outputs and inputs of the jth decision making unit (DMU), the technical efficiency of the kth member of the $j = 1, \ldots, n$ DMUs is:

$$\text{Max} \sum_{r=1}^{s} U_r y_{rk} \Big/ \sum_{i=1}^{m} V_i x_{ik},$$

$$\text{subject to} \sum_{r=1}^{s} U_r y_{rj} \Big/ \sum_{i=1}^{m} V_i x_{ij} \leq 1,\ j = 1, \ldots, n,$$

$$U_r \geq \epsilon > 0,\ r = 1, \ldots, s,$$

$$V_i \geq \epsilon > 0,\ i = 1, \ldots, m, \qquad (1)$$

where ϵ is defined as an infinitesimal constant (a Non-Archimedean quantity).[5] It is assumed that ϵ is sufficiently small, "e.g., 10^{-6}, so that its introduction will not appreciably perturb the solution obtained with no lower bounds" (Lewin and Morey [1981], p. 272).

To transform the nonlinear problem (1) to a tractable linear programming problem, Charnes, Cooper, and Rhodes [1978] set $u_r = tU_r$ ($r = 1, \ldots, s$), $v_i = tV_i$ ($i = 1, \ldots, m$), and $t^{-1} = \Sigma_i V_i x_{ik}$. Multiplying numerators and denominators in equation (1) by t and adding the consistency condition, $t\ \Sigma_i V_i x_{ik} = 1$, yields

$$\text{Max} \sum_{r=1}^{s} u_r y_{rk},$$

$$\text{subject to} \sum_{r=1}^{s} u_r y_{rj} - \sum_{i=1}^{m} v_i x_{ij} \leq 0, \; j = 1, \ldots, n,$$

$$\sum_{i=1}^{m} v_i x_{ik} = 1,$$

$$u_r \geq \epsilon > 0, \; r = 1, \ldots, s,$$

$$v_i \leq \epsilon > 0, \; i = 1, \ldots, m. \tag{2}$$

The dual to equation (2) is

$$\text{Min } h_k - \epsilon \left(\sum_{r=1}^{s} S_{rk}^{+} + \sum_{i=1}^{m} S_{ik}^{-} \right),$$

$$\text{subject to} \sum_{j=1}^{n} x_{ij}\lambda_j + S_{ik}^{-} = h_k x_{ik},$$

$$\sum_{j=1}^{n} y_{rj}\lambda_j - S_{rk}^{+} = y_{rk},$$

$$\lambda_j \; (j = 1, \ldots, n), \; S_{rk}^{+} \; (r = 1, \ldots, s), \; S_{ik}^{-} \; (i = 1, \ldots, m) \geq 0. \tag{3}$$

Chang and Guh [1988] have pointed out two important features of the DEA method. First, the DEA method is not strictly nonparametric as the literature claims. Second, although the Non-Archimedean quantity, ϵ, is useful in finding non-Pareto-Koopmans efficient DMUs, it cannot tell what the efficiency scores of those DMUs should be.

Regarding the first feature, from equation (1) it is known that linear functions are used to aggregate inputs and outputs; hence, both inputs and outputs are perfect substitutes for themselves. The first constraint of equation (2) indicates that the underlying production technology is a linear production function (the second constraint is a normalization condition). A two-input and one-output (x_1, x_2, y) example illustrates this result.[6]

Assume there are six DMUs: $P_1(1, 4, 1)$, $P_2(2, 2, 1)$, $P_3(4, 1, 1)$, $P_4(5, 1, 1)$, $P_5(3, 2, 1)$, $P_6(2, 3, 1)$. Substitute them into equation (3) with ϵ equal to 10^{-6}. The efficiency scores recorded in table 1 show that P_1, P_2 and P_3 are efficient. The efficiency measure of P_4 is approximately equal to 1, but the slack variable of the first input is nonzero, i.e.,

$S_{14}^{-*} = 1$ (figure 1). The *virtual* multipliers u^*, v_1^*, and v_2^*, derived from equation (2) are unique only up to a constant scaled-up factor (e.g., for P_1, P_2, and P_6, $(u^*, v_1^*, v_2^*) = (\alpha, \alpha/3, \alpha/6)$, where α is a real number). Moreover, as shown in figure 1, the DMUs that lie in four different regions are actually evaluated by the following four linear production frontiers:[7]

$$\text{region 1: } y \leq (1/3)\ x_1 + (1/6)\ x_2, \tag{4}$$
$$\text{for } P_1\text{: } [(1)(1)]/[(1/3)(1) + (1/6)(4)] = 1,$$
$$\text{for } P_2\text{: } [(1)(1)]/[(1/3)(2) + (1/6)(2)] = 1,$$
$$\text{for } P_6\text{: } [(1)(1)]/[(1/3)(2) + (1/6)(3)] = 6/7,$$

$$\text{region 2: } y \leq (1/6)\ x_1 + (1/3)\ x_2, \tag{5}$$
$$\text{for } P_2\text{: } [(1)(1)]/[(1/6)(2) + (1/3)(2)] = 1,$$
$$\text{for } P_3\text{: } [(1)(1)]/[(1/6)(4) + (1/3)(1)] = 1,$$
$$\text{for } P_5\text{: } [(1)(1)]/[(1/6)(3) + (1/3)(2)] = 6/7,$$

$$\text{region 3: } y \leq x_2, \tag{6}$$
$$\text{for } P_3\text{: } [(1)(1)]/[(0)(4) + (1)(1)] = 1,$$
$$\text{for } P_4\text{: } [(1)(1)]/[(0)(5) + (1)(1)] = 1,$$

$$\text{region 4: } y \leq x_1, \tag{7}$$
$$\text{for } P_1\text{: } [(1)(1)]/[(1)(1) + (0)(4)] = 1.$$

That is, the DEA method not only constructs a piecewise linear envelope, but also uses a particular linear segment of the envelope (i.e., a particular linear production function) to evaluate a given DMU's efficiency.[8]

Regarding the second feature of the DEA method, table 1 is helpful. Because the Non-Archimedean quantity, ϵ, is very close to zero, the efficiency score of P_4 cannot be distinguished from those of P_1, P_2, and P_3. However, P_4 should not be classified efficient (i.e., not Pareto-Koopmans efficient, see Charnes, Cooper, Golany, Seiford, and Stutz [1985]), because it uses one more unit of x_1 than P_3. The Non-Archimedean constant, ϵ, can be used to find non-Pareto-Koopmans efficient DMUs, e.g., for P_4, from (3), $S_{14}^{-*} = 1$, it is known that although the efficiency score of P_4 is (very close to) one, P_4 is not Pareto-Koopmans efficient. However, a problem still remains: What is P_4's efficiency score relative to other DMUs?[9] To solve this problem, we adopted Chang and Guh's [1991] remedy; that is, to find all the positive multiplier linear production functions and then, to assign each DMU to the production function that gives the highest efficiency score.[10] The remedy is consistent with the essence of Farrell's method: evaluating any given DMU under the most favorable conditions, i.e., giving any DMU the highest efficiency score under the available (the derived) production technologies. Hence, P_4 will be evaluated by equation (5) (rather than equation (4) because in figure 1, $OA/OP_4 > OB/OP_4$, and equations (6) and (7) will be dropped. The adjusted efficiency scores for P_i's are shown in table 1.[11]

Table 1. The efficiency scores and the multipliers.

	u^*	v_1^*	v_2^*	Efficiency score	Adjusted efficiency score[a]
P_1	1	1/3	1/6	1	1
P_2	1	1/3, 1/6	1/6, 1/3	1	1
P_3	1	1/6	1/3	1	1
P_4	1	10^{-6}	1	1	6/7
P_5	6/7	1/7	2/7	6/7	6/7
P_6	6/7	2/7	1/7	6/7	6/7

[a]The adjusted efficiency scores are calculated by using (4) and (5).

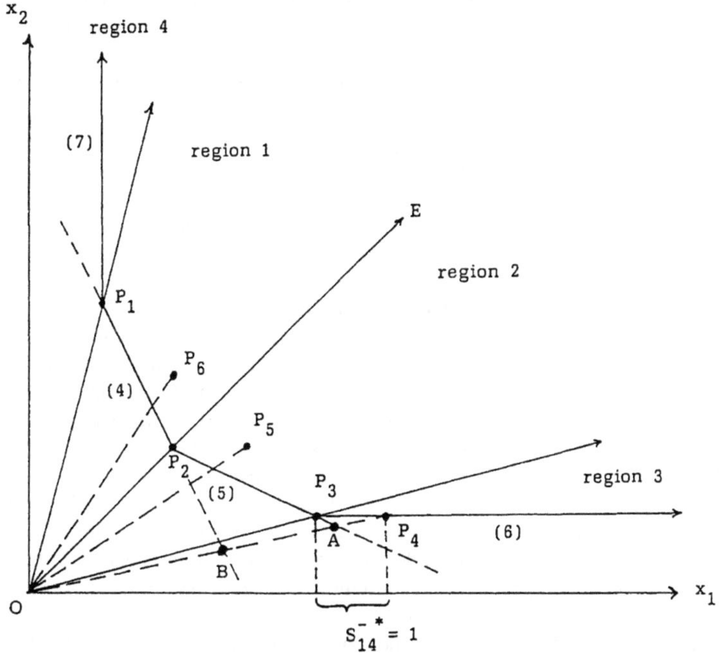

Figure 1. The efficiency scores and linear production functions.

3. Data and empirical results

The publicly owned TB started operation in 1945, and until 1969 it was the only bus firm in Taipei city. In 1969, the Taipei Municipal Government liberalized the urban bus market and entered four private firms: HH, TY, TN and KH. Right now, the publicly owned TB is still the dominant firm and is competing with the private firms. The basic data collected on the five bus firms came from publications of the Taipei Municipal Government. The time series data for TB are from 1956 to 1988; for the four private firms, from 1970 to

1988. Inputs include capital (X_1: the number of buses in operations), labor (X_2: the number of fulltime employees), and diesel fuel (X_3: measured in liters). Because of the difficulty of defining transportation output, three kinds of output measure were adopted. The first measure, vehicle kilometers (one output: Y_1), represents pure output. The second measure, revenue (one output: Y_2), represents the output including sale capability. The third measure (three outputs), which combines vehicle kilometers (Y_1), revenue (Y_2) and the number of bus traffic trips on routes (Y_3), should better measure the multidimensional nature of bus service.[12] Descriptive statistics of the variables are collected in table 2.

Our first task was to test whether the publicly-owned TB increased its efficiency after the government liberalized the urban bus market.[13] The time series data (1956–1988) of TB were used. The efficiency scores recorded in table 3a show that after 1969, TB's productivity increased in the one output: vehicle kilometers (Y_1) case, but not in the one output: revenue (Y_2) and three outputs cases. These results are validated by the parametric (t test) and nonparametric one-tailed tests (median and Wilcoxon, Mann, and Whitney tests) shown in table 7.[14] (Note that in the three outputs case, both t and Wilcoxon, Mann, and Whitney two-tailed tests conclude that TB's efficiency has decreased rather than increased after 1969.) The results are most likely caused by the fact that unlike the private firms, TB is not allowed to abandon unprofitable routes.[15]

The results of using the original DEA method (i.e., not using the Chang and Guh remedy) are recorded in table 3b. Comparing it with table 3a, it was found that (in terms of figure 1) many DMUs are located in region 3 or 4 and some DMUs are not Pareto-Koopmans efficient, e.g., in the one output: Y_1 case, the year 1956 is not Pareto-Koopmans efficient and except for the years 1979 and 1984–1987, all DMUs are in region 3 or 4. Table 7 also indicates that in the one output: Y_1 case, when the original DEA method is used. It will conclude that competition has no effect on TB's efficiency. In table 3a, the linear production functions used to measure efficiency were also listed. In the one output: Y_1 case, all the DMUs are evaluated by a linear production function: (A1). In the one output: Y_2 case, the DMUs of consecutive years are often evaluated by a particular production function, e.g., (B1) evaluates the years 1956–1976; (B2) evaluates the years 1986–1988; and (B3) evaluates the years 1968 and 1977–1987. In the three outputs case, (C1) evaluates the years 1956–1960 and 1962–1979; (C2) evaluates the years 1956, 1968 and 1980–1988; (C3) evaluates the years 1956, 1960–1961, 1968 and 1988. These results are consistent with the notion of the putty clay approach in production economics that states that in the short run, productive units or firms cannot change ex post technology.[16]

The second empirical test, examining the relative efficiency of TB versus the four private firms in the period 1970–1988, is summarized in tables 4a–6a. The statistical tests in table 7 indicate that in the one output: Y_1 and three outputs case, TB has performed substantially worse than the private firms. In the one output: Y_2 case, the null hypothesis that TB and the private firms have been equally efficient cannot be rejected. However, as shown in table 5, TB had the lowest efficiency scores in the years 1972–1975, 1980 and 1982–1988. Hence, it may be concluded that in the Taipei bus system, the beneficial effects of competition have not been sufficient to overcome the tendency toward inefficiency resulting from public ownership.[17] The results of using the original DEA method are recorded in tables 4b–6b. The efficiency scores in table 4b are very similar to those in table 4a, but the efficiency scores in tables 5a and 5b, and tables 6a and 6b, are different. Table 7 indicates that in the one output: Y_2 case, the result of t test is not consistent with those of the other two tests.

Table 2. Descriptive statistics of five bus firms*.

	X_1	X_2	X_3	Y_1	Y_2	Y_3
TB (1956–88):						
min	279	1530	476.3034	158.5912	1075.8758	219.0499
max	1701	5341	3333.0440	919.4089	7819.1122	1075.084
mean	858.27	3687.58	1777.2985	510.6912	3606.6815	633.6576
median	736	3842	1618.3510	468.2835	3012.4440	595.6734
standard deviation	475.61	970.62	937.3778	247.5382	2165.6909	263.4373
TB (1970–88):						
min	718	3803	1575.7300	448.9222	2867.4050	550.4709
max	1701	5341	3333.0440	919.4089	7819.1122	1075.084
mean	1158	4323.3200	2399.2465	675.7165	4836.3618	806.8605
median	962	4365	2195.8140	736.1424	3714.7945	789.4391
standard deviation	409.21	477.80	713.4860	187.5635	2053.9478	196.4135
TY (1970–88):						
min	155	622	383.1058	100.7328	594.7101	117.2703
max	317	1002	753.2803	223.2222	2145.0980	244.8091
mean	204.4211	778.4737	521.5650	144.4058	1049.1496	158.9612
median	190	757	477.6012	136.3522	835.2453	145.8636
standard deviation	50.6988	120.8113	125.5943	32.7344	471.4641	37.1640
TN (1970–88):						
min	100	530	255.0040	84.6634	461.6346	29.8598
max	236	879	529.8235	155.5399	1322.2279	188.5150
mean	168.3158	706.4211	410.2114	118.6336	827.6632	123.0050
median	156	725	386.4264	105.9252	633.4332	148.9764
standard deviation	47.4366	119.5855	94.8946	25.3983	296.1975	58.0765
HH (1970–88):						
min	192	1015	314.9661	75.2290	705.5534	51.1685
max	361	1616	890.5094	243.6632	2213.7057	377.6295
mean	290.7068	1260.158	726.4363	198.4650	1484.6674	263.0396
median	287	1235	786.1034	216.7216	1332.3133	327.9346
standard deviation	55.0604	198.1897	171.4378	48.5576	462.1928	113.1722
KH (1970–88):						
min	87	549	257.1393	87.0671	484.9367	38.0967
max	230	942	616.7583	167.7978	1664.3474	239.8160
mean	170.6316	695.368	479.5643	125.7485	982.5125	152.2585
median	165	661	461.7593	114.8286	767.8183	152.5519
standard deviation	42.1758	119.5418	97.0023	24.7802	359.6904	69.2073

*X_1 is the number of buses in operations; X_2 is the number of full-time employees; X_3 is the fuel measured in hundred thousands liters; Y_1 is measured in hundred thousands vehicle kilometers; Y_2 is the revenue measured in hundred thousands NT$ (1970 is the base period); Y_3 is measured in hundred thousands bus traffic trips on routes.

Table 3a. The efficiency scores of Taipei Municipal Bus (with the Chang and Guh remedy).*

Year	One Output Y_1	Y_2	Three Outputs
1956	0.8462 (A1)	0.8422 (B1)	1.0000 (C1, C2, C3)
1957	0.5595 (A1)	0.8038 (B1)	0.9273 (C1)
1958	0.6371 (A1)	0.8527 (B1)	1.0000 (C1)
1959	0.6205 (A1)	0.8616 (B1)	0.9846 (C1)
1960	0.6300 (A1)	0.8864 (B1)	1.0000 (C1, C3)
1961	0.6308 (A1)	0.8774 (B1)	0.9914 (C3)
1962	0.7718 (A1)	0.8749 (B1)	1.0000 (C1)
1963	0.6242 (A1)	0.8045 (B1)	0.9604 (C1)
1964	0.6417 (A1)	0.7640 (B1)	0.9493 (C1)
1965	0.6128 (A1)	0.8185 (B1)	0.9191 (C1)
1966	0.5960 (A1)	0.8195 (B1)	0.9086 (C1)
1967	0.6405 (A1)	0.8883 (B1)	0.9417 (C1)
1968	0.6996 (A1)	1.0000 (B1, B3)	1.0000 (C1, C2, C3)
1969	0.7691 (A1)	0.9351 (B1)	0.9687 (C1)
1970	0.7502 (A1)	0.7564 (B1)	0.8907 (C1)
1971	0.7333 (A1)	0.8069 (B1)	0.8828 (C1)
1972	0.7610 (A1)	0.8267 (B1)	0.9048 (C1)
1973	0.7568 (A1)	0.6964 (B1)	0.8581 (C1)
1974	0.7269 (A1)	0.6985 (B1)	0.8423 (C1)
1975	0.7298 (A1)	0.7405 (B1)	0.8583 (C1)
1976	0.7441 (A1)	0.7200 (B1)	0.8552 (C1)
1977	0.7920 (A1)	0.7266 (B3)	0.8932 (C1)
1978	0.7930 (A1)	0.7167 (B3)	0.8874 (C1)
1979	1.0000 (A1)	0.7558 (B3)	0.9614 (C1)
1980	0.7963 (A1)	0.8849 (B3)	0.8873 (C2)
1981	0.9447 (A1)	0.9418 (B3)	0.9559 (C2)
1982	0.9354 (A1)	0.8968 (B3)	0.9232 (C2)
1983	0.9812 (A1)	0.8511 (B3)	0.8823 (C2)
1984	1.0000 (A1)	0.8601 (B3)	0.8887 (C2)
1985	0.9706 (A1)	0.8963 (B3)	0.9088 (C2)
1986	0.9958 (A1)	1.0000 (B1, B2, B3)	1.0000 (C2)
1987	1.0000 (A1)	1.0000 (B2, B3)	1.0000 (C2)
1988	0.8826 (A1)	1.0000 (B1, B2)	1.0000 (C2, C3)

*The numbers in the brackets are the production functions used to measure efficiency:

(A1) $Y_1 \leq 0.08185\ X_1 + 0.11569\ X_2 + 0.07490\ X_3$

(B1) $Y_2 \leq 2.75155\ X_1 + 0.03163\ X_2 + 0.96851\ X_3$

(B2) $Y_2 \leq 2.51257\ X_1 + 0.19760\ X_2 + 0.86647\ X_3$

(B3) $Y_2 \leq 2.94070\ X_1 + 0.04961\ X_2 + 0.84543\ X_3$

(C1) $Y_1 + 0.03428\ Y_2 + 1.42083\ Y_3 \leq 1.23191\ X_1 + 0.00601\ X_2 + 0.40834\ X_3$

(C2) $Y_1 + 0.42065\ Y_2 + 0.13840\ Y_3 \leq 0.97404\ X_1 + 0.01067\ X_2 + 0.82739\ X_3$

(C3) $Y_1 + 0.56745\ Y_2 + 0.43588\ Y_3 \leq 1.17042\ X_1 + 0.00451\ X_2 + 1.20058\ X_3$

Table 3b. The efficiency scores of Taipei Municipal Bus (without the Chang and Guh remedy).

Year	One Output Y_1	Y_2	Three Outputs
1956	1.0000*	0.8583	1.0000
1957	0.7347	0.8217	0.9409
1958	0.8178	0.8712	1.0000
1959	0.8005	0.8719	1.0000*
1960	0.8409	0.9065	1.0000
1961	0.8233	0.8971	0.9995
1962	0.8532	0.8833	1.0000
1963	0.8757	0.8180	0.9886
1964	0.8193	0.7754	0.9583
1965	0.7823	0.8267	0.9245
1966	0.7780	0.8284	0.9139
1967	0.8094	0.8954	0.9442
1968	0.8627	1.0000	1.0000
1969	0.8673	0.9351	0.9920
1970	0.7978	0.7594	0.9197
1971	0.9359	0.8077	0.9739
1972	0.8097	0.8271	0.9360
1973	0.7851	0.6965	0.9011
1974	0.7807	0.6985	0.8685
1975	0.7882	0.7405	0.8826
1976	0.7759	0.7208	0.8965
1977	0.8185	0.7266	0.9511
1978	0.8213	0.7205	0.9492
1979	1.0000	0.7606	1.0000*
1980	0.8121	0.9153	0.9629
1981	0.9592	0.9652	1.0000*
1982	0.9373	0.8975	0.9540
1983	0.9875	0.8605	0.9913
1984	1.0000	0.8627	1.0000*
1985	0.9706	0.8994	0.9720
1986	0.9958	1.0000	1.0000
1987	1.0000	1.0000	1.0000
1988	0.9104	1.0000	1.0000

*means that the DMU is not Pareto-Koopmans efficient.

Table 4a. The efficiency scores of five bus firms (one output: Y_1; with the Chang and Guh remedy).*

Year	TB	TY	TN	HH	KH
1970	0.7278 (D3)	0.7809 (D3)	0.9448 (D1)	0.4357 (D3)	1.0000 (D1, D3)
1971	0.7213 (D3)	0.8427 (D3)	0.9198 (D3)	1.0000 (D3)	0.9738 (D1)
1972	0.7471 (D3)	0.9075 (D1)	0.8392 (D3)	0.4504 (D3)	0.8750 (D3)
1973	0.7279 (D3)	0.8779 (D1)	0.7456 (D3)	0.8450 (D3)	0.8180 (D1)
1974	0.7194 (D3)	0.8535 (D1)	0.7865 (D3)	0.8213 (D3)	0.8228 (D1)
1975	0.7256 (D3)	0.8452 (D1)	0.7444 (D3)	0.7792 (D3)	0.7766 (D1)
1976	0.7139 (D3)	0.8331 (D1)	0.7749 (D3)	0.7933 (D3)	0.7612 (D1)
1977	0.7608 (D3)	0.8056 (D1)	0.8033 (D1)	0.8291 (D1)	0.7854 (D1)
1978	0.7607 (D3)	0.8645 (D1)	0.8717 (D1)	0.8826 (D1)	0.8317 (D1)
1979	0.9390 (D3)	0.6629 (D3)	0.8340 (D1)	0.8148 (D1)	0.8241 (D1)
1980	0.7210 (D3)	0.8103 (D1)	0.7903 (D1)	0.7618 (D1)	0.8500 (D1)
1981	0.7839 (D1)	0.8790 (D1)	0.8304 (D1)	0.8087 (D1)	0.9165 (D1)
1982	0.7241 (D3)	0.8422 (D1)	0.8768 (D1)	0.7882 (D1)	0.9677 (D1)
1983	0.7271 (D1)	0.8452 (D1)	0.7857 (D1)	0.8126 (D1)	0.9245 (D1)
1984	0.7045 (D1)	0.7487 (D1)	0.7931 (D1)	0.8793 (D1)	0.9866 (D1)
1985	0.6854 (D1)	0.9250 (D2)	0.8705 (D1)	0.8236 (D1)	0.9832 (D1)
1986	0.6988 (D1)	1.0000 (D1, D2)	0.8307 (D1)	0.8945 (D1)	0.9399 (D1)
1987	0.7027 (D1)	1.0000 (D2)	0.8850 (D2)	0.9202 (D1)	0.8797 (D2)
1988	0.6036 (D3)	0.8690 (D2)	1.0000 (D1, D2, D3)	0.7822 (D1)	0.6928 (D2)

*The numbers in the brackets are the production functions used to measure efficiency:

(D1) $Y_1 \leq 0.58392\ X_1 + 0.06133\ X_2 + 0.00459\ X_3$

(D2) $Y_1 \leq 0.44770\ X_1 + 0.11666\ X_2 + 0.00086\ X_3$

(D3) $Y_1 \leq 0.42340\ X_1 + 0.02548\ X_2 + 0.13861\ X_3$

Table 4b. The efficiency scores of five bus firms (one output: Y_1; without the Chang and Guh remedy).

Year	TB	TY	TN	HH	KH
1970	0.7278	0.7809	0.9448	0.4357	1.0000
1971	0.7213	0.8427	0.9198	1.0000	0.9822
1972	0.7471	0.9075	0.8444	0.4504	0.8750
1973	0.7279	0.8779	0.7456	0.8450	0.8180
1974	0.7194	0.8535	0.7865	0.8213	0.8228
1975	0.7256	0.8452	0.7444	0.7792	0.7766
1976	0.7139	0.8331	0.7749	0.7933	0.7612
1977	0.7608	0.8056	0.8033	0.8291	0.7854
1978	0.7607	0.8645	0.8717	0.8826	0.8317
1979	0.9390	0.6629	0.8340	0.8148	0.8241
1980	0.7210	0.8103	0.7903	0.7618	0.8500
1981	0.7839	0.8790	0.8304	0.8087	0.9165
1982	0.7241	0.8422	0.8768	0.7882	0.9677
1983	0.7271	0.8452	0.7857	0.8126	0.9245
1984	0.7045	0.7487	0.7931	0.8793	0.9883
1985	0.6854	0.9465	0.8705	0.8236	0.9832
1986	0.6988	1.0000	0.8371	0.8945	0.9399
1987	0.7027	1.0000	0.9178	0.9202	0.8830
1988	0.6525	0.8942	1.0000	0.7822	0.7035

Table 5a. The efficiency scores of five bus firms (one output: Y_2; with the Chang and Guh remedy).*

Year	TB	TY	TN	HH	KH
1970	0.6263 (E3)	0.6585 (E3)	0.6164 (E3)	0.5754 (E3)	0.7044 (E3)
1971	0.6368 (E3)	0.7041 (E3)	0.8181 (E3)	0.8913 (E3)	0.5647 (E3)
1972	0.6509 (E3)	0.7177 (E3)	0.7928 (E3)	0.6866 (E3)	0.8093 (E3)
1973	0.5503 (E3)	0.5963 (E3)	0.6232 (E3)	0.5764 (E3)	0.6456 (E3)
1974	0.5474 (E3)	0.5826 (E3)	0.5992 (E3)	0.5783 (E3)	0.5993 (E3)
1975	0.5795 (E3)	0.5823 (E3)	0.5948 (E3)	0.6751 (E3)	0.6142 (E3)
1976	0.5717 (E3)	0.5407 (E3)	0.6085 (E3)	0.6718 (E3)	0.6136 (E3)
1977	0.5675 (E3)	0.5152 (E3)	0.5683 (E3)	0.6114 (E3)	0.5591 (E3)
1978	0.5573 (E3)	0.5254 (E3)	0.5627 (E3)	0.5997 (E3)	0.5604 (E3)
1979	0.5888 (E3)	0.5089 (E3)	0.4890 (E3)	0.6230 (E3)	0.6306 (E3)
1980	0.6772 (E3)	0.6877 (E3)	0.7387 (E3)	0.6960 (E3)	0.7322 (E3)
1981	0.7340 (E3)	0.7453 (E3)	0.7163 (E3)	0.8153 (E3)	0.7540 (E3)
1982	0.7180 (E3)	0.7791 (E3)	0.7497 (E3)	0.8014 (E3)	0.8089 (E3)
1983	0.6791 (E3)	0.7806 (E3)	0.7080 (E3)	0.7163 (E3)	0.8211 (E1)
1984	0.6943 (E3)	0.7725 (E3)	0.7253 (E3)	0.7425 (E3)	0.8749 (E1)
1985	0.7231 (E3)	0.8191 (E3)	0.7616 (E3)	0.7637 (E3)	0.9018 (E1)
1986	0.8107 (E3)	0.9817 (E1)	0.8944 (E3)	0.8608 (E3)	1.0000 (E1, E3)
1987	0.8093 (E3)	1.0000 (E1, E2)	0.8968 (E3)	0.9265 (E3)	1.0000 (E1, E2, E3)
1988	0.8430 (E3)	1.0000 (E1, E2)	0.9696 (E3)	0.9901 (E3)	1.0000 (E3)

*The numbers in the brackets are the production functions used to measure efficiency:

(E1) $Y_2 \leq 2.44468\ X_1 + 0.64265\ X_2 + 1.11713\ X_3$

(E2) $Y_2 \leq 1.28174\ X_1 + 1.00678\ X_2 + 1.24296\ X_3$

(E3) $Y_2 \leq 1.99542\ X_1 + 0.02979\ X_2 + 1.93609\ X_3$

Table 5b. The efficiency scores of five bus firms (one output: Y_2; without the Chang and Guh remedy).

Year	TB	TY	TN	HH	KH
1970	0.6134	0.6658	0.6379	0.5947	0.7703
1971	0.6445	0.7116	0.8266	0.9600	0.8785
1972	0.6586	0.7407	0.8056	0.6952	0.8450
1973	0.5564	0.6122	0.6308	0.5829	0.6670
1974	0.5540	0.6099	0.6070	0.5842	0.6602
1975	0.5867	0.6206	0.6012	0.6830	0.6475
1976	0.5780	0.5859	0.6162	0.6786	0.6430
1977	0.5736	0.5367	0.6096	0.6303	0.5735
1978	0.5632	0.5543	0.6133	0.6546	0.5851
1979	0.5946	0.5121	0.5360	0.6415	0.6883
1980	0.6827	0.6923	0.7452	0.7021	0.7934
1981	0.7377	0.7495	0.7214	0.8217	0.8323
1982	0.7204	0.7823	0.7523	0.8062	0.8683
1983	0.6803	0.7822	0.7101	0.7183	0.8308
1984	0.6947	0.7732	0.7269	0.7435	0.9428
1985	0.7235	0.8266	0.7616	0.7649	0.9414
1986	0.8112	0.9879	0.8944	0.8621	1.0000
1987	0.8097	1.0000	0.9111	0.9277	1.0000
1988	0.8940	1.0000	0.9743	0.9923	1.0000

Table 6a. The efficiency scores of five bus firms (three outputs: with the Chang and Guh remedy).*

Year	TB	TY	TN	HH	KH
1970	0.9072 (F20)	0.8585 (F2)	0.9390 (F6)	0.4855 (F13)	1.0000 (F1, F2, F4, F6, F7, F12–F14)
1971	0.8733 (F20)	0.9227 (F2)	0.9285 (F14)	1.0000 (F1–F3, F11–F13, F20, F21)	1.0000 (F7)
1972	0.8917 (F20)	0.9849 (F2)	0.8692 (F13)	0.6205 (F7)	0.9569 (F13)
1973	0.8583 (F20)	0.9457 (F2)	0.7642 (F13)	0.8698 (F1)	0.8507 (F7)
1974	0.8304 (F20)	0.9077 (F2)	0.8115 (F2)	0.8349 (F1)	0.8241 (F6)
1975	0.8419 (F20)	0.8944 (F2)	0.7589 (F1)	0.8133 (F13)	0.8057 (F7)
1976	0.8595 (F20)	0.8639 (F2)	0.7896 (F13)	0.8954 (F2)	0.7925 (F13)
1977	0.8774 (F20)	0.8459 (F2)	0.9320 (F2)	0.9667 (F11)	0.8766 (F2)
1978	0.8673 (F20)	0.8674 (F6)	1.0000 (F1–F3, F11)	0.9798 (F2)	0.8371 (F6)
1979	1.0000 (F1–F3)	0.7366 (F20)	0.9598 (F2)	0.9637 (F11)	0.8966 (F11)
1980	0.8232 (F11)	0.8779 (F2)	0.8895 (F12)	1.0000 (F20–F22)	0.9263 (F11)
1981	0.8504 (F11)	0.9151 (F12)	0.8998 (F2)	1.0000 (F11, F17, F20–F22)	0.9602 (F2)
1982	0.8039 (F20)	0.8755 (F12)	0.9056 (F1)	0.9724 (F21)	1.0000 (F1–F3, F6, F11–F12, F15–F18, F22, F23)
1983	0.7880 (F20)	0.8599 (F12)	0.8295 (F11)	0.9287 (F22)	0.9853 (F19)
1984	0.7666 (F20)	0.7882 (F17)	0.8281 (F11)	0.9507 (F16)	1.0000 (F4, F6–F8, F24)
1985	0.7406 (F18)	0.9546 (F5)	0.8893 (F5)	0.9243 (F16)	1.0000 (F4–F6, F7, F8, F10, F12–19, F23, F24)
1986	0.8000 (F18)	1.0000 (F4–F10 F13, F14	0.8926 (F19)	0.9507 (F17)	1.0000 (F4, F5, F7–F10, F13–F19, F23, F24)
1987	0.7733 (F18)	1.0000 (F5, F8–F10, (F24)	0.9795 (F5)	1.0000 (F2, F3, F15–F18)	1.0000 (F5, F9, F10, F19, F24)
1988	0.7011 (F20)	0.9260 (F9)	1.0000 (F1, F3 F5, F6, F9, F11–F21)	1.0000 (F15–F18, F20–F23)	1.0000 (F16, F18–F20, F22, F23)

*The numbers in the brackets are the production functions used to measure efficiency:

(F1) $Y_1 + 0.00327\ Y_2 + 0.23210\ Y_3 \leq 0.66167\ X_1 + 0.01143\ X_2 + 0.12985\ X_3$
(F2) $Y_1 + 0.00337\ Y_2 + 0.23780\ Y_3 \leq 0.67192\ X_1 + 0.01000\ X_2 + 0.13058\ X_3$
(F3) $Y_1 + 0.00251\ Y_2 + 0.25771\ Y_3 \leq 0.65565\ X_1 + 0.01124\ X_2 + 0.14080\ X_3$
(F4) $Y_1 + 0.10124\ Y_2 + 0.10334\ Y_3 \leq 1.41268\ X_1 + 0.00882\ X_2 + 0.04724\ X_3$
(F5) $Y_1 + 0.00595\ Y_2 + 0.56824\ Y_3 \leq 0.24416\ X_1 + 0.27235\ X_2 + 0.12917\ X_3$
(F6) $Y_1 + 0.00432\ Y_2 + 0.06518\ Y_3 \leq 0.63889\ X_1 + 0.05052\ X_2 + 0.02785\ X_3$
(F7) $Y_1 + 0.11597\ Y_2 + 0.08445\ Y_3 \leq 1.55803\ X_1 + 0.00688\ X_2 + 0.02737\ X_3$
(F8) $Y_1 + 0.03011\ Y_2 + 0.64317\ Y_3 \leq 0.62024\ X_1 + 0.33323\ X_2 + 0.01829\ X_3$
(F9) $Y_1 + 0.06068\ Y_2 + 0.45452\ Y_3 \leq 0.34964\ X_1 + 0.26322\ X_2 + 0.20349\ X_3$
(F10) $Y_1 + 0.00609\ Y_2 + 0.61464\ Y_3 \leq 0.26530\ X_1 + 0.30314\ X_2 + 0.10706\ X_3$
(F11) $Y_1 + 0.01836\ Y_2 + 0.68476\ Y_3 \leq 0.68134\ X_1 + 0.00221\ X_2 + 0.34884\ X_3$
(F12) $Y_1 + 0.03485\ Y_2 + 0.22699\ Y_3 \leq 0.80143\ X_1 + 0.00504\ X_2 + 0.15557\ X_3$
(F13) $Y_1 + 0.06447\ Y_2 + 0.18826\ Y_3 \leq 0.89987\ X_1 + 0.00101\ X_2 + 0.18135\ X_3$
(F14) $Y_1 + 0.06287\ Y_2 + 0.13576\ Y_3 \leq 0.87801\ X_1 + 0.01241\ X_2 + 0.15258\ X_3$
(F15) $Y_1 + 0.04172\ Y_2 + 1.03746\ Y_3 \leq 0.68838\ X_1 + 0.06223\ X_2 + 0.46592\ X_3$
(F16) $Y_1 + 0.02093\ Y_2 + 1.17746\ Y_3 \leq 0.54906\ X_1 + 0.10337\ X_2 + 0.47543\ X_3$
(F17) $Y_1 + 0.06077\ Y_2 + 0.88508\ Y_3 \leq 0.83126\ X_1 + 0.00991\ X_2 + 0.45997\ X_3$
(F18) $Y_1 + 0.03125\ Y_2 + 1.16544\ Y_3 \leq 0.57478\ X_1 + 0.10694\ X_2 + 0.48266\ X_3$
(F19) $Y_1 + 0.00010\ Y_2 + 1.10725\ Y_3 \leq 0.20961\ X_1 + 0.26786\ X_2 + 0.34168\ X_3$
(F20) $Y_1 + 0.00254\ Y_2 + 1.26742\ Y_3 \leq 0.37218\ X_1 + 0.00496\ X_2 + 0.68407\ X_3$
(F21) $Y_1 + 0.00791\ Y_2 + 1.21299\ Y_3 \leq 0.43289\ X_1 + 0.00330\ X_2 + 0.64927\ X_3$
(F22) $Y_1 + 0.00989\ Y_2 + 2.74297\ Y_3 \leq 1.18377\ X_1 + 0.08060\ X_2 + 0.89247\ X_3$
(F23) $Y_1 + 0.05059\ Y_2 + 1.71413\ Y_3 \leq 0.90901\ X_1 + 0.13093\ X_2 + 0.59877\ X_3$
(F24) $Y_1 + 0.00564\ Y_2 + 1.02418\ Y_3 \leq 0.38985\ X_1 + 0.49469\ X_2 + 0.01590\ X_3$

Table 6b. The efficiency scores of five bus firms (three outputs; without the Chang and Guh remedy).

Year	TB	TY	TN	HH	KH
1970	0.9101	0.8619	0.9448	0.6004	1.0000
1971	0.8572	0.9250	0.9716	1.0000	1.0000
1972	0.8922	0.9874	0.9195	0.8708	0.9696
1973	0.8592	0.9458	0.7663	0.8701	0.8512
1974	0.8350	0.9896	0.8115	0.8354	0.8259
1975	0.8465	0.8949	0.7589	0.8162	0.8067
1976	0.8607	0.8659	0.7956	0.8997	0.7931
1977	0.8819	0.8478	0.9379	0.9668	0.8766
1978	0.8714	0.8756	1.0000	0.9829	0.8436
1979	1.0000	0.7400	0.9670	0.9658	0.9105
1980	0.8232	0.8782	0.8920	1.0000	0.9319
1981	0.8504	0.9151	0.9002	1.0000	0.9793
1982	0.8039	0.8755	0.9256	0.9688	1.0000
1983	0.7891	0.8600	0.8321	0.9358	0.9950
1984	0.7645	0.7905	0.8305	0.9574	1.0000
1985	0.7406	0.9669	0.8920	0.9286	1.0000
1986	0.8235	1.0000	0.8997	0.9507	1.0000
1987	0.8222	1.0000	0.9936	1.0000	1.0000
1988	0.8982	1.0000*	1.0000	1.0000	1.0000

*means that the DMU is not Pareto-Koopmans efficient.

Table 7. Summary of test statistics.*

	Taipei Municipal Bus (before versus after 1969)			Five bus firms (public versus private firms)		
	One output		Three outputs	One output		Three outputs
	Y_1	Y_2		Y_1	Y_2	
With the Chang and Guh remedy:						
t test (t)	−5.5342	0.3269	3.7373	−4.5631	−1.8235	−3.0849
	(−2.042)	(−2.042)	(−2.042)	(−1.980)	(−1.980)	(−1.980)
Median test (x^2)	5.3694	0.2519	6.8444	16.4255	2.2134	12.5303
	(5.024)	(5.024)	(5.024)	(5.024)	(5.024)	(5.024)
Wilcoxon-Mann-Whitney test (Z)	−3.9522	0.9106	3.0780	−5.3080	−1.8096	−3.6968
	(−1.96)	(−1.96)	(−1.96)	(−1.96)	(−1.96)	(−1.96)
Without the Chang and Guh remedy:						
t test (t)	−1.5438	1.1294	1.4334	−4.4695	−2.3335	−3.3378
	(−2.042)	(−2.042)	(−2.042)	(−1.980)	(−1.980)	(−1.980)
Median test (x^2)	0.0412	0.0412	1.4560	16.4255	2.2134	12.5303
	(5.024)	(5.024)	(5.024)	(5.024)	(5.024)	(5.024)
Wilcoxon-Mann-Whitney test (Z)	−1.2021	1.0564	1.1474	−5.2893	−1.8096	−3.3897
	(−1.96)	(−1.96)	(−1.96)	(−1.96)	(−1.96)	(−1.96)

*The numbers in the brackets are the critical values for $\alpha = 0.025$.

The linear production functions listed in tables 4a–6a show that each firm usually employed a production technology for several, consecutive years. In the one output: Y_1 case (table 4a), it shows that all the five firms adopted (D3) first, then they moved to (D1) or (D2). In the one output: Y_2 case (table 5a), it shows that all the five bus firms have employed the same technology, (E3), for many years. In the three outputs case (table 6a), it shows that TB adopted (F20) first (1970–1978, 1982–1984), then it moved to (F18) (1985–1987) and back to (F20) (1988). The four private firms, on the other hand, were more flexible in adopting different technologies.[18]

4. Concluding remarks

Whether public firms are less efficient than private firms or not is an empirical question. This article has used the data envelopment analysis method to measure the efficiency scores of the five intracity bus firms in Taipei city. When vehicle kilometers (revenue or the measure combining vehicle kilometers, revenue and the number of traffic trips on routes) was used as the output measure, it concluded that the publicly owned TB had increased (not increased) its technical efficiency after the government liberalized the urban bus market. This article also found that in both the one output (vehicle kilometers) and three output cases, TB had, on an average, lower efficiency scores than the private firms, and that while each firm usually employed a (linear) production technology for several, consecutive years, the private firms were more flexible in adopting different technologies.

Acknowledgments

The authors wish to thank Professor C.A. Knox Lovell, participants in the Conference, and especially three anonymous referees for their very helpful comments and suggestions. The authors also appreciate the generous support of the R.O.C. National Science Council, NSC grant 78-0301-H00702.

Notes

1. For electricity utilities, Meyer [1975], Neuberg [1977], and Pescatrice and Trapani [1980] find that public firms are more efficient; Junker [1975], Färe, Grosskopf, and Logan [1985] and Atkinson and Halvorsen [1986] find no difference between public and private firms; Peltzman [1971] and De Alessi [1974, 1977] find that private firms are more efficient. For water delivery, Mann and Mikesell [1971] and Bruggink [1982] find that public firms are more efficient; Feigenbaum and Teeples [1983] and Byrnes, Grosskopf, and Hayes [1986] find no significant difference across ownership types; Cran and Zardkoohi [1978, 1980] find that private firms are more efficient. For transportation, Davies [1971, 1977] finds that private airlines are more efficient, but Jordan [1982] finds no difference between public and private airlines. Also, Caves and Christensen [1980] find no difference between private and public railroads. Pashigian [1976] and McGuire and Van Cott [1984] find that private nonrail transit firms are more efficient. Boardman and Vining [1989] point out that most of the empirical evidence is based on North American firms, and few empirical studies have tested the effect of ownership in a competitive environment. With data of international industrial firms, Boardman and Vining conclude that the public firms perform substantially worse than the private firms.

2. Chang [1987] has found that the publicly owned Chinese Petroleum Corp. (in Taiwan) has higher productivity than the U.S. privately owned petroleum firms. He suggests that this difference is due to the system of nationalized firms in Taiwan, which provides good fringe benefits and chances of promotion for its employees. (In the past twenty years, two Economic Ministers and one Premier have been chosen from the managers of these nationalized firms). Pryke [1986] also argued that publicly owned firms usually have lower risk, hence, lower costs of capital.
3. In 1977, five other private intercity bus firms also entered the market.
4. The bus fares are still regulated, but since only technical efficiency, i.e., the ratio of the output index to input index, was considered, the output price regulation should not affect our results.
5. Equation (1) presents the efficiency measure in a fractional form, which is consistent with the concept of the total factor productivity (TFP). The TFP measures developed in the economics literature, however, have either approximation errors or overly restrictive prior assumptions (such as assuming no allocative inefficiency). See Jorgensen and Griliches [1972], Diewert [1976], and Caves, Christensen, and Diewert [1982].
6. The results of this one output case can also be extended to a multioutput case.
7. Notice that in equation (1) the objective function is the same as one of the constraints. Hence, there might be multiple solutions, e.g., the DMUs on $\overline{P_2 E}$ of figure 1 are evaluated using the production functions:
$$y \leq v_1^* x_1 + v_2^* x_2, \text{ where } \begin{pmatrix} v_1^* \\ v_2^* \end{pmatrix} = \beta \begin{pmatrix} 1/3 \\ 1/6 \end{pmatrix} + (1 - \beta) \begin{pmatrix} 1/6 \\ 1/3 \end{pmatrix},$$
$$\text{and } 1 \geq \beta \geq 0.$$
8. This result, to some extent, refutes the statement of Farrell [1957, p. 262] that "the estimate (i.e., the efficiency measure) involves no assumptions about the shape of the isoquant."
9. Färe, Grosskopf, and Lovell [1985] and Färe, Grosskopf, and Logan [1985] do not use the Non-Archimedean quantity, ϵ, in their models, and they do not report the values of the slack variables, S_{ij}^- and S_{rj}^+. The Russell measure can also be used to measure P_4's efficiency (Färe and Lovell [1978], Russell [1990]). Thompson et al. [1990] have used the Assurance Region (AR) method to reduce the number of efficient DMUs. The AR method based on observational socioeconomic/environmental data and expert opinion may create different linear production functions to evaluate DMUs. For example, if we set $v_2/v_1 \leq 1.5$ in the preceding example (as in Thompson et al. [1990, p. 97], linear production frontiers (4) and (7) will remain the same, but (5) and (6) will be replaced by $(2/10)x_1 + (3/10)x_2 \geq y$, and P_3 will be termed inefficient, i.e., $h_3^* = (1)/[(2/10)(4) + (3/10)(1)] = 10/11$.
10. Although Bessent et al.'s [1988] remedy is equivalent to Chang and Guh's, the latter is much easier to apply.
11. The adjusted efficiency scores are calculated as follows. First, use a LP package (e.g., LINDO) to solve equations (2) or (3) for "efficient" DMUs (e.g., P_1, P_2, P_3, and P_4). Next, substitute these efficient DMUs into Steuer's [1989] ADBASE package, which is a vector maximum algorithm for generating extreme points and unbounded efficient edges, to obtain positive multiplier linear production frontiers, e.g., equations (4) and (5). Last, assign each DMU to the frontier that gives the highest efficient score.
12. Spady and Friedlaender [1978] have argued that the hedonic approach should be used to capture different facets of transportation output. Because in the Taipei bus system, the regulated price is equal for all bus firms and constant regardless of length of trip, our study uses revenue and the three outputs measure as proxies for revenue per passenger kilometer preferred by transportation economists, e.g., Berechman [1983].
13. Equations (1), (2) and (3) imply that the DMU's technology is a linear production function and that constant returns to scale are assumed. The published empirical results of scale economies of urban bus operations are mixed; e.g., Berechman [1983], and Williams and Dalal [1981] find scale economies, but Obeng [1985] finds scale diseconomies. If there are scale economies, improved scale efficiency will be an explanation for the increases in efficiency measures (Färe, Grosskopf, and Lovell [1985]). Because the econometric studies of Taipei bus system show only slight scale economies (Lin, H.C. [1986], Lin, H.S. [1986], this article assumes constant returns to scale, and does not adopt Färe, Grosskopf, and Logan's approach.
14. In the t (median) test the null hypothesis is that TB has the same mean (central tendency) efficient score before and after 1969. Wilcoxon, Mann and Whitney test, which serves as an alternative to the parametric t test, is used to test whether the two independent groups have been drawn from the same population (see Siegel and Castellan [1988] for the details). Unlike parametric tests, nonparametric tests do not assume particular distribution (such as normal distribution). Because the efficiency scores were restricted between 0 and 1, nonparametric tests should be more appropriate.

15. Some municipal councilmen "represent" the private bus firms and help them gain the more lucrative routes. The publicly owned TB, on the other hand, is forced to serve cost-inefficient social goals.
16. Although different production technologies listed in tables 3a–6a imply that the firm's technology has changed, the efficiency scores may include the effect of technological progress (or learning by doing). Färe, Grabowski, and Grosskopf [1985] have used Diewert and Parkan's [1983] technique to avoid confusing inefficiency with technological progress, i.e., with time series data, measuring efficiency of production in any given year only relative to production in that and earlier years. However, if the firm does *not* have technological progress in the next year, this technique may overestimate the firm's efficiency because in equation (2), reducing observations may increase the value of the objective function. We may also employ the technique often used in econometric studies: adding a time variable in the production function. Doing so implies that technological change is exogenous (Caves et al. [1982]) and the efficiency score will be higher (because in equation (3), adding an additional variable may increase the value of objective function).
17. The reasons why TB, unlike other public firms in Taiwan, has lower productivity may be two-fold. First, it is owned by the local government, so most of its employees do not have the chance to transfer to the (higher) positions of the central government. Second, TB is easier to be captured by the local representatives, and is required to serve cost-inefficient social goals; hence, it cannot provide good fringe benefits for its employees as other public firms.
18. The publicly owned TB, unlike the private bus firms, needs to obtain a (usually time consuming) approval from the city council to buy new vehicles.
19. An earlier version of the paper was presented in the "Productivity and Efficiency Analysis" sessions at the ORSA/TIMS 30th Joint National Conference, Philadelphia, U.S.A., 29–30 October 1990.

References

Alchian, A. (1965). "Some economics of property rights." *Politico* 30, pp. 816–829.

Atkinson, S.E., and R. Halvorsen. (1986). "The relative efficiency of public and private firms in a regulated environment: The case of U.S. electric utilities." *Journal of Public Economics* 29, pp. 291–294.

Berechman, J. (1983). "Costs, economies of scale and factor demand in bus transport." *Journal of Transport Economics and Policy* 17, pp. 7–24.

Bessent, A., W. Bessent, J. Elam, and T. Clark. (1988). "Efficiency frontier determination by constrained facet analysis." *Operations Research* 36, pp. 785–796.

Boardman, A. and A. Vining. (1989). Ownership and performance in competitive environments: a comparison of the performance of private, mixed and state-owned enterprises. *Journal of Law and Economics* 32, pp. 1–33.

Bruggink, T.H. (1982). "Public versus regulated private enterprise in the municipal water industry: a comparison of operating costs." *Quarterly Review of Economics and Business* 22, pp. 111–125.

Byrnes, P., S. Grosskopf, and K. Hayes. (1986). "Efficiency and ownership: further evidence." *Review of Economics and Statistics* 68, pp. 337–341.

Caves, D.W. and L. R. Christensen. (1980). "The relative efficiency of public and private firms in a competitive environment: the case of Canadian railroads." *Journal of Political Economy* 88, pp. 958–976.

Caves, D.W., L.R. Christensen, and W.E. Diewert. (1982). "The economic theory of index numbers and the measurement of input, output, and productivity." *Econometrica* 50, pp. 1393–1414.

Chang, K.P. (1987). "Productivity changes in the petroleum and natural gas industry: an international comparison." Paper presented at 9th Conference of the International Association of Energy Economists, Calgary, Canada.

Chang, K.P., and Y.Y. Guh. (1991). "Linear production functions and the data envelopment analysis." *European Journal of Operational Research* 52, pp. 215–223.

Chang, K.P. and Y.Y. Guh. (1988). "Functional forms in data envelopment analysis." Paper presented at the EURO IX and TIMS XXVIII Joint International Conference, Paris, France

Charnes, A., W.W. Cooper, and E. Rhodes. (1978). "Measuring the efficiency of decision making units." *European Journal of Operational Research* 2, pp. 429–444.

Charnes, A., W.W. Cooper, B. Golany, L. Seiford, and J. Stutz. (1985) "Foundations of data envelopment analysis for Pareto-Koopmans efficient empirical production functions." *Journal of Econometrics* 30, pp. 91–107.

Crain, W.M. and A. Zardkoohi. (1978). "A test of the property rights theory of the firm: water utilities in the United States." *Journal of Law and Economics* 21, pp. 395–408.

Crain, W.M. and A. Zardkoohi. (1980). "Public sector expansion: stagnant technology or attenuated property rights?" *Southern Economic Journal* 46, pp. 1069–1082.

Davies, D. (1971). "The efficiency of public versus private firms: the case of Australia's two airlines." *Journal of Law and Economics* 14, pp. 149–165.

Davies, D. (1977). "Property rights and economic efficiency: the Australian airlines revisited." *Journal of Law and Economics* 20, pp. 223–226.

De Alessi, L. (1974). "An economic analysis of government ownership and regulation: theory and the evidence from the electric power industry." *Public Choice* 19, pp. 1–42.

De Alessi, L. (1977). "Ownership and peak-load pricing in the electric power industry." *Quarterly Review of Economics and Business* 17, pp. 7–26.

Diewert, W.E. (1976). "Exact and superlative index numbers." *Journal of Econometrics* 4, pp. 115–145.

Diewert, W.E. and C. Parkan. (1983). "Linear programming tests of regularity conditions for production functions." In W. Eichhorn, R. Henn, K. Neumann, and R.W. Shephard (eds.) *Quantitative Studies on Production and Prices*. Würzburg: Physica Verlag.

Färe, R., R. Grabowski, and S. Grosskopf. (1985). "Technical efficiency of Philippine agriculture." *Applied Economics* 17, pp. 205–214.

Färe, R., S. Grosskopf, and C.A.K. Lovell. (1985). *The Measurement of Efficiency of Production*. Boston, MA: Kluwer-Nijhoff Publishing.

Färe, R., S. Grosskopf, and J. Logan. (1985). "The relative performance of publicly-owned and privately-owned electric utilities." *Journal of Public Economics* 26, pp. 89–106.

Färe, R. and W. Hunsaker. (1986). "Notions of efficiency and their reference sets." *Management Science* 32, pp. 237–243.

Färe, R. and C.A.K. Lovell. (1978). "Measuring the technical efficiency in production." *Journal of Economic Theory* 19, pp. 150–162.

Färe, R. and D. Njinkeu. (1989). "Computing returns to scale under alternative models." *Economics Letters* 30, pp. 55–59.

Farrell, M.J. (1957). "The measurement of productive efficiency." *Journal of Royal Statistical Society* 120, series A, part 3, pp. 253–281.

Feigenbaum, S. and R. Teeples. (1983). "Public versus private water delivery: a hedonic cost approach." *Review of Economics and Statistics* 65, pp. 672–678.

Jordan, W.A. (1982). "Performance of North American and Australian airlines." In W. Stanbury and F. Thompson (eds.) *Managing Public Enterprises*. New York: Praeger.

Jorgensen, D.W. and Z. Griliches. (1972). "Issues in growth accounting: a reply to Edward F. Denison." *Survey of Current Business* 52, part 2, pp. 65–94.

Junker, J.A. (1975). "Economic performance of public and private utilities: the case of U.S. electric utilities." *Journal of Economics and Business* 28, pp. 60–67.

Lewin, A. and R. Morey. (1981). "Measuring the relative efficiency and output potential for public sector organization: an application of data envelopment analysis." *International Journal of Policy Analysis and Information Systems* 5, pp. 267–285.

Lin, H.C. (1986). *Costs, Returns to Scale and Productivity:* A Case of Taipei Bus System. unpublished M.S. thesis, Department of Economics, National Taiwan Unviersity, Taiwan.

Lin, H.S. (1986). *Scale Economies of Urban Bus Service.* unpublished M.S. thesis, Department of Transportation and Communication Management, National Cheng Kung University, Taiwan.

McGuire, R.A. and T.N. Van Cott. (1984). "Public versus private economic activity." *Public Choice* 43, pp. 25–43.

Mann, P.C. and J.L. Mikesell. (1971). "Tax payments and electric utility prices." *Southern Economic Journal* 38, pp. 69–78.

Meyer, R.A. (1975). "Publicly owned versus privately owned utilities: a policy choice." *Review of Economics and Statistics* 57, pp. 391–399.

Millward, R. (1986). "The comparative performance of public and private ownership." In J. Kay, C. Mayer, and D. Thompson (eds.) *Privatisation and Regulation—the UK Experience*. New York: Oxford University Press.

Neuberg, L.G. (1977). "Two issues in the municipal ownership of electric power distribution systems." *Bell Journal of Economics* 8, pp. 303–323.

Obeng, K. (1985). "Bus transit cost, productivity, and factor substitution." *Journal of Transport Economics and Policy* 19, pp. 183–203.
Pashigian, B.P. (1976). "Consequences and causes of public ownership of urban transit facilities." *Journal of Political Economy* 84, pp. 1239–1260.
Peltzman, S. (1971). "Pricing in public and private enterprises: electric utilities in the United States." *Journal of Law and Economics* 14, pp. 109–147.
Pescatrice, D.R. and J.M. Trapani, III. (1980). "The performance and objectives of public and private utilities operating in the United States." *Journal of Public Economics* 13, pp. 259–276.
Pryke, R. (1986). "The comparative performance of public and private enterprise." In J. Kay, C. Mayer, and D. Thompson (eds.) *Privatisation and Regulation—the UK Experience*. New York: Oxford University Press.
Russell, R.R. (1990). "Continuity of measures of technical efficiency." *Journal of Economic Theory* 51, pp. 255–267.
Siegel, S. and N.J. Castellan, Jr. (1988). *Nonparametric Statistics: For the Behavioral Sciences*. New York: McGraw Hill.
Spady R. and A. Friedlaender. (1978). "Hedonic cost functions for the regulated trucking industry." *Bell Journal of Economics* 9, pp. 159–179.
Steuer, R.E. (1989). ADBASE operating manual, Department of Management Science and Technology, University of Georgia, Athens, GA 30602, U.S.A.
Thompson, R.G., L.N. Langemeier, C.T. Lee, E. Lee, and R.M. Thrall. (1990). "The role of multiplier bounds in efficiency analysis with application to Kansas farming." *Journal of Econometrics* 46, pp. 93–108.
Williams, M. and A. Dalal. (1981) "Estimation of the elasticities of factor substitution in urban bus transportation: a cost function approach." *Journal of Regional Science* 21, pp. 263–275.

The Journal of Productivity Analysis, 3, 85–101 (1992)

Productivity Changes in Swedish Pharamacies 1980–1989: A Non-Parametric Malmquist Approach

R. FÄRE
Department of Economics, Southern Illinois Unviersity, Carbondale, Illinois, U.S.

S. GROSSKOPF
Department of Economics, Southern Illinois Unviersity, Carbondale, Illinois, U.S.

B. LINDGREN
The Swedish Institute for Health Economics, Lund Sweden

P. ROOS*
The Swedish Institute for Health Economics, Lund Sweden

Abstract

In this article we develop a non-parametric (linear programming) approach for calculation of a Malmquist (input based) productivity index. The method is applied to the case of Swedish pharmacies.

1. Introduction

The purpose of this article is to develop an input based non-parametric methodology for calculating productivity growth and to apply it to a sample of Swedish pharmacies. Our methodology merges ideas from measurement of efficiency by Farrell [1957] and from measurement of productivity as expressed by Caves, Christensen, and Diewert [1982]. In his classic article, "The Measurement of Productive Efficiency," Farrell introduced a framework for efficiency gauging in which overall efficiency can be decomposed into the two component measures: allocative and technical efficiency. Technical efficiency is the reciprocal of the Shephard [1953] and Malmquist [1953] (input) distance function, which is the key building block in the Malmquist input based productivity index, which we use here.

Caves, Christensen, and Diewert [1982] define the input based Malmquist productivity index as the ratio of two, yet to be defined, input distance functions. When they impose overall efficiency by Farrell [1957] and a translog structure on the distance functions, they show how the Törqvist index can be derived from the geometric mean of two Malmquist indexes. Here, no such assumptions on behavior or technology will be imposed. Instead, we allow for inefficiencies and model technology as piecewise linear. Thus our Malmquist index of productivity can distinguish between changes in efficiency and changes in the production frontier. This distinction should prove useful for policy purposes.

*The authors thank three anonymous referees for their important comments.

In Sweden, the retail trade of pharmaceutical products has been the responsibility of a public monopoly since 1971. In their agreement with the Swedish Government, Apoteksbolaget (the National Corporation of Swedish Pharmacies) "is responsible for ensuring that an adequate supply of drugs is maintained in the country. For this purpose, the business shall be conducted to foster opportunities for taking advantage of pharmaceutical advances, while maintaining drug costs at the lowest possible level" (Act on Retail Trade in Drugs of May 27, 1970, No. 205, Sec. 4.). That is, Apoteksbolaget should meet demand while minimizing cost, which suggests that an input based productivity index using input distance functions is an appropriate approach.

At present, Apoteksbolaget calculates the productivity of a pharmacy as the ratio between a weighted sum of four outputs and the total number of hours worked for two categories of personnel. The weights assigned to the respective outputs are assumed to reflect differences in resource use, and in the calculation of total output aggregate, all pharmacies are assigned the same weights. Total labor input is obtained as the sum of hours worked by the two types of personnel. For each pharmacy, productivity is calculated every month by the headquarters of Apoteksbolaget in Stockholm and reported back to the pharmacy within a period of three months. The report to the pharmacy also includes comparisons with its own productivity one year earlier, as well as with the average pharmacy. The present method of calculating productivity is sensitive to the weights assigned to outputs and inputs, respectively. It also does not account for all inputs.

Our sample consists of 42 group (or regional) pharmacies operating in Sweden from 1980 to 1989. These group pharamacies (gruppapoteken) are a small part of the total number of pharmacies in Sweden (there were 816 pharmacies in 1989). We focus on these 42 group pharmacies for several reasons. First, we had data on these 42 over the entire time period. Second, the fact that they are all group pharmacies (as opposed to local or hospital pharmacies) means that their responsibilities and sizes are fairly similar. Third, this sample size was computationally feasible using a PC.

Relative to the method presently used by Apoteksbolaget, our method is different with respect to the degree of productivity change, as well as with respect to direction of change in some cases. For the sample as a whole we find productivity increasing in seven periods and productivity declining in two. The method presently used by Apoteksbolaget also yields progress in seven periods and regress in two. However, the important point to observe is that periods with progress/regress were not always the same using the two approaches. For example, on average our method showed regress between 1980 and 1981 and progress between 1985 and 1986. According to the Apoteksbolaget, the opposite occurred for these years. So, for a pharmacy or for the average of a group of pharmacies, the methodology suggested in this article may give quite different result of productivity changes with respect to level and/or direction of changes.

The method of calculating productivity and productivity changes presently used by Apoteksbolaget has many drawbacks, e.g.: (1) It assumes that the underlying pharmacy technology is of a very special form (which may not be an appropriate assumption for the pharmacy production technology); (2) It cannot distinguish between changes in efficiency and change in the frontier technology; (3) It cannot easily include more input variables other than labor and requires outputs to be measured in the same units; (4) It requires a priori chosen weights for the aggregation of inputs and outputs, respectively. All of these drawbacks can be relaxed using our non-parametric methodology for calculating productivity and productivity changes.

2. The productivity index

The production technology is defined at each period t, $t = 1, \ldots, T$, to be the set of all feasible input and output vectors. If $x^t \in R_+^N$ denotes an input vector at period t and $y^t \in R_+^M$ an output vector in the same period, then the technology is the set S^t, where $S^t = \{(x^t, y^t) : x^t \text{ can produce } y^t\}$. We also model the technology by the input correspondence or equivalently by the input requirement set

$$L^t(y^t) = \{x^t : (x^t, y^t) \in S^t\}, \; t = 1, \ldots, T. \tag{1}$$

The input requirement set $L^t(y^t)$, denotes all input vectors x^t capable of producing outputs y^t during period t. Here we assume that $L^t(y^t)$ is a closed convex set for all y^t, and that there is no free lunch, i.e., $0 \notin L^t(y^t)$ if $y^t \geq 0$, $y^t \neq 0$. Moreover, we impose disposability of inputs and outputs, i.e., $\hat{x}^t \geq x^t \in L^t(y^t) \Rightarrow \hat{x}^t \in L^t(y^t)$ and $\hat{y}^t \geq y^t \Rightarrow L^t(\hat{y}^t) \subseteq L^t(y^t)$, respectively.

In this article, we formalize equation (1) as a piecewise linear input requirement set or equivalently as an activity analysis model. The coefficients in this model consist of observed inputs and outputs. We assume that there are $k = 1, \ldots, K^t$ observations of $n = 1, \ldots, N$ inputs $x_n^{k,t}$ in each period $t = 1, \ldots, T$. These inputs are employed to produce $k = 1, \ldots, K^t$ of $m = 1, \ldots, M$ observed outputs, $y_m^{k,t}$, at period $t = 1, \ldots, T$, and we assume that the number of observations are the same for all t, i.e., $K^t = K$.

The input requirement set (1) is formed from the observations as (see Färe, Grosskopf, and Lovell [1985])

$$\begin{aligned} L^t(y^t) = \{x^t : \; & y_m^t \leq \sum_{k=1}^{K} z^{k,t} y_m^{k,t}, \; m = 1, \ldots, M, \\ & x_n^t \geq \sum_{k=1}^{K} z^{k,t} x_n^{k,t}, \; n = 1, \ldots, N, \\ & z^{k,t} \geq 0, \; k = 1, \ldots, K\}, \end{aligned} \tag{2}$$

where $z^{k,t}$ is an intensity variable familiar from activity analysis. The intensity variables serve to form technology, which here is the convex cone of observed inputs and outputs. Constant returns to scale is imposed on the reference technology, but other forms of returns to scale may be imposed by restricting the sum of the intensity variables (see Grosskopf [1986]). One may also show that $L^t(y^t)$ satisfies the properties introduced above (see Shephard [1970] or Färe [1988]).

The Malmquist input based productivity index is expressed in terms of four input distance functions. The first is defined as

$$D_i^t(y^t, x^t) = \sup\{\lambda > 0 : (x^t/\lambda) \in L^t(y^t)\}. \tag{3}$$

Clearly,

$$D_i^t(y^t, x^t) \geq 1 \text{ if and only if } x^t \in L^t(y^t),$$

as the following figure 1 illustrates.

In figure 1, the input vector x^t belongs to the input requirement set $L^t(y^t)$. The distance function $D_i^t(y^t, x^t)$ measures the largest possible contraction of x^t under the condition that (x^t/λ) is feasible, i.e., $(x^t/\lambda) \in L^t(y^t)$. In terms of figure 1, $D_i^t(y^t, x^t) = 0a/0b$.

For observation k', $k' = 1, \ldots, K$, the value of the distance function $D_i^t(y^{k',t}, x^{k',t})$ is obtained as the solution to the linear programming problem

$$[D_i^t(y^{k',t}, x^{k',t})]^{-1} = \min \lambda, \tag{4}$$

$$\text{subject to } y_m^{k',t} \leq \sum_{k=1}^{K} z^{k,t} y_m^{k,t}, \; m = 1, \ldots, M,$$

$$\lambda x_n^{k',t} \geq \sum_{k=1}^{K} z^{k,t} x_n^{k,t}, \; n = 1, \ldots, N,$$

$$z^{k,t} \geq 0, \; k = 1, \ldots, K.$$

Note that $x^{k',t}$ is an element of the input set which implies that the distance function takes values larger than or equal to one. The value one is achieved whenever the input vector belongs to the isoquant of the input set, and hence where it is technically efficient à la Farrell [1957].

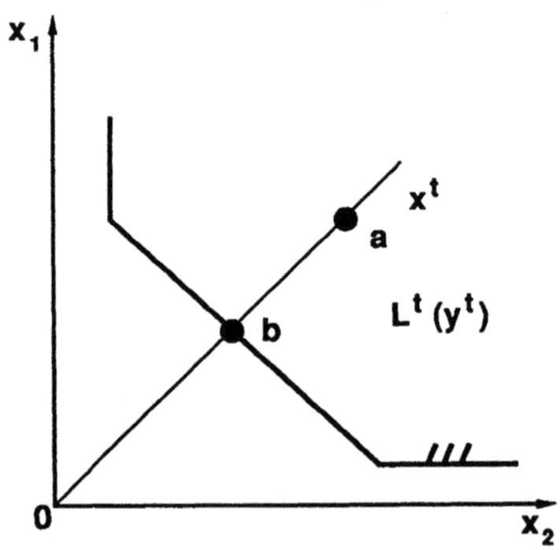

Figure 1. The input distance function.

We note the input distance function is the reciprocal of the Farrell technical efficiency measure, a fact which we have exploited to calculate the distance function.

In order to define the input based Malmquist productivity index by Caves, Christensen, and Diewert [1982], we need to relate the input output vectors (x^t, y^t) at period t to the technology L^{t+1} in the succeeding period. Therefore, we evaluate the input distance function for an input output vector (x^t, y^t) at period t relative to the input requirement set L^{t+1} in the following period.

$$D_i^{t+1}(y^t, x^t) = \sup\{\lambda > 0 : (x^t/\lambda) \in L^{t+1}(y^t)\}. \tag{5}$$

Again, $D_i^{t+1}(y^t, x^t) \geq 1$ if and only if $x^t \in L^{t+1}(y^t)$. However, (x^t, y^t) need not be feasible at $t + 1$, thus if equation (5) has a solution (i.e., supremum is a maximum), the value of $D_i^{t+1}(y^t, x^t)$ may be strictly less than one.

In our data set, the observed input $x_n^{k,t}$, $n = 1, \ldots, N$, is positive for each observation and each period. This together with strong disposability of inputs and constant returns to scale ensure that we can calculate the value of the input distance function (5) for k', $k' = 1, \ldots, K$, as the solution to the linear programming problem

$$[D_i^{t+1}(y^{k',t}, x^{k',t})]^{-1} = \min \lambda, \tag{6}$$

$$\text{subject to } y_m^{k',t} \leq \sum_{k=1}^{K} z^{k,t+1}\, y_m^{k,t+1},\ m = 1, \ldots, M,$$

$$\lambda x_n^{k',t} \geq \sum_{k=1}^{K} z^{k,t+1}\, x_n^{k,t+1},\ n = 1, \ldots, N,$$

$$z^{k,t+1} \geq 0,\ k = 1, \ldots, K.$$

We note that since $x^{k',t}$ need not be a member of the input requirement set $L^{t+1}(y^{k',t})$, the value of this distance function may be strictly less than one.

Two additional evaluations of the input distance function are required in order to define the productivity index. We need to evaluate observations at $t + 1$ relative to the technologies at t and $t + 1$. In particular,

$$D_i^{t}(y^{t+1}, x^{t+1}) = \sup\{\lambda > 0 : (x^{t+1}/\lambda) \in L^{t}(y^{t+1})\} \tag{7}$$

and

$$D_i^{t+1}(y^{t+1}, x^{t+1}) = \sup\{\lambda > 0 : (x^{t+1}/\lambda) \in L^{t+1}(y^{t+1})\} \tag{8}$$

The computation of equation (8) is identical to that of equation (3) so that in equation (4) we need only substitute $t + 1$ for t. The computation of equation (7) is parallel to that of equation (5), and again we need only substitute $t + 1$ for t and vice versa. We note of course that since (x^{t+1}, y^{t+1}) need not be feasible under the technology L^t, the input distance function $D_i^t(y^{t+1}, x^{t+1})$ may be strictly less than one.

Following Caves, Christensen, and Diewert [1982], we define the input based Malmquist productivity index as

$$M_i^{t+1}(y^{t+1}, x^{t+1}, y^t, x^t) = \left[\frac{D_i^t(y^{t+1}, x^{t+1})}{D_i^t(y^t, x^t)} \frac{D_i^{t+1}(y^{t+1}, x^{t+1})}{D_i^{t+1}(y^t, x^t)} \right]^{1/2}. \tag{9}$$

Actually, our definition is the geometric mean of two Malmquist indexes as defined by Caves, Christensen, and Diewert [1982]).

In their work, Caves, Christensen and Diewert [1982] make two assumptions. First, they assume that $D_i^t(y^t, x^t)$ and $D_i^{t+1}(y^{t+1}, x^{t+1})$ equal unity for each observation and period. In the terminology of Farrell [1957], this means that there is no technical inefficiency. Second, they assume that the distance functions are of translog form with identical second order terms. Here we follow Färe et al. [1989], and model the technology as piecewise linear and allow for inefficiencies. By allowing for inefficiencies, the productivity index can be decomposed into two components, one measuring change in efficiency and the other measuring technical change or equivalently change in the frontier technology. Equation (9) can be rewritten as

$$M_i^{t+1}(y^{t+1}, x^{t+1}y^t, x^t) = \frac{D_i^{t+1}(y^{t+1}, x^{t+1})}{D_i^t(y^t, x^t)} \left[\frac{D_i^t(y^{t+1}, x^{t+1})}{D_i^{t+1}(y^{t+1}, x^{t+1})} \frac{D_i^t(y^t, x^t)}{D_i^{t+1}(y^t, x^t)} \right]^{1/2}, \tag{10}$$

where the quotient outside the bracket measures the change in technical inefficiency and the ratios inside the bracket measure the shift in the frontier between periods t and $t + 1$ as figure 2 illustrates.

We denote the technology at t by S^t and at $t + 1$ by S^{t+1}, and note that $S^t = \{(x^t, y^t) : x^t \in L^t(y^t), y^t \geq 0\}$ and that S^{t+1} is similarly defined. The two observations (x^t, y^t) and (x^{t+1}, y^{t+1}) are both feasible in their respective periods. We may express the productivity index in terms of the above distances along the x-axis as

$$M_i^{t+1}(y^{t+1}, x^{t+1}, y^t, x^t) = \frac{0b/0a}{0d/0e} \left[\frac{0a}{0c} \frac{0f}{0e} \right]^{1/2}, \tag{11}$$

where (0b/0a)/(0d/0e) denotes the ratio of the Farrell measure of technical efficiency and the last part is the geometric mean of the shifts in technology at y^t and y^{t+1}. Note that the shifts in technology are measured locally for the observation at t and $t + 1$. This implies that: 1) the whole technology need not behave uniformly, and 2) that technolocial regress is possible.

In the literature on parametric modeling of productivity growth one can find decompositions comparable to the above (see e.g., Bauer [1990] or Nishimizu and Page [1982]).

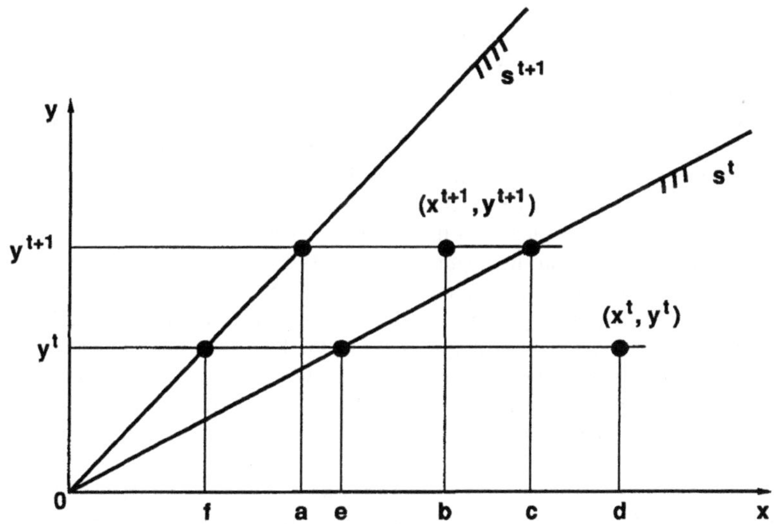

Figure 2. The input based Malmquist productivity index.

3. Results and comments

The data in this study consist of annual observations of outputs and inputs from 42 Swedish group pharmacies (gruppapoteken). The time period is 1980 to 1989. We specify four output variables and four input variables. Our four outputs: Drug deliveries to hospitals (SJHFANT); prescription drugs for outpatient care (RECFANT); medical appliances for the handicapped (FOLIANT); and over the counter goods (OTC). The first three outputs are measured in number of times. The volume of OTC is measured in 1980 prices. All pharmacies change the same output price for a given product.

Four separate inputs are used: Labour input for pharmacists (ARBTFT); labour input for technical staff (ARBTTT); building services (LOKY); and equipment services (AVSK). Labour input is measured in number of hours worked. Absence from work due to sickness, holiday, education, etc., is excluded. The flow of building services is assumed to be proportional to the floor space available, measured in square meters. The services flow from equipment is assumed to be proportional to the stock of equipment. By assumption, we have restricted changes in the stock of equipment to be either positive or unchanged, except when a pharmacy is completely rebuilt. As a proxy for the services flow from the stocks of equipment, we use annual depreciation of pharmacy equipment measured in 1980 prices. However, since we only allow for nonnegative changes in stocks of equipment, our series of annual depreciation measured in constant prices only shows increasing or unchanged values. Our main justification for making this assumption is that actual *lifeyears* of equipment is considerably longer than accounting *lifeyears*. For accounting purposes, equipment is assumed to provide services for only eight years.

The descriptive statistics of output and input variables are presented in Appendix A.

The number of hours worked by technical staff have decreased by 32 percent on average between 1980 and 1989 (see table A2). On the other hand, the number of hours worked by pharmacists is almost the same in 1989 as in 1980 (see table Al). However, on a year to year base, we observed small changes in the average number of hours worked by pharmacists on average. One reason for the decrease in hours worked by technical staff is that the pharmacies ceased to recruit new technical staff in the middle of the 1980's. Another reason is that some of the technical staff have been retrained to pharmacists. This retraining of technical staff started in the beginning of the 1980's.

Our estimation of services from equipment shows an increase for the average pharmacy during the observed time period by 16 percent (see table A3). We note that almost all pharmacies have changed from old to new equipment during the 1980's and that some pharmacies have been completely rebuilt. Looking at floor space we observe a decrease on average (see table A4). One reason for the decrease in floor space is that the pharmacies have eliminated unnecessary space. Another reason is that new pharmacies are smaller than the old ones.

On average, our statistics show a decrease over time in deliveries of drugs to hospitals (see table A5). A dramatic decrease of 57 percent occurred between 1983 and 1984, due mainly to reorganization.

Prescription of drugs for outpatient care has been fairly constant over time on average (see table A6). However, we observe a peak in 1983, which is due in part to an increase in the *out of pocket price* of prescription drugs that took place in December 1983. This increase led to an increase in sales of prescription drugs, i.e., prescription drugs that the patient should have purchased later but because of the increase in out of pocket price purchased earlier.

In the end of the 1970's, medical appliances for the handicapped were introduced as new products for the pharmacy. On average an increase in sales of medical appliances took place during the 1980's (see table A7). Here, we note that the number of products for the handicapped has increased over time, which may be one reason for the observed growth in medical appliances for the average pharmacy.

On average sales of over the counter goods have increased by 57 percent between 1980 and 1989 measured in fixed prices (see table A8). An increase in over the counter goods is in accordance with the development policy pursued by these pharmacies during the 1980's. The business of the pharmacies has gradually come to focus more and more on self medications. One may, however, find great variations among the pharmacies in the extent to which this policy has been pursued.

The mix of inputs and outputs has changed quite considerably during our observation period. We also note that in all years we find differences in input mix and output mix across pharmacies.

Computer costs and expenditures for energy, cleaning, stationery, etc. are not included among our input variables, because the data is not readily available. In addition, drugs and pharmaceuticals delivered to pharmacies have been excluded as inputs since the data is not readily available.

Tables 1 to 3 display our results. Table 1 shows calculated changes in relative input efficiency for each individual pharmacy and the overall average for the sample. In an input

Table 1. Changes[a] in pharamacy relative efficiency between time period *t* and *t* + 1, year 1980 to 1989, 42 Swedish pharmacies.

No.	1980/ 1981	1981/ 1982	1982/ 1983	1983/ 1984	1984/ 1985	1985/ 1986	1986/ 1987	1987/ 1988	1988/ 1989
1	1.0022	.8813	1.1521	1.0994	.9610	.9946	1.0205	1.0253	1.0000
2	1.0000	1.0000	1.0000	1.0000	1.0000	.9806	1.0198	1.0000	1.0000
3	1.0000	.9454	1.0577	1.0000	1.0000	1.0000	1.0000	1.0000	.8967
4	1.0085	.9131	1.0327	.9972	.9817	.9483	.9926	1.0541	1.0206
5	1.0687	.7166	1.1821	1.1876	.9659	.9279	.9990	1.0348	.9756
6	1.0442	.8887	1.2019	.9176	1.0110	.9984	.9593	1.0088	.9667
7	1.1588	1.0051	.9380	1.0833	.9984	.9720	.9946	1.0897	1.0000
8	1.5817	.7598	1.3162	1.0000	1.0000	1.0000	1.0000	1.0000	1.0000
9	.9708	.9708	1.0064	1.2077	.9910	.9116	.9705	.9959	.9971
10	1.0168	.8248	1.2097	.8932	1.0986	.9667	1.0317	1.0109	1.0408
11	.9657	.9299	1.2462	.8940	1.0305	1.0175	1.0025	1.0138	1.0496
12	.9949	1.0361	1.0000	.9714	.9696	.9567	1.0532	.8924	1.0342
13	1.0000	1.0000	1.0000	.9857	.9428	1.0446	.9734	1.0583	1.0000
14	1.0226	1.0000	1.0000	1.0000	1.0000	1.0000	1.0000	1.0000	1.0000
15	1.0000	1.0000	1.0000	1.0000	1.0000	1.0000	1.0000	1.0000	1.0000
16	1.0317	.9457	1.1174	1.0010	.9482	.9937	.9594	1.0376	1.0233
17	1.0000	.9347	1.0698	1.0000	1.0000	1.0000	1.0000	.9989	.9990
18	.9914	1.0087	1.0000	.8827	1.0663	1.0373	.9851	1.0396	.9131
19	1.1692	1.0000	.9760	1.0246	1.0000	1.0000	1.0000	1.0000	1.0000
20	.9634	1.0013	1.0210	1.0154	1.0000	1.0000	1.0000	1.0000	1.0000
21	1.0000	.8986	1.0704	.9956	.9098	.9030	1.0122	1.1707	.9927
22	.9306	.8545	1.1615	.9298	.9622	.9710	1.0481	1.0203	1.0519
23	1.0000	.8786	1.1382	1.0000	1.0000	1.0000	1.0000	1.0000	1.0000
24	1.0838	.9347	1.0139	.9430	1.0172	1.0803	.9405	1.0831	.9229
25	.9917	.9336	1.0126	1.0666	.9386	1.0654	1.0000	1.0000	1.0000
26	1.0000	1.0000	1.0000	1.0000	1.0000	.9363	1.0680	1.0000	1.0000
27	1.0908	.9264	1.0013	.9000	1.0228	.9368	1.0401	.9869	1.0658
28	1.0000	.8143	1.1384	.9974	.9691	.9845	1.0040	1.0587	1.0665
29	.9352	.8031	1.1935	1.0476	.9695	.9879	.9943	.9678	1.1612
30	1.0374	1.0000	1.0000	.8570	1.0630	.9925	1.0488	1.0545	1.0000
31	1.0000	1.0000	1.0000	.8428	.9912	1.0172	1.0553	.9703	1.0057
32	1.0000	1.0000	1.0000	1.0000	1.0000	1.0000	1.0000	1.0000	1.0000
33	1.0000	1.0000	1.0000	1.0000	1.0000	1.0000	1.0000	1.0000	1.0000
34	1.0839	1.0000	1.0000	1.0000	1.0000	1.0000	.8548	1.0888	1.0496
35	1.0000	1.0000	1.0000	1.0000	1.0000	1.0000	1.0000	1.0000	1.0000
36	1.0000	1.0000	1.0000	.9057	1.0517	1.0498	1.0000	1.0000	1.0000
37	1.1145	.9227	.9912	1.0098	1.0251	.7797	1.3060	.9867	1.0819
38	1.0000	1.0000	1.0000	.9813	1.0191	1.0000	1.0000	.9721	.9338
39	1.0000	1.0000	1.0000	1.0000	1.0000	1.0000	1.0000	1.0000	1.0000
40	.8441	.8561	1.0968	.9782	1.3138	.9892	.9970	1.0184	1.0138
41	1.0000	.9266	.9930	.9668	1.0103	1.1127	.8243	.9030	1.0625
42	1.0000	.9063	1.1034	1.0000	1.0000	.9509	.9896	1.0609	.9519
GE[b]	1.0220	.9353	1.0548	.9875	1.0039	.9868	1.0015	1.0133	1.0056

(a) In Table 1 to Table 3 a value over one mean progress, less than one mean regress and equal to one mean no change.
(b) Average geometrically of the sample (GE).

Table 2. Shifts[a] in pharamacy frontier technology. Averaged geometrically between time period *t* and *t* + 1, year 1980 to 1989, 42 Swedish pharmacies.

No.	1980/ 1981	1981/ 1982	1982/ 1983	1983/ 1984	1984/ 1985	1985/ 1986	1986/ 1987	1987/ 1988	1988/ 1989
1	.9049	1.1028	.9894	.9366	1.0497	.9793	1.0216	1.0163	1.0465
2	1.0077	1.1664	.9642	.9672	1.0365	1.0312	1.1683	1.1220	1.0587
3	.9927	1.1403	.9585	.9446	1.0511	1.1135	1.0285	1.0811	1.1033
4	.9600	1.1093	.9808	.9485	1.0411	1.0397	1.0937	1.0405	1.0299
5	.9550	1.4119	.8887	.7916	1.0651	1.1420	1.0598	1.0711	1.1243
6	.9140	1.1741	.9397	.8206	1.0486	1.0477	1.1035	1.0592	1.0250
7	.8587	1.0565	1.0258	.9019	1.0411	1.0489	1.1089	1.0350	1.0086
8	.9269	1.4032	.8190	1.1203	1.0555	1.1296	.9825	1.0550	1.0423
9	.9739	1.1573	.9866	.8380	1.0356	1.0960	1.0862	1.1068	1.0862
10	.9336	1.2912	.8815	1.0536	1.0560	1.0936	1.0597	1.0307	1.0268
11	.9129	1.1526	.9860	.7631	1.0473	1.0716	1.0945	1.0508	1.1222
12	1.0391	1.7107	.6985	1.0038	1.0927	1.0809	1.0928	1.0257	1.0093
13	1.0152	1.1443	.9576	.9966	.9832	1.0365	1.1483	.9819	1.0493
14	1.0673	1.1856	1.0425	1.0162	.9447	1.0674	1.0500	1.1283	.9680
15	1.0102	1.0694	.9214	1.0335	1.0280	.9859	.9945	.8965	1.0687
16	.9909	1.1352	.9583	.9409	1.0410	1.0096	1.0507	1.0514	1.0342
17	1.0518	1.0607	1.0158	.9377	1.0316	.9880	1.0583	.9019	1.0633
18	.9735	1.1271	.9304	.9699	1.0435	.9623	1.0262	.9522	10.450
19	.7989	1.1179	.9996	1.0828	1.0867	1.0730	.9842	.9494	.9882
20	.9809	1.1203	1.0440	1.0377	1.0856	1.0316	1.0161	.9800	1.0593
21	.9648	1.1718	.9460	1.0669	1.1073	1.0713	1.0695	1.0110	1.0336
22	1.0322	1.1324	.8821	.9954	1.0032	.9741	1.0015	.9526	1.0800
23	.6707	1.0935	.9154	.9819	1.0821	.9445	1.0519	1.0073	1.0325
24	.9185	1.0865	.9882	.9443	1.0488	1.0234	1.1721	1.0796	1.1412
25	.8829	1.2458	.9749	.9075	1.0597	.9404	1.1103	1.0295	1.0710
26	1.0291	1.0205	1.0123	.9696	1.1527	.8504	1.2002	1.0896	1.0918
27	.9230	1.0839	1.0380	.9297	1.0504	1.0292	1.0292	1.0524	1.0316
28	.9142	1.2740	.8912	.9196	1.0716	.9758	1.0407	1.0224	1.0588
29	.8946	1.2615	.8677	.9186	1.0452	1.0170	1.0511	1.0384	1.0392
30	.9193	1.1177	1.1205	.9220	1.0708	1.0505	1.0110	1.0401	1.0132
31	.9686	1.0888	1.0559	.8361	1.0848	1.0472	1.1086	1.0408	1.0450
32	.9816	1.0592	1.0603	.9641	1.0787	1.0178	1.1063	1.0124	.9756
33	1.0386	1.0372	1.0646	1.0512	1.0025	1.1112	1.1717	1.0163	1.1154
34	.8972	1.1140	1.0966	.9307	.9304	1.0105	.9013	1.0587	1.0321
35	1.3315	.7905	1.0253	1.0852	.9586	.9601	.9651	1.0019	.9190
36	.9829	1.0328	1.0409	.9244	1.0192	.9823	1.0634	1.0329	.9816
37	.9567	1.2328	1.0028	.9612	1.0661	1.0323	1.0420	.9903	1.0465
38	1.0247	1.1834	1.0265	.9247	1.0308	1.1278	1.0476	1.0904	1.1077
39	1.0223	1.0889	1.1285	.8541	.9857	1.0212	1.1630	1.0271	1.0096
40	1.1425	1.2353	.9352	1.0002	.9746	1.0977	1.0963	1.1015	1.0663
41	1.0933	.9847	.9698	1.0296	.9670	1.0719	1.1459	1.0069	1.0423
42	1.0829	1.3972	.9141	.9993	1.0435	1.0525	1.0251	1.0690	1.0557
GE[b]	.9698	1.1483	.9713	.9544	1.0395	1.0325	1.0649	1.0298	1.0455

(a) See Table 1.

(b) See Table 1.

Table 3. Productivity change[a] in pharamacies (annual change between time period t and $t + 1$, year 1980 to 1989, 42 Swedish pharmacies.

No.	1980/ 1981	1981/ 1982	1982/ 1983	1983/ 1984	1984/ 1985	1985/ 1986	1986/ 1987	1987/ 1988	1988/ 1989
1	.9069	.9719	1.1399	1.0297	1.0088	.9740	1.0425	1.0420	1.0465
2	1.0077	1.1664	.9642	.9672	1.0365	1.0112	1.1914	1.1220	1.0587
3	.9927	1.0780	1.0138	.9446	1.0511	1.1135	1.0285	1.0811	.9893
4	.9682	1.0129	1.0128	.9458	1.0220	.9859	1.0857	1.0968	1.0511
5	1.0206	1.0117	1.0505	.9401	1.0287	1.0596	1.0588	1.1084	1.0969
6	.9544	1.0435	1.1295	.7530	1.0601	1.0461	1.0586	1.0685	.9908
7	.9950	1.0619	.9622	.9770	1.0394	1.0196	1.1029	1.1279	1.0086
8	1.4661	1.0661	1.0780	1.1203	1.0555	1.1296	.9825	1.0550	1.0423
9	.9455	1.1235	.9929	1.0121	1.0263	.9992	1.0541	1.1022	1.0830
10	.9492	1.0650	1.0664	.9411	1.1601	1.0572	1.0933	1.0420	1.0687
11	.8815	1.0718	1.2288	.6822	1.0793	1.0905	1.0973	1.0653	1.1778
12	1.0338	1.7725	.6985	.9751	1.0595	1.0341	1.1509	.9153	1.0438
13	1.0152	1.1443	.9576	.9824	.9269	1.0827	1.1177	1.0391	1.0493
14	1.0915	1.1856	1.0425	1.0162	.9447	1.0674	1.0500	1.1283	.9680
15	1.0102	1.0694	.9214	1.0335	1.0280	.9859	.9945	.8965	1.0687
16	1.0222	1.0735	1.0707	.9418	.9870	1.0032	1.0081	1.0909	1.0583
17	1.0518	.9915	1.0867	.9377	1.0316	.9880	1.0583	.9009	1.0622
18	.9651	1.1369	.9304	.8562	1.1126	.9982	1.0109	.9899	.9542
19	.9341	1.1179	.9757	1.1093	1.0867	1.0730	.9842	.9494	.9882
20	.9450	1.1217	1.0659	1.0537	1.0856	1.0316	1.0161	.9800	1.0593
21	.9648	1.0530	1.0126	1.0622	1.0075	.9674	1.0825	1.1836	1.0261
22	.9606	.9676	1.0246	.9255	.9653	.9459	1.0496	.9719	1.1360
23	.6707	.9607	1.0419	.9819	1.0821	.9445	1.0519	1.0073	1.0325
24	.9954	1.0156	1.0019	.8905	1.0669	1.1056	1.1024	1.1693	1.0532
25	.8756	1.1630	.9873	.9679	.9946	1.0020	1.1103	1.0295	1.0710
26	1.0291	1.0205	1.0123	.9696	1.1527	.7963	1.2818	1.0896	1.0918
27	1.0069	1.0041	1.0394	.8366	1.0743	.9642	1.0705	1.0387	1.0995
28	.9142	1.0375	1.0145	.9172	1.0385	.9607	1.0449	1.0824	1.1292
29	.8367	1.0132	1.0355	.9623	1.0133	1.0046	1.0450	1.0050	1.2068
30	.9536	1.1177	1.1205	.7902	1.1383	1.0426	1.0603	1.0967	1.0132
31	.9686	1.0888	1.0559	.7046	1.0752	1.0652	1.1699	1.0099	1.0510
32	.9816	1.0592	1.0603	.9641	1.0787	1.0178	1.1063	1.0124	.9756
33	1.0376	1.0372	1.0646	1.0512	1.0025	1.1112	1.1717	1.0163	1.1154
34	.9724	1.1140	1.0966	.9307	.9304	1.0105	.7704	1.1527	1.0833
35	1.3315	.7905	1.0253	1.0852	.9586	.9601	.9651	1.0019	.9190
36	.9829	1.0328	1.0409	.8372	1.0719	1.0312	1.0634	1.0329	.9816
37	1.0663	1.1375	.9939	.9707	1.0929	.8049	1.3609	.9771	1.1322
38	1.0247	1.1834	1.0265	.9074	1.0505	1.1278	1.0476	1.0600	1.0344
39	1.0223	1.0889	1.1285	.8541	.9857	1.0212	1.1630	1.0271	1.0096
40	.9644	1.0576	1.0257	.9784	1.2804	1.0859	1.0930	1.1218	1.0810
41	1.0933	.9125	.9630	.9954	.9770	1.1927	.9445	.9092	1.1075
42	1.0829	1.2663	1.0086	.9993	1.0435	1.0008	1.0145	1.1342	1.0050
GE[b]	.9911	1.0740	1.0246	.9424	1.0435	1.0189	1.0665	1.0435	1.0513
AB[c]	1.023	1.056	1.020	.950	1.026	.994	1.082	1.070	1.072

(a) See Table 1.
(b) See Table 1.
(c) The present method used by Apoteksbolaget for calculating productivity of year t is given by:

$$P^t = SHFANT^t + RECFANT^t\ FOLIANT^t + 0.4{*}OTC^t \,/\, ARBTTT^t + ARBTFT^t$$

OTC is here transformed into number of customers by dividing OTC in real value (1980 prices) with average price in 1980. Productivity changes (AB), arithmetic average of the sample.

based model of productivity change, a number less than one will correspond to progress. However, in tables 1 to 3, for illustrative purposes we take the reciprocal numbers so that one equals no change, a number greater than one equals progress and less than one equals regress, which conforms to standard interpretation in the productivity literature. We also note that the linear programming model chosen yields pharmacy specific result. We report averages which are calculated as the geometric mean of the 42 individual results.

The results reported in table 1 represent the terms outside the bracket in equation (10), i.e., changes in efficiency. A pharmacy which has been efficient in time period t and time period $t + 1$, will naturally show no change in relative efficiency. We found five pharmacies (nos. 15, 32, 33, 35, and 39) to be efficient in all time periods. With the exception of pharmacy no. 39, these efficient pharmacies are all of middle size; in contrast, no. 39 is a small pharmacy. For the other 37 pharmacies we found periods with declines in efficiency as well as periods with improvements in efficiency. We found no pharmacy with only progress or only regress in efficiency during the period 1980 to 1989. For the sample as a whole, six periods showed average improvement in efficiency and three periods should average decline in efficiency. Between 1981 and 1982 the overall average fall in efficiency was 6.5 percent. This was followed by a 5.5 percent improvement in efficiency. For the remaining periods we found small changes in efficiency.

Table 2 presents calculated technical progress/regress as measured by average shifts in the pharmacy frontier from time period t to time period $t + 1$. This corresponds to the term in the bracket in equation (10). Our results showed on average six periods with progress and three periods with regress. Between 1981 and 1982 almost all phramacies showed technical progress. Here, we note that on average the number of hours worked by technical staff decreased by 6.5 percent, which may be one explanation for the calculated positive shift in the frontier. The large shifts in the frontier between 1981 and 1982 for a few pharmacies (nos. 5, 8, 12, and 42) may be due to errors in reported data. On the other hand, for more than half of the pharmacies our calculations showed technical progress of more than 10 percent between 1981 and 1982. Only one pharmacy (no. 33) showed technical progress for all periods 1980 to 1989. On average, we found progress in all periods for the latter part of the 1980's.

Table 3 displays calculated productivity changes in pharmacies, as represented by the Malmquist input based productivity index in equation (10), which is a combination of the efficiency and technical change components discussed above. According to our results, we have had on average productivity gains in seven periods and productivity losses in two periods. Again, only one pharmacy (no. 33) showed progress in all periods. The overall fall in productivity that took place between 1983 to 1984 may be connected to the change in out of pocket price for prescriptions introduced in December 1983. However, ten pharmacies showed productivity gains between 1983 and 1984. For all pharmacies and all periods we found productivity gains in 259 cases and productivity losses in 119 cases, i.e., progress in 68 percent of all cases. For the period 1985 to 1989 we found progress in 78 percent of all cases. We note that the on average, progress in productivity during the latter part of the 1980's is mainly explained by positive shifts of the frontier.

Compared to the method presently used by Apoteksbolaget (see Section 1) our method different both with respect to degree of change as well as with respect to direction in some cases. Table 3 displays our results as well as the result of the present method for the average of the sample as a whole. Our findings suggest that there were productivity gains in seven periods and productivity losses in two. The present method used by Apoteksbolaget also yields progress in seven periods and regress in two. However, the important point to observe is that periods with progress/regress were not always the same in the two approaches. For example, on average our method showed regress between 1980 and 1981, and progress between 1985 and 1986, respectively. According to Apoteksbolaget, the opposite results were found.

Our decomposition of the productive index in equation (10) allows us to distinguish between change in efficiency and change in frontier technology. This distinction should prove useful for policy purposes. Inefficiency of a pharmacy may partly be explained by, for example, divergence between individual pharmacy managers and the overall purpose of the organization (Apoteksbolaget). This divergence in goals may in turn give differences in *the way of doing things* at a pharmacy. In explaining inefficiency, one can search for differences between efficiency pharmacies and inefficiency pharmacies. Table 4 shows the frequency with which a pharmacy has been used as a reference in forming a frontier (input isoquant) for a given pharmacy. These are the model pharmacies relative to which inefficient pharmacies are compared. Our results showed that some pharmacies have been used as reference pharmacies in all or almost all time periods; for example pharmacies no. 14, 23, 32, and 39. However, we also found pharmacies that have never belonged to the frontier technology; pharmacies no. 4, 5, 9, 10, 16, 29, 37, and 40. Further research can hopefully identify what is typical for the efficient pharmacies compared to the inefficient pharmacies. Furthermore, it is the frontier pharmacies that move the frontier. One may study what characterizes movements in the frontier, for example effects of new forms of organization, new equipment or computerization.

A final note of caution is reading our results is that our model does not contain quality variables on outputs. Of course, exlcusions of possible changes in quality might have affected our results. Further research will, hopefully, show how quality variables could be included in the model.

4. Summary

In this article we calculate total factor productivity for a sample of Swedish regional pharmacies over the 1980–1989 period. The technique we use is non-parametric; the index of productivity we use is the input-based Malmquist productivity index introduced by Caves, Christensen, and Diewert [1982]. As shown by Caves, Christensen and Diewert, if it is assumed that technology is translog (and second order terms are identical over time) and firms are technically and allocatively efficient (profit maximizers), then the Malmquist index is equivalent to the Törnqvist, and is in turn a *superlative* index.

Instead of assuming translog technology and efficiency, we directly calculate the Malmquist index which, because it is constructed from distance functions, allows us to aggregate inputs and outputs without price or data and explicitly allows for (technical) inefficiency. In fact, since input distance functions are reciprocal to Farrell technical efficiency of the input saving variety, we use Farrell technical efficiency measures to construct the Malmquist productivity index. This allows us to decompose productivity growth into efficiency change and technical change.

In our empirical application, we compose our Malmquist total factor productivity indexes to the labor productivity measures currently used by the Swedish pharmacy sector to assess their nonperformance.

Table 4. Frequency with which a pharmacy has been used as a reference in forming an input frontier.

Nr.	1980	1981	1982	1983	1984	1985	1986	1987	1988	1989
1	0	0	0	0	3	0	0	0	1	1
2	7	11	18	3	3	2	0	6	9	9
3	17	12	0	1	1	11	10	2	2	0
4	0	0	0	0	0	0	0	0	0	0
5	0	0	0	0	0	0	0	0	0	0
6	0	0	0	1	0	0	0	0	0	0
7	0	0	0	1	0	0	0	0	0	0
8	0	3	0	2	11	13	23	9	5	3
9	0	0	0	0	0	0	0	0	0	0
10	0	0	0	0	0	0	0	0	0	0
11	0	0	0	13	0	0	0	0	0	3
12	0	0	25	1	0	0	0	0	0	0
13	1	1	3	1	0	0	0	0	1	2
14	0	8	5	13	14	8	10	14	11	7
15	2	4	5	3	5	7	6	5	2	5
16	0	0	0	0	0	0	0	0	0	0
17	1	3	0	1	1	1	1	2	0	0
18	2	0	3	3	0	0	0	0	3	0
19	0	1	3	0	5	10	17	10	4	6
20	2	0	0	0	2	3	6	9	8	3
21	3	12	0	0	0	0	0	0	0	0
22	1	0	0	0	0	0	0	0	0	0
23	18	5	0	7	10	13	13	13	11	7
24	0	0	0	0	0	0	0	0	2	0
25	11	0	0	0	1	0	2	4	1	2
26	1	2	5	2	1	9	0	14	11	15
27	0	1	0	0	0	0	0	0	0	0
28	2	7	0	0	0	0	0	0	0	10
29	0	0	0	0	0	0	0	0	0	0
30	0	2	7	12	0	0	0	0	2	2
31	1	1	3	1	0	0	0	0	0	0
32	6	6	4	8	18	15	6	16	5	4
33	2	4	7	3	5	1	5	6	3	6
34	0	2	8	12	5	2	3	0	0	0
35	1	9	3	2	5	3	2	4	3	3
36	2	1	1	1	0	0	1	1	1	1
37	0	0	0	0	0	0	0	0	0	0
38	2	2	1	1	0	2	3	1	0	0
39	6	1	6	8	13	16	12	15	15	14
40	0	0	0	0	0	0	0	0	0	0
41	1	2	0	0	0	0	2	0	0	0
42	3	3	0	3	3	5	0	0	0	0

Note: Zero implies that the pharmacy for that year has been inefficient. One means that a pharmacy only has been a reference pharmacy for itself. A value more than one implies that the pharmacy has been efficient for that year and used as a reference for other pharmacies. For example, a number of 7 means that the pharmacy has been used as a reference for 6 other pharmacies.

Appendix A: Descriptive statistics of input and output variables

Table A1. Descriptive statistics of input variable ARBTFT (number of hours worked).

Year	Arithmetic mean	Min	Max
1980	17581	5520	26316
1981	17359	7248	26328
1982	17523	5292	29796
1983	18712	8856	36396
1984	16504	6957	24962
1985	16870	7578	25336
1986	17900	7195	26276
1987	18237	7729	26371
1988	18223	8349	25324
1989	17260	7107	25512

Table A2. Descriptive statistics of input variable ARBTTT (number of hours worked).

Year	Arithmetic mean	Min	Max
1980	28802	6456	43332
1981	26940	7236	45564
1982	25904	7104	47712
1983	26446	5436	49980
1984	24863	6375	46918
1985	24256	6994	46138
1986	24194	6713	47420
1987	22626	7043	45244
1988	21289	6333	36793
1989	19657	6068	32040

Table A3. Descriptive statistics of input variable AVSK ('000 of Swedish kronor).

Year	Arithmetic mean	Min	Max
1980	212	40	560
1981	224	40	560
1982	222	40	560
1983	231	40	560
1984	230	50	560
1985	228	50	560
1986	243	50	560
1987	246	75	560
1988	246	75	560
1989	246	75	560

Table A4. Descriptive statistics of input variable LOKY (square meter).

Year	Arithmetic mean	Min	Max
1980	634	271	1400
1981	639	271	1400
1982	637	271	1400
1983	638	271	1400
1984	619	271	1400
1985	612	271	1400
1986	610	271	1400
1987	604	271	1400
1988	608	271	1400
1989	608	271	1400

Table A5. Descriptive statistics of output variable SJHFANT (number of items).

Year	Arithmetic mean	Min	Max
1980	20524	0	142536
1981	20307	0	143728
1982	20393	0	140088
1983	20719	0	144082
1984	13212	0	125644
1985	13605	0	129841
1986	14548	0	128356
1987	14788	0	127715
1988	14427	0	133398
1989	12721	0	125437

Table A6. Descriptive statistics of output variable RECFANT (number of items).

Year	Arithmetic mean	Min	Max
1980	143372	22632	242460
1981	134406	33444	238452
1982	137982	33888	266580
1983	145889	34776	314440
1984	126677	24501	223447
1985	126513	26061	234927
1986	124591	25724	231117
1987	129187	28330	229953
1988	131563	26005	236991
1989	131577	26456	225934

Table A7. Descriptive statistics of output variable FOLIANT (number of items).

Year	Arithmetic mean	Min	Max
1980	3723	961	6312
1981	3973	1176	7680
1982	4687	1452	9156
1983	5125	1562	10019
1984	4933	1850	9914
1985	5177	2019	10537
1986	5487	2396	11038
1987	6023	2465	12134
1988	5879	2054	9587
1989	5832	1951	9991

Table A8. Descriptive statistics of output variable OTC ('000 of Swedish kronor).

Year	Arithmetic mean	Min	Max
1980	2156	238	4072
1981	2312	318	5152
1982	2453	355	6219
1983	2640	389	6464
1984	2490	359	6262
1985	2649	385	6189
1986	2842	401	6780
1987	3060	415	7023
1988	3294	336	7571
1989	3388	335	7673

References

Bauer, P. (1990). "Decomposing TFP Growth in the Presence of Cost Inefficiency, Nonconstant Returns Scale, and Technological Progress." *Journal of Productivity Analysis* 1, pp. 287–299.

Caves, D., L. Christensen, and E. Diewert. (1982). "The Economic Theory of Index Numbers and the Measurement of Input, Output, and Productivity." *Econometrica* 50, pp. 1393–1414.

Färe, R. (1988). *Fundamentals of Production Theory,* Berlin: Springer-Verlag.

Färe, R., S. Grosskopf, and C.A.K. Lovell. (1985). *The Measurement of Efficiency of Production,* Boston: Kluwer-Nijhoff.

Färe, R., S. Grosskopf, B. Lindgren, and P. Roos. (1989). "Productivity Developments in Swedish Hospitals: A Malmquist Output Index Approach." Department of Economics, Southern Illinois University, Carbondale.

Farrell, M.J. (1957). "The Measurement of Productive Efficiency." *Journal of The Royal Statistical Society.* Series A, General, 120, part 3 pp. 2553–281.

Malmquist, S. (1953). "Index Numbers and Indifference Surfaces." *Trabajos de Estatistica* 4, pp. 209–242.

Nishimizu, M. and J.M. Page. (1982). "Total Factor Productivity Growth, Technological Progress and Technical Efficiency Change: Dimensions of Productivity Change in Yugoslavia. 1967–1978." *Economic Journal* 92, pp. 920–936.

Shephard, R.W. (1953). *Cost and Production Functions.* Princeton: Princeton University Press.

Shephard, R.W. (1970). *Theory of Cost and Production Functions.* Princeton: Princeton University Press.

The Journal of Productivity Analysis, 3, 103-117 (1992)

Variation in Productive Efficiency in French Workers' Cooperatives*

JACQUES DEFOURNY
University of Liège and CIRIEC

C.A. KNOX LOVELL
University of North Carolina

AKÉ G.M. N'GBO
University of Abidjan and CIRIEC

Abstract

In this study, we explore the distribution of productive efficiency among workers' cooperatives operating in each of four sectors of French manufacturing. We use stochastic frontier panel data techniques to estimate production relationships in each sector, and to decompose output variation into input variation, variation in the effects of two indicators of the degree of worker participation in management, variation in productive efficiency, and an unexplained residual. In all four sectors we find that conventionally measured capital and labor inputs make a significant contribution to productivity. In only one sector do participation indicators contribute significantly. Variation in productive efficiency contributes significantly in all four sectors.

1. Introduction

The purpose of this study is to explore the distribution of productive efficiency among workers' cooperatives operating in each of four sectors of French manufacturing. Productive efficiency is one component of overall productivity, and although the measurement of productivity change (or variation) in European cooperatives has attracted much attention recently, for a variety of reasons the technical efficiency component of productivity change has been almost completely neglected. This study is an effort to remedy that neglect.

We have recent data on output, inputs, and other relevant variables for a number of workers' cooperatives operating in each of four sectors of French manufacturing for the two adjacent years 1987 and 1988. The sectors are architecture, printing, furniture, and public works. Thus we have four short two-year panels containing 24, 55, 22 and 42 firms, respectively.

We use recently developed stochastic frontier panel data techniques to estimate the production relationships within each sector. These techniques provide a decomposition of output variation into input variation, variation in a pair of variables representing the degree of participation of workers in management, variation in technical efficiency, and an unexplained residual.[1]

*Earlier versions of this article were presented at the ORSA/TIMS Joint National Meeting in Philadelphia, PA, October 1990, and at the Allied Social Science Associations meetings in Washington, DC, December 1990. Helpful comments from discusants at both meetings, and from two good referees, are gratefuly acknowledged, as is financial support of AUPELF and the UNC University Research Council.

The decomposition of productivity variation into input variation and participation variation is not new in this literature; see Jones and Svejnar [1985], Defourny, Estrin and Jones [1987], Defourny [1987] and Estrin, Jones and Svejnar [1987] for applications of this technique. The introduction of an additional component—efficiency variation—is new. Only Defourny [1988] and Sterner [1990] have sought to measure the technical efficiency of workers' cooperatives, in several sectors of the French economy and in the Mexican cement industry, respectively. However, Defourny estimated the mean technical efficiency, rather than individual efficiencies, over all cooperatives and over all capitalist firms in each sector. Consequently, he did not use efficiency variation to explain any part of intra-sectoral productivity variation.[2] Sterner compared technical efficiencies of individual plants with different ownership structures, but there were only two cooperatives in his sample.[3]

In all four sectors we find that conventionally measured capital and labor inputs make a significant contribution to productivity. In only two sectors do participation indicators contribute significantly. Variation in technical efficiency contributes significantly in all four sectors. One conclusion to be drawn from these findings is that it is risky to analyze productivity variation under the assumption of technical efficiency. To do so leads to an erroneous allocation of productivity variation to its other sources, which in turn can lead to inappropriate policy decisions, particularly those that may be designed to influence participation.

This article is organized as follows: in Section 2 we outline the production frontier model, its characteristics and its estimation; Section 3 contains a brief description of the data, and a discussion of the empirical results; and Section 4 concludes with a summary of the study and suggestions for further related research.

2. The Production Frontier Model

For a single cross section, Aigner, Lovell, and Schmidt [1977], Battese and Corra [1977] and Meeusen and van den Broeck [1977] all showed how to estimate a stochastic production frontier model of the form

$$\ln y_i = \alpha_0 + \sum_{j=1}^{K} \alpha_j \ln x_{ji} + v_i + u_i, \qquad i = 1, \ldots, I, \tag{1}$$

where y_i is observed output in the ith firm, x_{ji} is the observed amount of the jth input employed in the ith firm, $(\alpha_0, \alpha_1, \ldots, \alpha_K)$ is a vector of technology parameters to be estimated, $v_i \sim N(0, \sigma_v^2)$ is an error term capturing the random effects of noise, measurement error and the like, and u_i is a nonpositive error term, distributed independently of v_i, capturing the effects of technical inefficiency in production. Once a particular distribution is assigned to u_i—half normal, truncated normal, exponential and gamma have been used—its parameter(s) can be estimated and mean technical efficiency in the sample can be estimated. This is what Defourny [1988] did, using least squares methods.

Now we consider a time series of cross sections, and write the panel data extension of the cross section production frontier model (2.1) as

$$\ln y_{it} = \alpha_0 + \sum_{j=1}^{K} \alpha_j \ln x_{jit} + v_{it} + u_i, \qquad i = 1, \ldots, I, \; t = 1, \ldots, T_i, \qquad (2)$$

where y_{it} is observed output of the *i*th firm in the *t*th period, and x_{jit} is observed usage of the *j*th input in the *i*th firm in the *t*th period. We have I firms and $T = \max \{T_i\}$ periods, although not all firms must be observed in all periods. Note that technical inefficiency is captured by the "firm effect," and is time-invariant. Models of this nature have been considered by several authors recently; this particular unbalanced panel version is adapted from Battese, Coelli, and Colby [1989].

In this study we use a standard Cobb-Douglas production function[4]

$$y_{it} = AK_{it}^{\alpha}L_{it}^{\beta}, \qquad (3)$$

and incorporate the following institutional features of the cooperatives

$$K_{it} = K_{it}^{I} + K_{it}^{E} \qquad (4)$$

and

$$L_{it} = L_{it}^{N} + L_{it}^{M}, \qquad (5)$$

where K_{it}^{I} and K_{it}^{E} denote the amounts of fixed assets financed internally and externally, respectively, and where L_{it}^{N} and L_{it}^{M} denote the number of employees who are non-members and members of the cooperative, respectively, all in firm i in period t.[5] We now rewrite equation (3) as

$$y_{it} = AK_{it}^{\alpha}[(1 + (d - 1)(K_{it}^{E}/K_{it})]^{\alpha} L_{it}^{\beta}[(1 + (c - 1)(L_{it}^{N}/L_{it})]^{\beta}, \qquad (6)$$

where d and c are parameters that allow for productivity differentials between K_{it}^{E} and K_{it}^{I}, and between L_{it}^{N} and L_{it}^{M}, respectively. In the event that $d = c = 1$, equation (6) collapses to equation (3), while if $d \neq 1$ or $c \neq 1$ there is a productivity differential between externally and internally financed fixed assets, or between nonmember and member employees. Following Brown and Medoff [1978], we take the logarithm of equation (6) and take linear approximations to the two bracketed terms to generate[6]

$$\ln y_{it} = \ln A + \alpha \ln K_{it} + \beta \ln L_{it} + \alpha(d - 1)(K_{it}^{E}/K_{it}) + \beta(c - 1)(L_{it}^{N}/L_{it}). \qquad (7)$$

After reparameterization our stochastic production frontier model becomes

$$\ln y_{it} = a_0 + a_1 \ln K_{it} + a_2 \ln L_{it} + a_3(K_{it}^{E}/K_{it}) + a_4(L_{it}^{N}/L_{it}) + v_{it} + u_i. \qquad (8)$$

The disturbance component v_{it} is assumed to be independently and identically distributed as $N(0, \sigma_v^2)$, independent of the disturbance component u_i, which is assumed to be independently and identically distributed as the nonpositive part of a $N(\mu, \sigma^2)$ distribution truncated above at zero. Both components are also assumed to be distributed independently of the exogenous variables in the model.

Firm-specific but time-invariant estimates of technical efficiency are obtained by following Jondrow et al. [1982] and Battese and Coelli [1988] to obtain

$$TE_i = E[\exp(u_i | v_{it} + u_i)] = \left\{ \frac{1 - F(\sigma_i^* + (\mu_i^*/\sigma_i^*))}{1 - F(\mu_i^*/\sigma_i^*)} \right\} \exp(\mu_i^* + ½\, \sigma_i^{*2}), \quad (9)$$

where F(•) is the cumulative distribution function of the standard normal variable and μ_i^* and σ_i^{*2} are the parameters of the conditional normal distribution of $(u_i | v_{it} + u_i)$. The mean technical efficiency of all firms in a sector is given by

$$TE = \left\{ \frac{1 - F[\sigma + (\mu/\sigma)]}{1 - F(\mu/\sigma)} \right\} \exp(\mu + ½\, \sigma^2). \quad (10)$$

Equation (8) is the model to be estimated, after which equations (9) and (10) are used to estimate time-invariant efficiency by observation and as a sample mean.

There are eight parameters to be estimated. The three technology parameters (a_0, a_1, a_2) describe the contribution of conventionally measured capital and labor inputs to output. The two participation parameters (d and c) measure the contribution of two popular indicators of participation to output. The three efficiency parameters [μ, $\tilde{\sigma}^2 = \sigma^2 + \sigma_v^2$ and $\gamma = \sigma^2/\tilde{\sigma}^2$] describe the contribution of technical efficiency to output. All eight parameters are estimated using maximum likelihood techniques described in Battese, Coelli, and Colby [1989] and Coelli [1989].

3. The data and the results

We use panel data covering 1987 and 1988 for cooperatives in four sectors: in Architecture we have 24 firms and 45 observations, in Printing, we have 55 firms and 110 observations, in Furniture we have 22 firms and 41 observations, and in Public Works we have 42 firms and 81 observations. Output y_{it} is value added in thousand FF, capital K_{it} is the value of fixed assets in thousand FF, labor L_{it} is the number of employees, and K_{it}^E/K_{it} and L_{it}^N/L_{it} are ratios of external capital to total capital and non-member workers to total workers, respectively. The data were obtained from CGSCOP [1989], and are summarized in table 1.

Having only two years of data, we think the fixed effects model gives reliable estimates of technical efficiency. We use maximum likelihood methods to obtain estimates of a_0, a_1, a_2, a_3, a_4, μ, $\tilde{\sigma}^2$ and γ and their standard errors.[8] The participation parameters c and d are also identified, and so we estimate them and their standard errors as well.[9] The results for each of the four sectors are presented in tables 2–5. Each table reports the results of four model specifications, in which different restrictions are imposed on the parameters. Student t-statistics are reported beneath parameter estimates. The χ^2 statistic provides a test of the hypothesis that variation in technical efficiency contributes nothing to productivity variation; the hypothesis is that $\gamma = 0$.

Table 1. Data.

	y (Thousand FF)	K (Thousand FF)	L (Number of Employees)	K^E/K	L^N/L
Furniture					
Mean	4373.92	3128.02	28	0.13	0.26
Min	96.12	144.18	3	0.0	0.0
Max	93133.51	83150.54	409	0.46	0.70
Printing					
Mean	3659.63	2941.38	20	0.12	0.23
Min	61.00	80.64	2	0.0	0.0
Max	20206.99	21105.36	88	0.75	0.69
Public Works					
Mean	8276.71	4189.22	44	0.16	0.43
Min	390.94	26.80	2	0.0	0.0
Max	66123.66	44846.77	343	0.99	0.90
Architecture					
Mean	1100.46	227.51	5	0.10	0.15
Min	253.23	8.96	2	0.0	0.0
Max	3217.74	1037.63	18	0.43	0.55

As mentioned in the introduction, we seek to quantify the contributions of three sources of productivity variation. Although there are clear differences across the four sectors, we provide a functional summary of the results by focusing on the contributions of inputs, participation and efficiency to output in the four sectors.

The role of inputs: Estimated output–capital elasticities are stable across models, with values in the (0.1, 0.2) range, and are frequently significantly greater than zero. Estimated output–labor elasticities are also stable across models, with values in the (0.9–1.0) range, and are always significantly greater than zero. Consequently, scale economies appear to play a role in all four sectors, with estimated scale elasticities falling in the (1.0–1.2) range, although they are only occasionally significantly greater than unity.

The role of participation: One way of measuring the impact of participation is to examine the estimated coefficients on the two participation variables. These estimated coefficients are not significantly different from zero in two sectors (Architecture and Public Works); they are suggestively close to being significantly different from zero in the Furniture sector; and they are clearly significantly different from zero in the Printing sector. Where significant, these estimated coefficients are negative, suggesting that increased participation leads to increases in output. A second way of measuring the impact of participation on output is through use of likelihood ratio tests, which we leave to the reader. These tests tell much the same story. A third way of measuring the impact of participation is to derive estimates of $(d - 1)$ and $(c - 1)$ from the coefficient estimates, and then to calculate approximate standard errors of the estimated values of $(d - 1)$ and $(c - 1)$, respectively. Results of these calculations are consistent with the first two sets of tests, and suggest that participation indicators exert a significantly positive impact on output in the Printing sector, and they come close to doing so in the Furniture sector. They do not have a significant

Table 2. Panel frontier results for architecture cooperatives. Dependent Variable: ln y_{it}

		MLE Parameter Estimates			
		Model			
Independent Variable	Coefficient	1	2	3	4
Constant	a_0	4.2310 (12.5588)	4.1966 (12.6411)	4.2294 (12.6588)	4.1955 (12.5725)
ln K_{it}	a_1	0.2144 (4.1791)	0.2060 (4.3046)	0.2143 (4.1762)	0.2060 (4.3086)
ln L_{it}	a_2	1.0215 (5.7717)	1.0544 (6.5458)	1.0242 (6.2137)	1.0566 (7.0454)
$(K^E/K)_{it}$	a_3	−0.1881 (−0.4508)	—	−0.1879 (−0.4502)	—
$(L^N/L)_{it}$	a_4	0.0128 (0.0431)	0.0108 (0.0363)	—	—
	$\tilde{\sigma}^2$	0.1212 (2.4415)	0.1210 (2.4440)	0.1214 (2.4577)	0.1212 (2.4755)
	γ	0.2288 (0.5281)	0.2210 (0.5022)	0.2306 (0.5379)	0.2230 (0.5134)
	μ	0	0	0	0
	ln £	−12.7418	−12.8439	−12.7427	−12.8445
	$\chi^2_{(1)}$	5.5029	4.3492	4.3960	3.2799
	RTS	1.2359 (1.4908)	1.2604 (1.7528)	1.2385 (1.6411)	1.2626 (1.9150)
	$d - 1$	−0.8773 (−0.6235)	—	−0.8768 (−0.4495)	—
	$c - 1$	0.0125 (0.0313)	0.0102 (0.0361)	—	—
Mean Efficiencies by Cooperative					
Firm	NOBS				
1	2	0.8930	0.8898	0.8926	0.8893
2	2	0.8910	0.8933	0.8904	0.8927
3	2	0.9105	0.9107	0.9101	0.9103
4	2	0.8902	0.8923	0.8900	0.8920
5	2	0.9017	0.9050	0.9013	0.9047
6	2	0.9283	0.9273	0.9280	0.9269
7	2	0.7928	0.7875	0.7913	0.7859
8	2	0.8818	0.8875	0.8816	0.8871
9	2	0.9032	0.8981	0.9032	0.8980
10	2	0.9048	0.9065	0.9044	0.9060
11	1	0.9008	0.9031	0.9003	0.9026
12	2	0.8884	0.8931	0.8880	0.8926
13	2	0.8825	0.8821	0.8822	0.8818

Table 2. continued

Mean Efficiencies by Cooperative		MLE Parameter Estimates			
		Model			
Firm	NOBS	1	2	3	4
14	2	0.8674	0.8731	0.8675	0.8731
15	1	0.8775	0.8808	0.8767	0.8800
16	2	0.8653	0.8682	0.8644	0.8673
17	2	0.8421	0.8498	0.8417	0.8493
18	2	0.8607	0.8664	0.8603	0.8659
19	2	0.8842	0.8848	0.8836	0.8841
20	2	0.8011	0.8062	0.7995	0.8045
21	2	0.8537	0.8612	0.8527	0.8602
22	2	0.8326	0.8380	0.8322	0.8375
23	2	0.9233	0.9230	0.9233	0.9229
24	1	0.9353	0.9357	0.9353	0.9357
Overall Mean Score		0.8798	0.8818	0.8793	0.8813

effect in the two remaining sectors. Our finding of a significant positive effect of participation in the Printing sector is consistent with results of Defourny, Estrin, and Jones [1987]. Among the six sectors in which they studied the performance of cooperatives, Printing also emerged as a sector in which the productivity enhancing effect of workers' participation was particularly important. This common finding may be linked to the fact that the cooperative movement has long been very active in Printing, with its skilled workers, strong personal involvement, and militancy.

The role of efficiency: Efficiency plays a substantial, and statistically significant, role in all four sectors. Estimated values of γ, the ratio of the variance of the efficiency element in the composed error term to the variance of the composed error term itself, are statistically significant in the majority of models. More to the point, the chi-square statistics, which test the improvement in explanatory power of MLE over OLS, suggest that the parameters of the one-sided component of the composed error structure are statistically significant in all cases. In all sectors the impact of inefficiency is captured by two parameters, σ^2 and γ; in no sector did the model converge with a statistically significant value of μ.

The time-invariant estimates of technical efficiency for each cooperative enterprise in each sector are reported in the lower half of tables 2–5. These efficiencies show little variation across models, suggesting that the specification is robust to variation in the participation component of the model. The efficiencies vary substantially across sectors, with sample means declining from 0.88 in Architecture to 0.80 in Printing, 0.77 in Public Works, and 0.74 in Furniture. The efficiencies also vary substantially within each sector, with scores in Model 1 ranging from 0.79 to 0.93 in Architecture, from 0.59 to 0.93 in Printing, from 0.45 to 0.94 in Furniture, and from 0.45 to 0.96 in Public Works. This variation in productive efficiency goes a long way toward explaining observed variation in output within each sector.

Table 3. Panel frontier results for printing cooperatives. Dependent Variable: ln y_{it}

Independent Variable	Coefficient	MLE Parameter Estimates — Model 1	2	3	4
Constant	a_0	4.8581	4.8552	4.6858	4.5776
		(21.7339)	(21.8062)	(21.0673)	(19.9383)
ln K_{it}	a_1	0.0802	0.0693	0.1196	0.1331
		(2.2724)	(1.9017)	(3.5449)	(3.8013)
ln L_{it}	a_2	1.0253	1.0446	0.9504	0.9373
		(15.3438)	(15.1135)	(16.8060)	(15.7294)
$(K^E/K)_{it}$	a_3	−0.4920	—	−0.6823	—
		(−1.8197)		(−2.6805)	
$(L^N/L)_{it}$	a_4	−0.5284	−0.6613	—	—
		(−2.6885)	(−3.4813)		
	$\tilde{\sigma}^2$	0.2151	0.2188	0.2319	0.2686
		(3.5142)	(3.5430)	(3.8753)	(3.6509)
	γ	0.4016	0.3800	0.4329	0.5021
		(2.0924)	(1.8650)	(2.5470)	(3.0339)
	μ	0	0	0	0
	ln £	−53.7778	−55.9284	−56.2136	−59.9991
	$\chi^2_{(1)}$	7.4121	6.6459	7.1295	7.9143
	RTS	1.1055	1.1139	1.0700	1.0704
		(1.8178)	(1.9213)	(1.3142)	(1.2023)
	d − 1	−6.1347	—	−5.7048	—
		(−1.5102)		(−2.0517)	
	c − 1	−0.5154	−0.6331	—	—
		(−1.2105)	(−8.4719)		
Mean Efficiencies by Cooperative					
Firm	NOBS				
1	2	0.7972	0.8115	0.7824	0.7694
2	2	0.8336	0.8260	0.8398	0.8093
3	2	0.8061	0.8225	0.7891	0.7839
4	2	0.7971	0.8082	0.7923	0.7853
5	2	0.7874	0.8031	0.7829	0.7810
6	2	0.8926	0.8881	0.8925	0.8771
7	2	0.8768	0.8813	0.8739	0.8705
8	2	0.7469	0.7629	0.7442	0.7328
9	2	0.8096	0.8106	0.7873	0.7520
10	2	0.6837	0.6736	0.6804	0.6131
11	2	0.5921	0.6174	0.5670	0.5432
12	2	0.8388	0.8394	0.8111	0.7772
13	2	0.8941	0.8954	0.8849	0.8761

Table 3. continued

Mean Efficiencies by Cooperative		MLE Parameter Estimates			
		Model			
Firm	NOBS	1	2	3	4
14	2	0.8053	0.8222	0.7690	0.7578
15	2	0.7370	0.7250	0.7546	0.7033
16	2	0.8049	0.8182	0.7994	0.7971
17	2	0.8289	0.8287	0.8324	0.8115
18	2	0.7786	0.7925	0.7690	0.7554
19	2	0.8907	0.8159	0.8222	0.8191
20	2	0.7393	0.7541	0.7365	0.7190
21	2	0.8710	0.8577	0.8407	0.7770
22	2	0.7443	0.7185	0.7593	0.6787
23	2	0.7122	0.7219	0.7287	0.7111
24	2	0.8503	0.8544	0.8492	0.8396
25	2	0.7336	0.7566	0.7155	0.7134
26	2	0.8782	0.8311	0.8832	0.7912
27	2	0.8504	0.8567	0.8575	0.8563
28	2	0.8534	0.8713	0.7891	0.7862
29	2	0.7436	0.7688	0.7095	0.7025
30	2	0.6572	0.6967	0.5904	0.5719
31	2	0.8565	0.8301	0.8578	0.7966
32	2	0.8356	0.8475	0.8147	0.8079
33	2	0.7985	0.7690	0.8233	0.7666
34	2	0.9286	0.9330	0.9080	0.9091
35	2	0.9290	0.9261	0.9295	0.9276
36	2	0.8071	0.8184	0.8117	0.8120
37	2	0.8825	0.8891	0.8538	0.8455
38	2	0.7539	0.7717	0.7292	0.7200
39	2	0.8467	0.8566	0.8386	0.8399
40	2	0.8467	0.8534	0.8531	0.8542
41	2	0.7825	0.7892	0.7441	0.7074
42	2	0.6584	0.6454	0.5786	0.4752
43	2	0.8559	0.8229	0.8713	0.8112
44	2	0.8426	0.8496	0.8460	0.8414
45	2	0.9256	0.9260	0.9274	0.9278
46	2	0.7928	0.8043	0.8023	0.8033
47	2	0.7444	0.7556	0.7673	0.7625
48	2	0.8367	0.8509	0.8118	0.8133
49	2	0.8113	0.8248	0.8048	0.8027
50	2	0.7278	0.6855	0.6937	0.5591
51	2	0.7418	0.7638	0.6928	0.6776
52	2	0.8895	0.8951	0.8731	0.8706
53	2	0.8358	0.7778	0.7960	0.6113
54	2	0.6595	0.6907	0.6251	0.6126
55	2	0.7516	0.7110	0.7216	0.5923
Overall Mean Score		0.8028	0.8059	0.7901	0.7632

Table 4. Panel frontier results for furniture cooperatives. Dependent Variable: $\ln y_{it}$

Independent Variable	Coefficient	MLE Parameter Estimates Model 1	2	3	4
Constant	a_0	3.7444 (4.0135)	4.1210 (4.2149)	3.5304 (5.3755)	3.9651 (6.7151)
$\ln K_{it}$	a_1	0.2759 (1.2024)	0.1726 (0.4705)	0.2795 (2.1170)	0.1411 (1.2536)
$\ln L_{it}$	a_2	0.8866 (3.5658)	0.9717 (1.2200)	0.8840 (8.9588)	1.0293 (10.9101)
$(K^E/K)_{it}$	a_3	−0.8206 (−0.8183)	—	−0.9007 (−1.5425)	—
$(L^N/L)_{it}$	a_4	−0.6856 (−2.2005)	−0.7385 (−1.9891)	—	—
	$\tilde{\sigma}^2$	0.1920 (2.7934)	0.2219 (0.6404)	0.1826 (1.2874)	0.2308 (1.4005)
	γ	0.8353 (8.0606)	0.8719 (3.2549)	0.7262 (2.5192)	0.7700 (3.4276)
	μ	0	0	0	0
	ln £	−3.7674	−4.0023	−7.4889	−8.7876
	$\chi^2_{(1)}$	13.2057	16.6850	8.6422	9.3057
	RTS	1.1625 (2.6144)	1.1443 (0.3041)	1.1635 (1.7275)	1.1704 (1.9329)
	d − 1	−2.9743 (−0.9180)	—	−3.2225 (−1.7608)	—
	c − 1	−0.7733 (−0.6660)	−0.7600 (−1.8176)	—	—
Mean Efficiencies by Cooperative					
Firm	NOBS				
1	2	0.7713	0.6654	0.8498	0.7782
2	2	0.8799	0.8910	0.7445	0.7193
3	2	0.6407	0.5520	0.7674	0.6640
4	2	0.7467	0.7359	0.8220	0.8077
5	1	0.7638	0.7265	0.8151	0.7622
6	2	0.9477	0.9294	0.9213	0.8837
7	2	0.7522	0.6462	0.7935	0.6839
8	2	0.9046	0.9099	0.9165	0.9139
9	2	0.6628	0.7382	0.7289	0.7850
10	2	0.6301	0.5965	0.6277	0.5792
11	1	0.8902	0.8986	0.8989	0.8897
12	2	0.8536	0.8973	0.8533	0.8725
13	2	0.9025	0.8785	0.9034	0.8719

Table 4. continued

Mean Efficiencies by Cooperative		MLE Parameter Estimates			
		Model			
Firm	NOBS	1	2	3	4
14	2	0.5893	0.6092	0.6803	0.7064
15	2	0.8219	0.8440	0.8927	0.9056
16	2	0.4884	0.4256	0.5799	0.4832
17	2	0.8859	0.8861	0.7992	0.7664
18	2	0.8473	0.8879	0.7846	0.8187
19	2	0.6662	0.7279	0.6213	0.6595
20	2	0.5275	0.4745	0.5131	0.4721
21	1	0.4531	0.4089	0.5547	0.5117
22	1	0.6477	0.6987	0.7083	0.7607
Overall Mean Score		0.7422	0.7271	0.7648	0.7359

Overall impressions: Output variation across cooperative enterprises is significantly related to input variation across enterprises in all four sectors. But that is only part of the story. Output variation is also significantly and positively affected by increases in participation in one sector. Output variation is also significantly affected by variation in productive efficiency in all four sectors. The conclusion is that any model that attempts to explain productivity performance exclusively in terms of conventionally measured inputs is bound to generate misleading results concerning the absolute and relative importance of those inputs. It is sometimes necessary to examine the extent to which members of the cooperative finance or supply these inputs, and it is always necessary to examine the efficiency with which management coordinates the employment of these variables.

4. Summary and suggestions

In this article we have employed stochastic frontier panel data techniques to investigate the magnitude and distribution of productive efficiency in samples of producer cooperatives operating in four sectors of French industry. The economic finding of primary interest concerns the role of efficiency variation in explaining observed output variation. That role is statistically significant in all four sectors. In addition, the role of two popular indicators of worker participation is significantly positive in one sector. This suggests that conclusions about productivity variation, and policy recommendations emanating therefrom, based on econometric analysis with symmetric error structures and without participation variables, may be very misleading.

It would be of interest to reanalyze the same data using nonparametric, nonstochastic techniques to compare the performance of the two approaches. The nonparametric construction and decomposition of the Malmquist index into productivity variation and efficiency variation recently developed by Färe et al. [1989] would provide an ideal counterpart to our stochastic parametric approach.

Table 5. Panel frontier results for public works cooperatives. Dependent Variable: ln y_{it}

Independent Variable	Coefficient	MLE Parameter Estimates Model 1	Model 2	Model 3	Model 4
Constant	a_0	4.1330 (4.8408)	4.5860 (4.7209)	4.2925 (22.3826)	4.5013 (26.1761)
ln K_{it}	a_1	0.2009 (1.8209)	0.1634 (1.3118)	0.1665 (5.1396)	0.1435 (4.4837)
ln L_{it}	a_2	0.8595 (11.5334)	0.8689 (15.0722)	0.9514 (12.2352)	0.9636 (24.0603)
$(K^E/K)_{it}$	a_3	0.3656 (1.1580)	—	0.2960 (1.2083)	—
$(L^N/L)_{it}$	a_4	0.3683 (0.8930)	0.2730 (1.0726)	—	—
	$\tilde{\sigma}^2$	0.1475 (7.2110)	0.2247 (4.6128)	0.1781 (2.6249)	0.1917 (2.7814)
	γ	0.8262 (13.9386)	0.8886 (20.3922)	0.8100 (8.3282)	0.8300 (9.4723)
	μ	0	0	0	0
	ln £	−4.1414	−5.7854	−6.0338	−8.2930
	$\chi^2_{(1)}$	16.4122	22.7723	16.9051	16.7397
	RTS	1.0604 (1.0307)	1.0323 (0.2843)	1.1179 (1.9815)	1.1071 (3.5581)
	d − 1	1.8198 (2.1567)	—	1.7778 (1.0974)	—
	c − 1	0.4285 (0.8399)	0.4058 (1.3410)	—	—
Mean Efficiencies by Cooperative					
Firm	NOBS				
1	2	0.7481	0.7252	0.7416	0.7407
2	2	0.6879	0.5891	0.7270	0.6745
3	2	0.6448	0.6227	0.7046	0.6337
4	2	0.7258	0.6664	0.6859	0.6740
5	2	0.6488	0.6043	0.6437	0.6232
6	2	0.6633	0.5881	0.6361	0.6555
7	2	0.6966	0.6601	0.6473	0.6260
8	2	0.6167	0.5479	0.6139	0.5743
9	2	0.9102	0.8964	0.9171	0.9232
10	2	0.7739	0.7162	0.7050	0.6810
11	2	0.6608	0.5664	0.5917	0.5642
12	2	0.7200	0.6300	0.6797	0.6551
13	2	0.9299	0.3515	0.8765	0.9291

Table 5. continued

Mean Efficiencies by Cooperative		MLE Parameter Estimates			
		Model			
Firm	NOBS	1	2	3	4
14	2	0.7997	0.6726	0.7550	0.7092
15	2	0.7666	0.7883	0.8245	0.8547
16	2	0.9615	0.9532	0.9620	0.9602
17	2	0.8797	0.9560	0.3672	0.8525
18	2	0.8647	0.7737	0.8157	0.7864
19	2	0.7921	0.6647	0.7450	0.6879
20	2	0.8713	0.7365	0.7927	0.7446
21	2	0.8543	0.9261	0.8262	0.9006
22	2	0.7733	0.6746	0.7613	0.7210
23	2	0.8974	0.9293	0.8921	0.9411
24	2	0.6994	0.6271	0.6240	0.6126
25	2	0.6925	0.5804	0.6719	0.6239
26	2	0.9484	0.9092	0.8991	0.8758
27	2	0.8680	0.7605	0.8020	0.7528
28	2	0.7746	0.6493	0.7581	0.7051
29	2	0.4529	0.3944	0.4856	0.4689
30	2	0.9290	0.8730	0.8767	0.8510
31	1	0.8830	0.8365	0.8794	0.8608
32	2	0.5077	0.4479	0.4879	0.4777
33	2	0.5691	0.5480	0.6036	0.6292
34	2	0.8852	0.7765	0.8211	0.7724
35	2	0.8984	0.8049	0.7920	0.7543
36	2	0.6442	0.5377	0.6434	0.5861
37	2	0.9271	0.7857	0.9095	0.8442
38	2	0.8640	0.7504	0.7938	0.7507
39	1	0.7011	0.5484	0.7089	0.6295
40	2	0.5049	0.4844	0.5395	0.5592
41	2	0.6545	0.5281	0.6810	0.6220
42	1	0.4631	0.4126	0.5028	0.4972
Overall Mean Score		0.7727	0.7238	0.7567	0.7471

Notes

1. Our model is parametric, and so the decomposition we obtain is conditional on both the functional form of the production function we estimate (Cobb–Douglas) and the functional form of the error component intended to capture productive inefficiency (half-normal).
2. However, by segmenting his sample into size classes, Defourny was able to test hypotheses concerning variation of technical efficiency over size classes.
3. One can also mention Côté [1989], who measured technical efficiency in private, public and cooperative U.S. electric utilities, but his sample included only consumer cooperatives, and he estimated only mean technical efficiencies.
4. The Cobb–Douglas functional form is used in this study because single equation translog rarely works, and did not work with these data.

5. Since internal and external capital resources are used together to finance most types of asset purchases, it is impossible to know precisely what proportion of fixed assets is internally financed. We took the percentage of equity capital held by workers (as opposed to the percentage held by nonworkers) as an approximation to this proportion.
6. This approximation has been applied before in this literature, by Jones and Svejnar [1985] and Defourny [1987], but only for the labor input. The approximations are obtained by taking Taylor series expansions of the two nonlinear participation terms in equation (6) around the points $d = 1$ and $c = 1$ respectively, and truncating each expansion at the first-order term. Lovell, Sickles, and Warren [1988] have shown that if $c = d = 1$ the linear approximations are exact, and equation (7) correctly shows that participation has no effect on productivity. However if $c \neq 1$ or $d \neq 1$, then although equation (7) correctly identifies the directions of the participation effects, it overstates their magnitudes, and the approximation errors increase in magnitude as c or d depart from unity. Of course it would be possible to embed the nonlinear model (6) directly into a stochastic frontier panel data framework and avoid the approximation error issue altogether. We have not done so. Consequently, we interpret our empirical findings as establishing upper bounds on the likely impacts of participation on productivity in these sectors.
7. Initially we tried a two-stage formulation. In the first stage, we estimated a stochastic Cobb-Douglas production frontier (2). In the second stage, we attempted to use the two participation variables to explain variation in measured efficiency by performing regressions of the general form

$$\hat{u}_i = f(E(K_{it}^E/K_{it}),\ E(L_{it}^N/L_{it})),$$

where the expectation is taken over time. When we found no significant correlation between $\hat{u}_i$ and the means of the two participation indicators, we turned to the single stage formulation (8). In this formulation participation influences productivity not by influencing efficiency, but by altering production possibilities.
8. We use a computer program written by Coelli [1989].
9. $(d - 1) = a_3/a_1 = f(a_1, a_3)$ and $(c - 1) = a_4/a_2 = g(a_2, a_4)$. The functions f and g are nonlinear, and so we use linear approximations to obtain estimated standard errors of the estimated values of d and c. If we have $\hat{b} = h(\hat{a})$, where $\hat{a}$ is a vector and $\hat{b}$ is a scalar and if ∇h is the gradient vector and Σ is the variance-covariance matrix, then by approximation we have

$$h(\hat{a}) - h(a) \approx [\nabla h(a)]^T(\hat{a} - a),$$

and the variance of $\hat{b}$ is given by

$$\mathrm{var}(\hat{b}) = [\nabla h(a)]^T\ \Sigma[V\nabla h(a)].$$

See also N'Gbo [1991].

References

Aigner, D., C.A.K. Lovell, and P. Schmidt. (1977). "Formulation and Estimation of Stochastic frontier Production Function models." *Journal of Econometrics* 6(1), pp. 21–37.

Battese, G.E. and T.J. Coelli (1988). "Prediction of Firm-Level Technical Efficiencies with a Generalized Frontier Production Function and Panel Data." *Journal of Econometrics* 38, pp. 387–99.

Battese, G.E., T.J. Coelli, and T.C. Colby (1989). "Estimation of Frontier Production Functions and the Efficiencies of Indian Farms Using Data from ICRISAT's Village Level Studies." *Journal of Quantitative Economics* 5 (2), pp. 327–48.

Battese, G.E. and G.S. Corra (1977). "Estimation of a Production Frontier Model: With Application to the Pastoral Zone of Eastern Australia." *Australian Journal of Agricultural Economics* 21, pp. 169–79.

Brown, C. and J. Medoff (1978). "Trade Unions in the Productive Process." *Journal of Political Economy* 86 (3) pp. 355–78.

Coelli, T.J. (1989). "Estimation of Frontier Production Functions: A Guide to the Computer Program 'Frontier'." Working Paper No. 34, Department of Econometrics, University of New England, Armidale, NSW, Australia.

Confédération Générale des SCOP (1989). *Bilans et Comptes de Résultat 1987 et 1988.* Fichiers de la Centrale des Bilans, Paris.

Côté, D. (1989). "Firm Efficiency and Ownership Structure: The Case of U.S. Electric Utilities Using Panel Data." *Annals of Public and Cooperative Economics* 60 (4), pp. 431-50.

Defourny, J. (1987). "La Performance économique comparée des coopératives de travailleurs: La cas des SCOP francaises." Thèse de doctorat, Unversité de Liège, Faculté de Droit, d'Economie et de Sciences Sociales.

Defourny, J. (1988). "Comparative Measures of Technical Efficiency for 500 French Workers' Cooperatives." Working Paper 88/07, CIRIEC, The University of Liege, Liege, Belgium. Forthcoming in D.C. Jones, and J. Svejnar (eds.), *Advances in the Economic Analysis of Participatory Labor-Managed Firms,* Volume 4. Greenwich, CT: JAI Press.

Defourny, J., S. Estrin, and D.C. Jones (1987. "The Effects of Workers' Participation on Enterprise Performance: Empirical Evidence from French Cooperatives." *International Journal of Industrial Organization* 3, pp. 197–217.

Estrin, S., D.C. Jones, and J. Svejnar (1987). "The Productivity of Worker Participation: Producer Cooperatives in Western Economies." *Journal of Comparative Economics* 11 (1), pp. 40–61.

Färe, R., S. Grosskopf, B. Lindgren, and P. Roos (1989). "Productivity Developments in Swedish Hospitals: A Malmquist Output Index Approach." Paper presented at a Conference on New Uses of DEA in Management, IC² Institute, The University of Texas, Austin, TX, September 27–29.

Jondrow, J., C.A.K. Lovell, I. Materov, and P. Schmidt (1982). "On the Estimation of Technical Inefficiency in the Stochastic Frontier Production Model." *Journal of Econometrics* 19 (2/3), pp. 233–38.

Jones, D.C. and J. Svejnar (1985). "Participation, Profit-Sharing, Worker Ownership and Efficiency in Italian Producer Cooperatives." *Economica* 52 (208), pp. 449-65.

Lovell, C.A.K., R. Sickles, and R. Warren (1988). "The Effect of Unionization on Labor Productivity: Some Additional Evidence." *Journal of Labor Research* 9 (1), pp. 55–63.

Meeusen, W. and J. van den Broeck (1977). "Efficiency Estimation from Cobb–Douglas Production Functions with Composed Error." *International Economic Review* 18, pp. 435–44.

N'Gbo, A.G.M. (1991). "Elasticité-prix de la demand de cacao et test d'exogeneité." *Economie Appliquée* 44 (1), pp. 123–40.

Sterner, T. (1990). "Ownership, Technology and Efficiency: An Empirical Study of Cooperatives, Multinationals and Domestic Enterprises in the Mexican Cement Industry." *Journal of Comparative Economics* 14 (2), pp. 286–300.

The Journal of Productivity Analysis, 3, 119–133 (1992)

Technical Inefficiency and Productive Decline in the U.S. Interstate Natural Gas Pipeline Industry Under the Natural Gas Policy Act

ROBIN C. SICKLES
Rice University, P.O. Box 1892, Houston, Texas 77251

MARY L. STREITWIESER
Center For Economic Studies, U.S. Bureau of the Census, Washington, D.C. 20233

Abstract

Firm-specific and temporal patterns of technical efficiency of the interstate natural gas transmission industry during the implementation of the Natural Gas Policy Act are estimated by two alternative methodologies. A new panel stochastic frontier systems estimator exploits the potential exogeneity of certain regressors from firm effects. This allows for heterogeneity in slopes, as well as in intercepts. Patterns of technical efficiency based on the structural stochastic model are compared with those based on deterministic programming methods, data envelopment analysis. Concordant findings based on these alternative methodologies suggest a perversive pattern of declining technical efficiency in the industry during the period of phased in well-head price deregulation.

1. Introduction

The U.S. natural gas industry has undergone substantial change in the past decade. Enactment of the Natural Gas Policy Act of 1978 (NGPA) set initial ceiling well-head prices and escalation schedules for over two dozen categories of natural gas.[1] The deregulation of well-head gas prices covered in the NGPA applied both to purchases by inter- and intrastate pipeline companies even though state regulated intrastate pipeline companies were not subject to other forms of federal regulation, such as rate of return regulation. By January 1985, between 55 and 60 percent of flowing natural gas had been released from field price control. The transmission industry experienced serious price competition, both from within the industry and from alternative fuels (residual fuel oil, nuclear, and coal) as the relative prices of substitute energy sources fell, due to rising natural gas field prices under deregulation, declining oil prices after U.S. crude price control was ended in 1981, and due to technological innovation. Demand declined due to general energy conservation and the disappearance of traditional industrial users with multi-fuel boilers. Supporters of partial deregulation argued that the new regulatory environment would allow the price of gas to reflect market conditions and would enhance competition and efficiency in the industry. Although the major focus of the NGPA was to deregulate the price of natural gas at the well-head, the natural gas transmission industry was profoundly affected by changes in the relative prices of competing fuels and contractual relationships among producers, transporters, distributors and end-users.

The scope of the NGPA and its distributional effects on end-use consumers has been vast. Estimates by Streitwieser [1989] indicate that over $100 billion was redistributed to primarily industrial consumers through partial decontrol during the period 1977–1985. It is quite remarkable therefore, that no empirical study of the impact of the NGPA on the natural gas transmission industry has been undertaken at the firm level. This is the first study, to our knowledge, that assesses the impact of the NGPA on the technical efficiency of natural gas transmission firms. We focus on the distortionary effects that resulted in the industry during a period in which changes in regulatory policy could neither anticipate changing market conditions nor rapidly adjust to those changes. The measurement of distortionary effects of the NGPA follows from two alternative estimating methodologies, stochastic frontier production analysis and data envelopment analysis. The implications of our findings are strengthened by relying on concordant findings from these alternative methodologies.

The plan of this article is as follows: in Section 2 we briefly discuss the structure of the industry and its recent regulatory history, Section 3 discusses the models with which the technical inefficiency will be measured. We introduce a new systems estimator for the stochastic frontier panel data model which allows for time varying technical efficiency that is firm specific and potentially correlated with the regressors in a simultaneous system based on a translog production function and cost-minimizing share equations. We also outline the standard programming alternatives for the deterministic panel frontier. Section 4 provides a discussion of the data and variable construction. Estimation results are discussed in Section 5 while Section 6 concludes.

2. Structure and regulation of the transmission industry

The U.S. natural gas industry is composed of a vertically linked set of firms which produce, transport, and distribute natural gas. The firms that provide transmission services have traditionally served as merchant and shipper and are linked upstream to producers and downstream to local distribution companies. The regulatory history of the natural gas transmission industry is long and complicated, beginning in the early 1880's as state and municipal authorities established rate of return regulation over local transmission firms. Interstate transmission was regulated in the 1938 passage of the Natural Gas Act (NGA), which also created the Federal Power Commission (FPC), later to become the Federal Energy Regulatory Commission (FERC). The basic charge of the FPC was to define service areas, to certify any changes in pipeline capacity, and to set transport rate schedules to allow fair rates of return. In 1954, federal price regulation was extended to the well-head for gas destined to the interstate market in order to smooth regional price variations. Large discoveries of easily accessible natural gas along with promotion of natural gas as an alternative to coal or petroleum based fuels lent stability to an industry which showed steady productivity growth through the early 1960's. The oil price shocks of the 1970's abruptly changed this relatively peaceful industrial setting. The NGA prevented well-head prices of natural gas sold in interstate markets from rising at a fast enough pace to keep a dual intra/interstate market from developing. Substantial curtailments of shipments of both industrial and residential customers resulted and the Natural Gas Policy Act of 1978 was passed to allow partial decontrol of the well-head price of natural gas. By 1985, natural gas prices had risen 218 percent. The combination of falling demand for natural gas during the early 1980's due to the recession, a fall in the quantity demanded and thus in need of transport because of the increased price, and an increase in the cost of a key variable input in transport, pipeline compressor fuel, impacted the transmission industry greatly. At a time when rapid adjustment to changing economic conditions was essential, FERC regulatory proceedings often lagged by up to two years in ruling on an original filing for rate changes.

The empirical models we outline below will allow us to examine patterns of technical efficiency among firms in the transmission industry over the period 1977-85, the period during which the NGPA was enacted and changes in natural gas prices were mandated by Congress instead of being left to market forces. We analyze the productive performance of a newly constructed panel of 14 natural gas transmission firms that comprise almost 50 percent of the total interstate sales of the industry. Our empirical results point to a substantial and pervasive fall in technical efficiency during the period in which the NGPA was enacted and its pricing mandate implemented.

3. Models

We measure the firm specific levels of technical inefficiency using both stochastic frontier and data envelopment analysis. We base our panel stochastic frontier model on a simultaneous equations extension of the single equation panel production frontier model introduced by Schmidt and Sickles [1984] and by Cornwell, Schmidt, and Sickles [1990]. Our data envelopment analysis is carried out using an approach outlined in Gong and Sickles [1992] which modifies the efficiency scores from the standard piece-wise linear programming problem of Charnes, Cooper, and Rhodes (CCR) [1978, 1981] to accommodate a panel deterministic frontier that is changing over the sample period.

Our motivation for modeling as we do technical distortions due to FERC regulation in light of the NGPA is grounded in the extremely complicated and often contradictory regulatory process itself. For example, figure 1 provides us with the maximum ceiling price schedules from 1978 to 1985 which give 24 different combinations of prices over the period for different categories of natural gas. Over the ceiling price schedules are layered regulations dealing with rate filings, lagged rate hearings and final disposition of cases for each firm over a nine year period. The information requirements to allow a formal structural analysis of the distortionary effects of such regulation renders its feasibility moot. The stochastic frontier and data envelopment analyses can be viewed as parsimonious approaches to reduced form estimation of the effects that distortions had on firms' abilities to pursue average frontier or best practice technologies.

The panel stochastic frontier production model was first considered by Schmidt and Sickles [1984]. In their original model the production function was written as

$$y_{it} = \alpha + X_{it}'\beta + \nu_{it} - u_i, \qquad (1)$$

where y_{it} is output, X_{it} is a vector of factor inputs, ν_{it} is standard statistical noise, and $u_i > 0$ is a firm specific effect that is interpreted as technical inefficiency. Alternative estimators of u_i were proposed which were based on the time invariance of technical inefficiency.

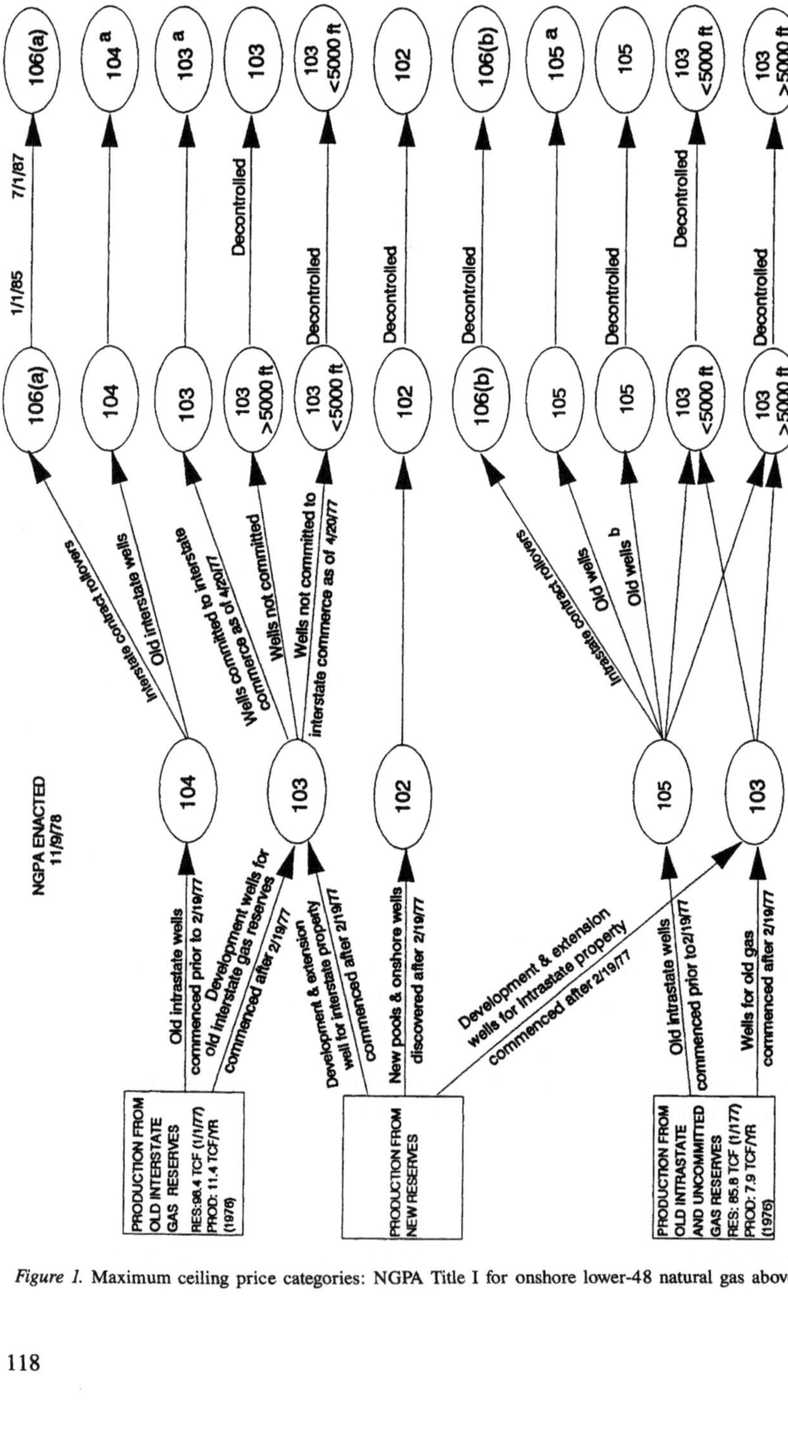

a. Not decontrolled.
b. Price greater than $ 1.00 per million Btu under a definite escalator clause.
Note: Stripper wells and high cost gas omitted.
Source: U.S. Energy Information Administration, Natural Gas Market (1981), p. 16.
Reprinted From: Teece, David J., "Structure and Organization of the Natural Gas Industry," The Energy Journal, 11 (1989), p. 17.

Figure 1. Maximum ceiling price categories: NGPA Title I for onshore lower-48 natural gas above 15,000 feet.

In subsequent work, Cornwell, Schmidt, and Sickles [1990] generalized the panel frontier production model to allow for consistent estimation of firm-specific and time-varying technical inefficiency and introduced a class of efficient instrumental variables estimators for use when technical inefficiencies were uncorrelated with selected regressors. Here we generalize the panel frontier production model further by nesting it in a system of equations and specify a class of efficient three stage least squares estimates of the production system in which (1) firm-specific technical inefficiency is time-varying (2) technical inefficiency may be correlated with selected regressors (3) right-hand-side variables may be correlated with statistical noise.

We begin with a variant of the model considered by Cornwell, Schmidt, and Wyhowski [1992] in which the *j*th structural equation of a G–equation system is written as

$$y_j = Y_j\delta_j + X_j\beta_j + Z_j\gamma_j + W_j\alpha_j + \epsilon_j, \qquad j = 1, \ldots, G, \tag{2}$$

where observations are ordered as, e.g., $y_j' = (y_{j11} \ldots y_{j1T} \ldots y_{jN1} \ldots y_{jNT})$. Time-varying right-hand-side endogeneous variables and exogenous variables are in the data matrices Y_j and X_j, time-invariant exogenous variables are in Z_j, and W_j is a matrix of exogenous variables whose coefficients may exhibit heterogeneity over time and over the cross-section. Individual effects are allowed to vary over the cross-sectional observations but not over time. However, since time can be a regressor in W_j and since heterogeneity in slopes and intercepts is allowed for in this model, firm-specific technical inefficiency can vary over time if we interpret the individual effects as technical inefficiency. The model can be rewritten by letting $\alpha_j = \alpha_{j0} + u_j$ in which case equation (2) becomes

$$y_j = Y_j\delta_j + X_j\beta_j + Z_j\gamma_j + W_j\alpha_{j0} + v_j,$$

$$v_j = Q_j u_j + \epsilon_j, \tag{3}$$

where $Q_j = \mathrm{Diag}(W_{ji})$, $i = 1, \ldots, N$. Next write the *j*th structural equation as

$$y_j = R_j\xi_j + v_j, \tag{4}$$

where $R_j = (Y_j, X_j, Z_j, W_j)$ and $\xi_j' = (\delta_j', \beta_j, \gamma_j', \alpha_{j0}')$. Stacking the G equations gives us the system

$$y_* = R_*\xi_* + v_*. \tag{5}$$

We assume that the covariance matrix for each u_j is block diagonal in Δ_j, that the u_{ji}'s are iid with zero mean and covariance Σ_u, that $(\epsilon_{1it}, \ldots, \epsilon_{Git})$ is iid with zero mean and covariance matrix Σ_ϵ and that the terms u_j and ϵ_j are uncorrelated. This implies that the $(GNT \times GNT)$ covariance matrix for v_* takes the form

$$\Omega = \Sigma_\epsilon \otimes I_{NT} + \Sigma_u \otimes Q(I_N \otimes \Delta)Q' \tag{6}$$

We distinguish between the exogenous variables in the system being uncorrelated with both statistical noise and the firm effects and those which are uncorrelated with statistical noise but correlated with the firm effects (Breusch, Mizon, and Schmidt, [1988]). Partition these into $X = [X_{(1)}, X_{(2)}]$, $Z = [Z_{(1)}, Z_{(2)}]$, $W = [W_{(1)}, W_{(2)}]$. Let M_A be the projection into the null space of an arbitrary matrix A. Then the efficient IV estimator can be written as

$$\hat{\xi}_* = (R_*'\Omega^{-1/2}P_{A*}\Omega^{-1/2}R_*)^{-1}R_*'\Omega^{-1/2}P_{A*}\Omega^{-1/2}y_*, \tag{7}$$

where $A_* = \Omega^{-1/2}(M_Q, X_{(1)}, Z_{(1)}, W_{(1)})$ and $P_{A*} = I - M_{A*}$. The covariance matrix for $\hat{\xi}_*$ is $\mathrm{Cov}(\hat{\xi}_*) = (R_*'\Omega^{-1/2}P_{A*}\Omega^{-1/2}R_*)^{-1}$.

The panel stochastic frontier production system with which we estimate time-varying technical efficiency levels for our sample firms is a special case of (7). We follow Aigner, Lovell, and Schmidt [1977], Schmidt and Sickles [1984], and Cornwell, Schmidt, and Sickles [1990] who use the Zellner, Kmenta, and Dreze [1966] assumption that firms in the industry are maximizing expected profit and specify a stochastic frontier production function. We also assume that firms are cost-minimizing and that any allocatively inefficient errors in setting factor proportions are nonsystematic. Costs are required to be well documented and reasonable, and FERC did disallow some expenses. Moreover, once the rate structure was set, the firm had incentives to minimize costs since any shortfall or excess profit was considered a windfall loss or gain. Previous to the study period the regulatory lag more often than not benefited the firm since output continually expanded. Since output generally fell through the study period, firms could not get their rates adjusted quickly enough to reflect their increasing input costs and declining throughput. Thus the regulatory process imposed discipline on the pipelines as the regulatory lag increased during the study period. Stich and Smith [1984], for example, found that the time required to process rate cases increased from 405 days in 1973 to 697 days in 1978.

We specify the firm effect by a linear function of time, in which case W_j is composed of the constant term and a time trend. The factor inputs are labor, energy, and pipeline and compressor station services. Construction of quantities and prices for output and for the factor inputs is discussed in the next section. Much of the capacity of the transmission firms was in place by mid to late 1970's and to the extent that take-or-pay contract provisions and FERC regulations prevented an optimal downward adjustment of pipeline and compressor station services as demand for natural gas fell during the sample period, technical efficiency and changes therein may be correlated with the two capital inputs. Our seemingly unrelated regressions production system is composed of a homogeneous translog production function and the associated cost-minimizing factor input requirements which are expressed in expense share form (c.f. Aivazian, et al. [1987]). Fixed effects in the production function are time varying and allowed to be correlated with both compressor and pipeline services. Disturbances in the share equations are assumed to be iid with zero mean.

Previous econometric studies of productivity in the natural gas transmission industry have been typically based on estimates from a Cobb-Douglas engineering function (Chenery [1949]; Cookenboo [1952]; Callen [1978]). We lift the assumption that substitution elasticities are unity and specify a flexible translog production function along with the cost minimizing input shares derived from it. We allow for technical change to be factor biasing and for neutral technical change to be quadratic in time. We also include dummy variables to represent three different regulatory epochs. The first (D_1) is the period 1977–1978 before the NGPA went into effect. The second (D_2) is for the years after the NGPA was passed, but before the natural gas spot market developed (1979–1983). The third (D_3) is for the years when the spot market was in operation after 1983. The production function and associated share equations are given by:

$$\ln Y_{it} = \beta_o + \Sigma_k \beta_k \ln x_{it}^k + 1/2\, \Sigma_k \Sigma_l \beta_{kl} \ln x_{it}^k \ln x_{it}^l + \Sigma_k \delta_k \ln x_{it}^k t + \delta_t^t$$

$$+ 1/2\, \delta_{tt} t^2 + \rho_2 D_2 + \rho_3 D_3 + \nu_{it} - u_i,$$

$$M_{it}^j = (\beta_j + \Sigma_k \beta_{jk} \ln x_{it}^k + \delta_j t)/(\Sigma_k \beta_k) + \epsilon_{it}^j, \quad j = 1, \ldots, 4. \tag{8}$$

Homogeneity ($\Sigma_k \beta_{kl} = 0 \;\forall\; l$) and symmetry ($\beta_{kl} = \beta_{lk} \;\forall\; k \neq l$) are imposed in estimation. Time-varying firm efficiency levels are derived from the efficient three-stage least squares estimates based on equation (7). We first estimate α_{li} (the fixed effects in equation (1), the production function) by regressing the residuals for firm i on the W_{lit} vector containing the constant term and the time trend. These provide us with consistent ($\forall$ i, t as $t \to \infty$) estimates of the α_{lit}. Following the arguments of Cornwell, Schmidt, and Sickles [1990] we identify the most efficient firm in period t by $\hat{\alpha}_{lt} = \max_j (\hat{\alpha}_{ljt})$ and relative technical efficiencies by $TE_{it} = \exp\{\hat{\alpha}_{lit} - \hat{\alpha}_{lt}\}$.

The statistical approach to efficiency measurement imposes strong distributional assumptions and economic structure on the data. Programming approaches such as data envelopment analysis (DEA) use piece-wise linear approximations to model the best practice reference technology and are an attractive alternative to stochastic frontier analysis in that more robust, and presumably more policy relevant inferences and forecasts can be made from concordant results based on differing methodologies. The presence and relative variation of statistical noise vis-a-vis deterministic movements in the frontier over the sample is problematic, however, since DEA assumes a deterministic frontier and hence assumed that the data is free from measurement error.

The generic DEA model was introduced to measure the productive efficiency of decision making units (DMU's), or for our purposes, firms, (Charnes, Cooper, and Rhodes [1978, 1981]). Consider a specific firm i at time t which produces an S-vector of outputs (Y_{it}) and an M-vector of inputs (X_{it}). Using the Charnes and Cooper [1985] transformation of fractional programming, the primal linear programming problem (DEA) is set up to

$$\text{Minimize } (\Lambda - \epsilon \ell^T s^+ - \epsilon \ell^T s^-)$$

$$\Lambda, \lambda, s^+, s^-$$

$$\text{subject to } Y\lambda - s^+ = Y_{it},\; \Lambda X_{it} - X\lambda - s^- = 0,\; \lambda, s^+, s^- \geq 0,$$

$$y_{it} > 0,\; X_{it} > 0,\; \forall\; i, t,\; \lambda \ell^T = 1, \tag{9}$$

and where ϵ is a non-Archimedean infinitesimal.[2] The primal problem (9) minimizes the intensity (Λ) of the input under the constraint that the output vector Y_{it} is enveloped from above and the input vector X_{it} is enveloped from below. We adopt the convention used by Charnes and Cooper [1985] and define a firm to be technically efficient if and only if, minimizing (or optimal) values of the primal problem satisfy $\Lambda^* = 1$, $s^{*+} = 0$ and $s^{*-} = 0$, i.e., the intensity is unity and all slacks equal zero, where an optimal solution to equation (9) is denoted by $(\Lambda^*, \lambda^*, s^{*+}, s^{*-})$. Inefficient firms are projected onto their efficient frontier (or efficient facet) by means of the transformation, $X_{it} \rightarrow X'_{it} = \Lambda^* X_{it} - s^{*-}$ and $Y_{it} \rightarrow Y'_{it} = Y_{it} + s^{*+}$. The differences, $\Delta X_{it} = X_{it} - X'_{it} = (1 - \Lambda) X_{it} + s^{*-}$, $\Delta Y_{it} = Y'_{it} - Y_{it} = s^{*+}$, represent the estimated amounts of technical inefficiency at the point (X_{it}, Y_{it}). The index of technical inefficiency for a specific firm i is constructed by regressing the technical efficiencies for each firm against a constant term and a time trend. We then normalize efficiency scores to unity for the most efficient firm in each year just as we do with the panel stochastic frontier estimates discussed above. In principle a weak law of large numbers argument should be applicable to prove weak convergence of the DEA estimate of technical inefficiency as T becomes large.[3]

4. Data

The technology of the natural gas pipeline industry is fairly straightforward in that the firm acts as a merchant and/or carrier of natural gas. As a merchant it buys natural gas from the producing fields, compresses and transports it through long distance pipelines, and resells the gas at the point of delivery to local distributors (sales for resale) or industrial users (mainline sales). The firm also transports gas for others without being a gas merchant. Transport for others became an important activity for the transmission industry as FERC sought to unbundle transport and merchant services. The volume of natural gas transported for others in our sample increased from 20.3 percent of total volume transported in 1977 to 42.8 percent in 1985. The major factor inputs are the pipeline itself, compressor stations to regulate the flow of gas, energy to fuel the compressors (primarily natural gas), and labor. We have collected data on fourteen major interstate natural gas pipe-line companies for nine years, 1977–1985. The firms are: Algonquin Gas, ANR Pipeline, Colorado Interstate, Columbia Gas, Columbia Gulf, Florida Gas, Mississippi River, Northern, Sea Robin, Southern, Texas Eastern, Texas Gas, Transwestern, and Trunkline Gas. These are major interstate natural gas pipeline companies, each with combined gas sales for resale, transport, or storage exceeding 50 billion cubic/year, and have combined sales that amount to almost half of interstate deliveries in 1985.

We measure the output and input variables with a similar methodology as Aivazian, et al. [1987] in order to allow for comparisons between their study of the natural gas transmission industry during its year of expansion prior to the NGPA and our study of a mature industry coping with shrinking markets and a different regulatory environment. Data are from the 1977–1985 firm specific FERC Form–2: Annual Report of Major Natural Gas Pipeline Company, supplemented with the Annual Statistics of Interstate Natural Gas Pipeline Companies (ASI) unless otherwise indicated. Both are available from the Federal Energy Regulatory Commission. The FERC Form–2 contains very detailed information on the financial and operating expenses of the pipeline company, as well as a breakdown of types of output and sources of revenues earned. These reports are not generally distributed, but are available through the Public Information Office at FERC.

Output is measured in trillion cubic feet-miles, derived by multiplying the total volume of gas delivered under *sales for resale, mainline sales*, and *transport of gas of others* by the miles transported. Aivazian, et al. [1987] did not include transport for others or consider the distance transported in their measurement of output. We have included transport for others because of its increasing importance to the industry during the 1977–1985 period. Gas quantities were extracted from the *Gas Accounts-Deliveries* schedule. As miles transported are not reported for resale and mainline sales, we use the average length of the major transmission trunklines from the main production area(s) to the major delivery point(s) for these two categories. The mileage figures are calculated with the use of firm specific pipeline system maps. The weighted average miles transported for gas transported for others is calculated from the *Revenue from Transportation of Gas of Others* schedule.

The quantity of labor is calculated by multiplying the total number of firm employees by the proportion of transmission labor expenses relative to total labor expenses, from the *Distribution of Wages and Salaries* schedule. Energy (natural gas) consumed in production is measured in thousand cubic feet (mcf), as reported in the *Gas Used by the Utility* schedule. The expenses for energy consumed are from the Transmission Expense section of the *Operations and Maintenance Expense* schedule. The prices of labor and energy are derived by dividing total labor and energy expenses by their respective quantities.

Two measures of capital input are used: total horsepower ratings of transmission compressor stations as a proxy for compressor capital services and tons of steel as a proxy for pipeline services. In measuring the quantity of compressor and pipeline capital services used in production, we had to draw on additional data sources as the horsepower rating and pipeline diameters are often not explicitly reported in the FERC Form–2 after 1979. To determine the post–1979 total horsepower and pipeline diameter we turned to the *Pipeline Economics Report* published in the Oil and Gas Journal (OGJ). The OGJ *Pipeline Economics Report* is published once a year, usually in November, and contains data on the configuration and cost of current pipeline and compressor station construction. Data are by state for specific projects. By comparing the location of the individual projects in the OCJ with the areas of operation for each firm and information from the FERC Form–2, we can determine which company is undertaking which project.

Beginning with the horsepower total for 1979, this quantity is updated for each successive year by close examination of information in the *Compressor Stations* schedule and Section 5 of the *Important Changes During the Year*, both in the FERC Form–2. This information is checked against the information given in the OGJ. In a similar fashion, we are able to obtain the weighted average diameter of the pipelines after 1979. The size and length of additional transmission lines, or abandon segments, was often specified in the FERC Form–2 *Transmission Lines* or *Important Changes During the Year* schedules, or the pipeline projects from the OCJ. Thus the miles of transmission pipeline is multiplied by the weighted average diameter, and then by Callen's proportionality constant for converting size and length into ton-miles.[4] Since the firms have not significantly expanded their pipeline systems during the period of study, the method of calculating horsepower and pipeline diameter is not as cumbersome as might be expected.

Neither prices nor expenses for capital services are directly reported; we rely on the value added methodology. First, total revenues from sales for resale, mainline sales, and transport of gas of others are obtained from the *Gas Operating Revenues* schedule. The

Table 1. Parameter estimates for the stochastic frontier model.*

Coefficient	Estimate	T-statistic
β_1	0.072	5.01
β_2	0.074	4.48
β_3	0.201	4.98
β_4	0.806	3.21
β_{11}	0.029	4.16
β_{12}	−0.014	−3.30
β_{13}	−0.008	−1.07
β_{14}	−0.007	−0.75
β_{22}	0.040	4.10
β_{23}	−0.014	−1.24
β_{24}	−0.012	−0.97
β_{33}	0.132	3.42
β_{34}	−0.110	−3.09
β_{44}	−0.129	−3.63
δ_1	0.001	1.15
δ_2	0.006	3.29
δ_3	0.002	0.57
δ_4	−0.009	−2.66
δ_t	*0.047*	*1.02*
δ_{tt}	−0.018	−1.98
ρ_2	0.028	0.42
ρ_3	0.131	1.56

*The order of the factor inputs is labor, energy, compressor services, pipeline services.

cost of labor, energy, and gas purchased are netted out. This net revenue was allocated between compressor and pipeline services based on the ratio of book value cost and operating costs of compressors to pipelines (referred to as *mains*). End of year book value costs are from the Transmission Plant section of the *Gas Plant in Service* schedule. The operating and maintenance costs are from the Transmission Expenses section of the *Gas Operation and Maintenance Expenses* schedule. The resulting two residuals are divided by the appropriate quantity, horsepower or pipeline steel tons, to obtain user prices for the two capital categories.

5. Estimation results

Coefficient estimates for the panel stochastic frontier systems estimator are found in Table 1. The system contains the production function, labor, energy, and compressor services share equations. The system $\bar{R}^2 = 0.892$. Estimates of the derived own- and cross-demand elasticities, Morishima substitution elasticities, and average total factor productivity growth rate are given in Table 2. Table 3 contains χ^2 Wald statistics for various tests of hypotheses regarding returns to scale, homogeneity of the regulatory regimes, efficiency differentials, presence of technological change, the appropriateness of the Cobb-Douglas functional form as a special case of the translog production function, and Hausman-Wu test results for the correlatedness of regressors and statistical noise.

Table 2. Summary statistics.

Average Demand Elasticities

$\eta_{labor} = -1.634$
$\eta_{energy} = -1.674$
$\eta_{comp} = -3.621$
$\eta_{pipe} = -0.942$

Cross Demand Elasticities

	Energy	Compressor	Pipeline
Labor	0.536	0.561	0.536
Energy		0.792	0.485
Compressor			3.003

Morishima Substitution Elasticities

	Labor	Energy	Compressor	Pipeline
Labor	—	2.201	4.172	1.479
Energy	2.170	—	4.403	1.428
Compressor	2.195	2.465	—	3.946
Pipeline	2.170	2.159	6.613	—

Average Annual Total Factor Productivity Growth ($\dot{TFP}$)

$\text{TFP} = -0.0118$

Table 3. Results of Wald and Hausman-Wu hypothesis tests.

I. H_0: Constant returns to scale

$\chi^2_3 = 0.51$

II. H_0: No differential regulatory regimes

$\chi^2_2 = 2.93$

III. H_0: No efficiency differential among firms

$\chi^2_{28} = 502.1$

IV. H_0: No technical change

$\chi^2_5 = 36.1$

V. H_0: Cobb-Douglas technology

$\chi^2_6 = 27.1$

VI. H_0: Factor inputs labor and energy are exogeneous

$\chi^2_{10} = 2.17$

VII. H_0: All factor inputs are exogeneous

$\chi^2_{14} = 11.10$

We begin by pointing out that monotonicity conditions are met for all but three of the 126 sample observations using our stochastic panel systems estimator. These violations were for firm 1 (Algonquin Gas) for years 1,2, and 3 and related specifically to a negative estimate for the energy share. Given the wide fluctuations in the price of energy during the period it is surprising that more violations did not occur. Convexity conditions were not met for 14 of the 126 sample observations. Firms 1 (Algonquin), 6 (Florida Gas), and 7 (Mississippi) failed convexity for several years early in the sample. Estimation of a single equation translog (or even Cobb-Douglas) model without the cost minimizing share equations resulted in negative returns to scale and/or failure of regularity over much of the sample space. Our estimates of derived own-demand elasticities (Table 2) indicate near unitary elasticity of demand for pipelines with substantial firm responsiveness to price variations in the other three inputs. Cross-demand elasticities are all positive and are generally inelastic although pipeline demand is quite responsive to changes in the prices of compressor services. Morishima substitution elasticities indicate substantial scope for substitution among the factor inputs. The results in Table 3 indicate that technical change is significant. Our estimates indicate that factor biases are .6 percent/year for energy and −.9 percent/year for pipeline services, the later a possible artifact of the patterns of pipeline capacity utilization toward the end of the sample period. The hypothesis of no efficiency differentials are strongly rejected as was that of no technical change, a Cobb-Douglas technology, and the presence of correlation between selected inputs and statistical noise. The hypotheses of no scale economies and no differential regulatory regimes were not rejected at conventional significance levels.

Tables 4 and 5 provide estimates of the temporal pattern of firm efficiencies relative to the average frontier and firm efficiencies relative to the best practice frontier. Although the levels and relative rankings of efficiencies are often not the same for the two methods, there is an unambiguous downward trend in firm efficiency levels during the sample period. Concordance in these trends is further highlighted by considering the temporal pattern of efficiency levels in the industry. If we weight the relative efficiencies by the firm's share in

Table 4. Technical efficiency relative to the stochastic frontier.

Firm/Year	1977 %	1978 %	1979 %	1980 %	1981 %	1982 %	1983 %	1984 %	1985 %
Aloqonquin Gas	67.48	67.46	67.44	67.42	67.40	67.37	67.35	67.33	67.31
ANR Pipeline	65.93	65.14	64.37	63.61	62.85	62.10	61.37	60.64	59.92
Colorado Interstate	89.99	88.17	86.39	84.65	82.93	81.26	79.62	78.01	76.43
Columbia Gas	93.67	91.46	89.31	87.22	85.17	83.16	81.21	79.30	77.44
Columbia Gulf	58.69	58.30	57.91	57.52	57.13	56.75	56.37	56.00	55.62
Florida Gas	100.00	100.00	100.00	100.00	100.00	100.00	100.00	100.00	100.00
Mississippi River	80.38	78.78	77.21	75.67	74.16	72.68	71.23	69.81	68.42
Northern Natural	63.31	62.91	62.52	62.12	61.73	61.34	60.95	60.57	60.19
Sea Robin Pipeline	69.80	67.66	65.58	63.57	61.62	59.73	57.89	56.12	54.39
Southern Natural	60.58	59.58	58.61	57.65	56.71	55.78	54.87	53.97	53.09
Texas Eastern	91.43	90.66	89.90	89.14	88.40	87.65	86.92	86.19	85.46
Texas Gas	67.73	67.14	66.56	65.98	65.41	64.84	64.28	63.72	63.17
Transwestern	93.83	92.31	90.82	89.36	87.91	86.49	85.09	83.72	82.37
Trunkline Gas	85.19	83.49	81.82	80.19	78.59	77.01	75.48	73.97	72.49

Table 5. Technical efficiency relative to the best practice technology.

Firm/Year	1977 %	1978 %	1979 %	1980 %	1981 %	1982 %	1983 %	1984 %	1985 %
Aloqonquin Gas	100.00	99.50	98.67	97.84	96.76	95.24	93.73	92.26	90.26
ANR Pipeline	74.99	75.85	76.46	77.07	77.48	77.52	77.56	77.60	77.17
Colorado Interstate	83.70	82.91	81.85	80.80	79.55	77.94	76.37	74.83	72.88
Columbia Gas	99.99	96.35	92.52	88.85	85.10	81.11	77.31	73.68	69.81
Columbia Gulf	87.50	88.97	90.15	91.35	92.31	92.84	93.37	93.90	93.88
Florida Gas	78.86	81.87	84.71	87.65	90.45	92.89	95.39	97.96	100.00
Mississippi River	95.06	92.64	89.99	87.41	84.67	81.63	78.69	75.87	72.70
Northern Natural	68.47	69.57	70.45	71.35	72.06	72.43	72.80	73.17	73.10
Sea Robin Pipeline	83.89	79.10	74.33	69.84	65.46	61.05	56.94	53.10	49.23
Southern Natural	67.29	66.53	65.56	64.60	63.49	62.10	60.73	59.40	57.75
Texas Eastern	99.66	100.00	100.00	100.00	99.73	98.99	98.25	97.51	96.20
Texas Gas	70.74	70.99	70.99	70.99	70.79	70.26	69.74	69.22	68.29
Transwestern	98.95	95.95	92.74	89.63	86.39	82.87	79.49	76.25	72.71
Trunkline Gas	96.98	98.04	98.78	99.52	100.00	100.00	100.00	100.00	99.40

total industry output, in which case the technical efficiency scores from DEA intuitively become closer in spirit to the average efficiency construct of stochastic frontiers and further from the best practice efficiency construct of DEA, then the evidence from the two methodologies become strikingly similar. Best practice relative efficiencies for the industry were 85 percent in 1977 and declined to 82 percent in 1985 while relative efficiencies for the average frontier declined from 78 percent to 74 percent. A representative firm in the industry, or alternatively an industry comprised of these sample firms, found its efficiency falling at a rate averaging 0.55 percent per year during the period in which the NGPA was implemented.

5. Conclusions

In this article we have examined the patterns of technical efficiency change in the natural gas transmission industry during a period in which a major regulatory intervention was implemented, the Natural Gas Policy Act of 1978. We have examined firm-specific and temporal patterns of technical efficiency for a newly constructed panel of fourteen firms in the industry. These firms comprise almost half of the total output of major natural gas transmission firms. We have introduced a new panel stochastic frontier systems estimator which exploits the potential exogeneity of certain regressors from firm effects which can cause heterogeneity in slopes as well as in intercepts. Our systems estimator also can accommodate a simultaneous equations structure. Patterns of technical efficiency based on our structural stochastic model are compared with those based on deterministic programming methods involving data envelopment analysis. Concordant findings based on these alternative methodologies suggest a perversive pattern of declining technical efficiency in the industry during the period in which this major regulatory intervention was introduced and implemented. The broad policy implications from the rather robust industry trends suggest that the NGPA had a substantial distortionary effect on the productive performance of the natural gas transmission industry.

Acknowledgments

The authors would like to thank William A. Johnson and C.A.K. Lovell for helpful comments and suggestions. The findings and conclusions expressed herein are the authors and do not necessarily reflect the views of the Census Bureau. The authors are grateful to Purvez Captain for invaluable research assistance.

Notes

1. Natural gas is classified according to well vintage, commitment to intra- or interstate markets, type of geological formation, rate of production, and the provision of existing gas sale contracts. For a summary of the NGPA gas categories and their respective pricing regulation see *The Natural Gas Regulation Handbook*, Pierce [1980].
2. We experimented with several different values for ϵ. The correlation between efficiency scores for $\epsilon = 1.0 \times 10^{-3}$ and $\epsilon = 1.0 \times 10^{-6}$ was 0.99. Estimates are based on $\epsilon = 1.0 \times 10^{-6}$.
3. Modifications of the CCR or Banker, Charnes, and Cooper (BCC) [1984] programming set up can be made in which a nonconvex technology is allowed for due to the presence of increasing economies of scale. Although our estimates do not indicate scale economies, previous studies of the natural gas transmission industry (Robinson [1972]; Callen [1978]; Aivazian and Callen [1981]; Aivazian, et al., [1987] have indicated the presence of scale economies with an engineering upper bound estimated by Robinson of 2.07. As pointed out by several authors, efficiency estimates based on either BCC or CCR are inconsistent with the nonconvex technology set implied by increasing returns to scale. Recently Peterson [1990] and Cooper and Sinha [1990] have discussed alternatives to the CCR and BCC when the technology set exhibits increasing returns to scale, i.e., it is nonconvex. By specifying convex input and output sets and with a suitable modification of the standard linear program used in the CCR or the BCC formulation, efficiency measures for a technology set exhibiting increasing returns to scale can be obtained by a two stage program which provides a nonconvex spanning of the piecewise linear reference technology.
4. See equation A8, page 320 of Callen [1978]: $P = 0.382d^2L$. where P = pipeline capital services, d = weighted average diameter, and L = miles of transmission pipelines.

References

Aigner, D., C.A.K. Lovell, and P. Schmidt. (1977). "Formulation and Estimation of Stochastic Frontier Production Function Models." *Journal of Econometrics* 6, pp. 21–37.

Aivazian, Varouj A., Jeffrey L. Callen, M.W. Luke Chan, and Dean C. Mountain. (1987). "Economies of Scale Versus Technological Change in the Natural Gas Transmission Industry." *Review of Economics and Statistics* 69, pp. 556-561.

Aivazian, Varouj A. and Jeffrey L. Callen. (1981). "Capacity Expansion in the U.S. Natural Gas Pipeline Industry." Thomas G. Cowing and Rodney E. Stevenson, *Productivity Measurements in Regulated Industries. New York: Academic Press.*

Banker, R.D., A. Charnes, and W.W. Cooper. (1984). "Some Models for Estimating Technical and Scale Inefficiencies in Data Envelopment Analysis." *Management Science* 30, pp. 1078–1092.

Breusch, T.S., G. E. Mizon, and P. Schmidt. (1989). "Efficient Estimation Using Panel Data." *Econometrica* 57, 695–700.

Callen, Jeffrey L. (1978) "Production Efficiency, and Welfare in the Natural Gas Transmission Industry." *American Economic Review* 68, pp. 311–323.

Charnes, A. and W.W. Cooper. (1985). "Preface to Topics in Data Envelopment Analysis." *Annals of Operations Research* 2, pp. 59–94.

Charnes, A., W.W. Cooper, and E. Rhodes. (1978). "Measuring Efficiency of Decision Making Units." *European Journal of Operations Research* 2, pp. 429–444.

Charnes, A., W.W. Cooper, and E. Rhodes. (1981). "Evaluating Program and Managerial Efficiency: An Application of Data Envelopment Analysis to Program Follow Through." *Management Science* 27, pp. 668–697.

Chenery, Hollis, B. (1949). "Engineering Production Functions." *Quarterly Journal of Economics* 63, pp. 507–531.

Cookenboo, Leslie Jr. (1955). "Production and Cost Functions for Oil Pipe Lines." *Crude Oil Pipelines and Competition in the Oil Industry,* Cambridge, Mass.: Harvard University Press, pp. 13–32.

Cooper, W.W. and K.K. Sinha. (1990). "A Note on Petersen's Relaxed Assumptions for DEA." mimeo, IC^2 Institute, University of Texas, Austin.

Cornwell, C., Peter Schmidt, and Robin C. Sickles. (1990). "Production Frontiers with Cross-Sectional and Time-Series Variation in Efficiency Levels." *Journal of Econometrics* 46, pp. 185–200.

Cornwell, C. Peter Schmidt, and D. Wyhowski. (1992). "Simultaneous Equations and Panel Data." forthcoming in *Journal of Econometrics* 51, pp. 151–181.

Federal Energy Regulatory Commission, U.S. Department of Energy. (1977–1985). *FERC Form No. 2: Annual Report of Natural Gas Companies (Class A and Class B),* Washington, D.C.: U.S. Government Printing Office.

Federal Energy Regulatory Commission, U.S. Department of Energy. (1978–1986). *Statistics on Interstate Natural Gas Pipeline Companies,* Washington, D.C.: U.S. Government Printing Office.

Gong, B-H, and Robin C. Sickles. (1992). "Finite Sample Evidence on the Performance of Stochastic Frontiers and Data Envelopment Analysis Using Panel Data." *Journal of Econometrics* 51, pp. 259–284.

Natural Gas Monthly (1978–1980). Merrill Lynch, Pierce, Fenner & Smith Incorporated, various issues.

Natural Gas Policy Act of 1978 (1980). U.S. Code, Supp. 5, Title 15.

Petersen, N.C. (1990). "Data Envelopment Analysis on a Relaxed Set of Assumptions." *Management Science* 36, pp. 305–314.

Pierce, Jr., Richard J. (1980). *Natural Gas Regulation Handbook.* New York: Executive Enterprises Publication.

Robinson, S.T. (1972). "Powering of Natural Gas Pipelines." *Journal of Engineering for Power* 94, pp. 181–186.

Schmidt, Peter, and Robin C. Sickles. (1984). "Production Frontiers and Panel Data." *Journal of Business and Economic Statistics* 2, pp. 367–374.

Stich, Robert S. and L. Douglas Smith. (1984). "Federal Regulation of Gas Pipeline Rates, 1973–1982." *Public Utilities Fortnightly,* pp. 34–38.

Streitwieser, Mary L. (1989). *Productivity in the U.S. Interstate Natural Gas Transmission Industry Under the Natural Gas Policy Act of 1978,* unpublished Ph.D. dissertation, Rice University, Houston, Texas.

Zellner, A., J. Kmenta, and J. Dreze. (1966). "Specification and Estimation of Cobb-Douglas Production Function Models." *Econometrica* 34, pp. 784–795.

The Journal of Productivity Analysis, 3, 135–151 (1992)

Measuring Technical Efficiency in European Railways: A Panel Data Approach

HENRY-JEAN GATHON AND SERGIO PERELMAN
Department of Economics, University of Liège

Abstract

We estimate a factor requirement frontier for European railways using a panel data approach in which technical efficiency is assumed to be endogeneously determined. This approach has two main outcomes. On one hand, it allows the identification of factors influencing technical efficiency, and on the other hand, it allows the estimation of alternative efficiency indicators free of these influences. In the case under study, a particular attention is devoted to an *autonomy* indicator representing the managerial freedom, with respect to public authorities, experienced by firms, that appears to be positively correlated with technical efficiency.

1. Introduction

Beginning with Klein's [1953] seminal econometric study on the US railway companies, the applied economic literature has given considerable attention to the rail activity. This interest can be explained by the special nature of this transportation activity, which can be considered at first glance as rather simple and easy to formalize. Nevertheless, the experience shows that this is a difficult task, especially because of the multi-output character of the production process and the heavily regulated environment in which these companies operate.

This is particularly the case of the European railway sector which is the object of this article. All the companies we observe, except one, are state-owned. They hold a natural monopoly position on the rail transportation, but in return, their activity is constrained by the public authorities. They have to face various regulations concerning, for instance, their fare policy, their investments, the structure of their network, the management of their workforce, etc.. This means that these firms do not enjoy the same autonomy in order to respond to the changing environmental conditions.

Our main concern in this article is to estimate and compare the levels of technical efficiency reached by each of these railway companies over the last thirty years, taking into account the institutional context in which they operate.

With this context in view we estimate a *factor requirement frontier* for the railway transportation, using a panel data approach. This approach is an extension of the methodology proposed by Schmidt and Sickles [1984] who assumed that specific individual effects can be good indicators of technical efficiency when panel data on productive units are available. These authors so apply an old proposition made by Mundlak in 1961, to the context of recent frontier analysis developments.

Nevertheless, one shortcoming of this approach is that the efficiency indicator, like the other estimated parameters, will be biased if performance is correlated with other variables in the model. To overcome this difficulty it is possible to adopt the Hausman and Taylor [1981] approach that consists in a test and an instrumental variables estimation technique. We use this technique, but paying a particular attention to the possible correlation between the technical efficiency, assumed to be endogenous, and the other explanatory variables in the model, among which we include an *autonomy* indicator representing the managerial freedom experienced by each railway company with respect to the public authorities supervision.

Furthermore, as suggested by Mundlak [1978], this last relation is estimated on the basis of an auxiliary equation allowing to obtain some insight into the process leading to inefficiency and to get an alternative measure of performance, free of the influence of factors that are beyond the firm control.

The results obtained for European railways confirm the case of a high correlation between the individual efficiency indicators and the exogeneous factors and illustrates the pertinence of the suggested approach in measuring performance within a panel of firms.

In this article we proceed as follows: in the second section we present some methodological considerations; then, in the third section we deal with the data and the specification of the input constrained frontier; finally, in the last section we report the main results of our estimations.

2. The panel data approach

We begin with the specification of a parametric function representative of the railway activity, to be estimated on the basis of available pooled cross-section and time-series data. For reasons we are going to explain below, we adopt here a factor requirements function (Diewert [1974]) of the form:

$$\begin{aligned} y_{it} &= \alpha_0 + X_{it}'\beta + r_t\tau + Z_i'\gamma + \epsilon_{it}, \qquad (1)\\ \epsilon_{it} &= u_i + \nu_{it}, \end{aligned}$$

where $i = 1, \ldots, I$ and $t = 1, \ldots, T$, indicate firms and periods, respectively; y_{it} is the endogenous input and X_{it} is a vector of exogeneous variables that includes, besides the outputs, some variables characterizing the outputs and the technology; r_t and Z_i indicate time-varying and cross-section variables, respectively; α, β, τ, and γ are the parameters to be estimated; and finally ϵ_{it} is a composed error term that combines the time-invariant latent individual effects u_i and the disturbance terms ν_{it}, assumed to be normally distributed and uncorrelated neither with u_i nor with the explanatory variables in the model.

Following Schmidt and Sickles [1984], we assume that the individual effects u_i are indicators of the firm's efficiency. Furthermore, if we assume $u_i \geq 0$, equation (1) corresponds to a special case of the stochastic frontier model introduced by Aigner, Lovell, and Schmidt [1977], and by Meusen and van den Broek in 1977. The difference lies in the fact that for panel data, equation (1) provides a natural way to discriminate between the efficiency indicator and the noise.

Then, in order to be able to apply the main results of the panel data literature, we transform equation (1) into:

$$y_{it} = X_{it}'\,\beta + r_t\,\tau + Z_i'\,\gamma + \alpha_i + \nu_{it}, \tag{2}$$

where $\alpha_i = \alpha_0 + u_i$.

The two traditional and alternative methods proposed to deal with latent individual effects are the so called *fixed* and *random effects* models. Each of them allows us to calculate an alternative and specific measure of efficiency.

2.1. Fixed and random effects models

In the first case we obtain the *Within group* estimators, indicated by the subscript *W*, by estimating the following equation:

$$\tilde{y}_{it} = \tilde{X}_{it}'\,\beta_W + \tilde{r}_t\,\tau_W + \epsilon_{W,it} \tag{3}$$

and

$$\hat{\alpha}_{W,i} = \bar{Y}_{i.} - \bar{X}_{i.}'\,\hat{\beta}_W,$$

where $\bar{k}_{i.}$ indicates mean values within groups; ~ indicate deviations from individual means, and ∧ estimated values; and $\epsilon_{W,it} = \tilde{\nu}_{it}$ is the normal disturbance term.

The estimated levels of performance $\hat{\mu}_{W,i}$ are then obtained on basis of the estimated fixed effects $\hat{\alpha}_{W,i}$ by assuming that the most efficient firm in the sample corresponds to $\min(\hat{\alpha}_{W,i})$ and that the inefficiency level is given by the distance $\hat{\mu}_{W,i} = \hat{\alpha}_{W,i} - \min(\hat{\alpha}_{W,i})$. Note that when the input requirement function adopts a logarithmic shape—as it will be in our application—the corresponding measure of efficiency will be: $\hat{\mu}_{W,i} = \exp[\hat{\alpha}_{W,i} - \min(\hat{\alpha}_{W,i})]$. Then $\hat{\mu}_{W,i} = 1$ will indicate the most labor efficient firm identified by $\min(\hat{\alpha}_{W,i})$; otherwise, $\hat{\mu}_{W,i} > 1$ will indicate the degree of labor overutilization with respect to the requirement frontier.

In the case of the random effects model, we obtain generalized least squares (GLS) estimators by performing ordinary least squares (OLS) on the transformed variables:

$$(y_{it} - \theta\,\bar{y}_{i.}) = (X_{it} - \theta\,\bar{X}_{i.})'\,\beta_{GLS} + (r_t - \theta\,\bar{r}_.)\,\tau_{GLS} + (1-\theta)\,Z_i'\gamma_{GLS} + \epsilon_{GLS,it}, \tag{4}$$

where

$$\theta = 1 - (\hat{\sigma}_\nu^2/(\hat{\sigma}_\nu^2 + T\,\hat{\sigma}_\alpha^2))^{1/2},\quad \epsilon_{GLS,it} = (1-\theta)\,\alpha_i + (\nu_{it} - \theta\,\bar{\nu}_{i.}),$$

and $\hat{\sigma}_\nu^2$ and $\hat{\sigma}_\alpha^2$ can be estimated, for instance, by performing OLS on equation (2) as suggested by Wallace and Hussein [1969].

The random effects are computed as $\hat{\alpha}_{GLS,i} = 1/T\,\Sigma_t\,\hat{\epsilon}_{it}$ on basis of the estimated mean firms residuals obtained also by applying OLS to equation (2). As before, the performance levels are obtained by: $\hat{\mu}_{GLS,i} = \hat{\alpha}_{GLS,i} - \min(\hat{\alpha}_{GLS,i})$.

As expected, these two alternative models yield different results. We thus have to choose the one that most fits the sample and the purpose of the analysis. A way to proceed is to rely on the statistical properties of the sample, in which case we would apply the random effects model for random samples and the fixed effect model otherwise. However, this criteria may be misleading, as shown by Mundlak [1978] when the possibility of correlation between the latent individual effects, α_i, and the other variables in the model is introduced.

Following Mundlak [1978], this relation can be formalized through an auxiliary equation, that in the present case takes the form:

$$\alpha_i = \bar{X}_{i.}' \pi + Z_i' \xi + \omega_i \tag{5}$$

where π and ξ are parameters and ω_i is an error term with the normal properties.

Considering the aim of this article (performance assessment) it is clear that this last relation may have a special interest. Recall that we have chosen to assume (equation 2) that the α_i's are indicators of efficiency free from the noise which is caught by the ν_i error term. Indeed, among all the variables included in equation (2), we can reasonably consider that those of them characterizing the technology and the environment, including regulation, may affect the technical efficiency of the firm.[1]

Furthermore, as Mundlak showed, the random effects model (4) and the fixed effects model (3) are special cases of the general model described by equations (2) and (5). The first one corresponding to the special case of absence of correlation, i.e., $E[\alpha_i \mid X_{it}, Z_i] = 0$ (or $E[\mu_i \mid X_{it}, Z_i] = 0$), and the second one corresponding to the opposite case in which the α_i (or μ_i) are correlated with all the variables in the model.

Then we have to determine the most suited model to handle this problem. Hausman and Taylor [1981] (hereafter H&T) provide a method for that purpose. On one hand, they presented a specific test on the correlation between individual-specific effects and explanatory variables, and on the other hand they introduced an instrumental variable estimation technique in order to obtain non-biased and efficient estimators in the case that not all variables will be correlated with the individual effects.

The test performed by H&T is based on the Within and GLS estimators. As mentioned before, these estimators correspond to the extreme cases in which all or none of the variables are correlated with the individual latent effects. We perform:

$$\hat{m} = \hat{q}' \operatorname{cov}(\hat{q})^{-1} \hat{q} \tag{6}$$

where $\hat{q} = \hat{\beta}_{GLS} - \hat{\beta}_w$ and $\operatorname{cov}(\hat{q}) = \operatorname{cov}(\hat{\beta}_w) - \operatorname{cov}(\hat{\beta}_{GLS})$. We test the null hypothesis $H_0 = E[\alpha_i \mid X_{it}, Z_i] = 0$ against the alternative $H_1 = E[\alpha_i \mid X_{it}, Z_i] \neq 0$ hypothesis on basis of a χ^2 test. If the null hypothesis is accepted, then IV estimation procedure is required.

2.2. *The GLS-Instrumental Variable model*

The advantage of the GLS-IV model proposed by H&T is twofold. First, all the instrumental variables can be selected within those already present in the original model. Second, we can estimate the γ parameters for the variables of Z_i type, estimation which is not possible with the Within effects model.[2]

In fact, the problem of potential correlation between individual latent effects and the explanatory variables is limited, by definition, to the cross sectional level. This is the reason why in panel data analysis the IV model, designed to deal with this problem, can be applied without adding supplementary variables. The IV technique can be implemented by introducing a distinction between the exogeneous ($X1_{it}$, $Z1_i$)—non-correlated with α_i—variables[3] and the endogenous ($X2_{it}$, $Z2_i$) ones. We then apply the instrumental variable technique to equation (4) in the GLS model using ($\bar{X}1_{it}$, $\tilde{X}1_{it}$, $\tilde{X}2_{it}$, $Z1_i$) as instruments. The only difference is that the variance components are estimated from a previous two stage least squares procedure in which consistent estimators of β and γ can be obtained. Furthermore, in order to avoid identification problems, it is necessary to check that $k_1 > g_2$, where k_1 and g_2 indicate the number of variables in $X1_{it}$ and $Z2_i$, respectively.

Proceeding in this way, we obtain consistent and efficient estimators when the effects are correlated with the explanatory variables (H&T [1981]). Indicating by a suffix IV these estimators, we calculate the individual effects by performing:

$$\hat{\alpha}_{IV,i} = \bar{Y}_{i.} - \bar{X}_{i.}' \hat{\beta}_{IV} - Z_i' \hat{\gamma}_{IV}, \tag{7}$$

and the corresponding measures of efficiency: $\hat{\mu}_{IV,i} = \hat{\alpha}_{IV,i} - \min(\hat{\alpha}_{IV,i})$.

2.3. *Measuring net efficiency*

Summing up, once we have decided which of the three alternative models will be used to estimate performances, we turn to the analysis of the factors influencing technical efficiency. One possibility, however, is that individual effects may be uncorrelated with the exogeneous variables present in the model. In that case the GLS estimators will be consistent and efficient and the $\hat{\mu}_{GLS,i}$ will be the univocal measures of performance. Otherwise, we turn to the estimation of the auxiliary function (5).

Here, we adapt the estimation procedure proposed by Mundlak [1978] to the case of incomplete correlation, by performing an OLS regression between estimated individual effects ($\hat{\alpha}_{IV,i}$) and all the variables identified as factors influencing technical efficiency, that is $\bar{X}2_{i.}$ and $Z2_i$:

$$\hat{\alpha}_{IV,i} = \bar{X}2_{i.}' \pi + Z2_i' \xi + \omega_i. \tag{8}$$

Then, equation (8) can be used in order to analyze the influence of the factors on efficiency and, as far as these factors are believed to be out of control of the managers, it is possible to re-estimate net efficiency measures purged from these influences by doing: $\bar{\mu}_{N,i} = \hat{\omega}_i - \min(\bar{\omega}_i)$. Where the suffix *N* indicates the net character of these measures.

Finally, when the hypothesis of correlation between the individual effects and all the explanatory variables in the model cannot be rejected, the net indicators of efficiency must be estimated on the basis of the Within model estimators as indicated by equation (5).[4]

It is important to note that, at this point, our approach differs radically from Schmidt and Sickles [1984]. Dealing with a traditional production function, these authors assume that mismanagement affects the choice of the input intensity. In other words, the causality between technical inefficiency and explanatory variables is assumed to go in the opposite direction as we suppose here. As a consequence, for these authors the efficiency measures obtained under the random effects model ($\hat{\mu}_{GLS,i}$) must be considered as definitive.

Our claim is that the alternative measures of performance presented here are free of bias caused by internal correlation. Therefore we can rank all the firms as if they were free from the constraints imposed by exogeneous conditions. At the same time these evaluations stress the potential capacity of policies designed to lighten these constraints.

2.4. Maximum-Likelihood estimators

We also present the results obtained from the estimation of equation (2) under the assumption that technical efficiency is half-normally distributed. As well known, this type of distribution is generally used for efficiency measurement in the stochastic frontier literature (e.g. Jondrow et al. [1982]). In the present case, we focus on the results obtained by a Maximum Likelihood (ML) procedure proposed by Battese and Coelli [1988]. Specially designed to deal with panel data, this procedure amounts to estimate the conditional expectation, $\mu_{ML,i}$, of the individual efficiencies, as follows:

$$\mu_{ML,i} = E[\exp(\alpha_i) \mid \alpha_i + \nu_{it}] = 2 \exp(\sigma_\alpha^2/2)[1 - \Phi(\sigma_\alpha)], \qquad (9)$$

where $\Phi(.)$ indicates the standard normal distribution function.[5]

These estimations will be performed under the assumption of absence of correlation between the α_i and the other variables present in the model. Nevertheless, they will be included here in order to be compared with those obtained with the alternative procedures described above.

3. Model specification and data

Our main purpose is to estimate an indicator of technical efficiency within a panel composed of 19 European railway companies observed over the period 1961–1988. In table 1, we present the main characteristics of these companies.

As indicated before, we adopt here a parametric approach based on the estimation of a so-called *factor requirement function* (Diewert [1973, 1974]) with labor units as the dependent variable.[6] Even if it is not a usual way to modelize production activities, it appears to us as a promising field for railways which produce multiple outputs and operate in heavily regulated conditions. In fact, we prefer using this type of function instead of a usual production function because of the problems encountered in obtaining functional forms for multiple output production functions. We could alternatively use a dual cost function. Unfortunately, the cost function approach requires data on the railways' input prices, data which are not very reliable in the present—international and heavily regulated—context.

Table 1. Sample descriptive statistics (mean values over the period 1961–1988)[1]

			Train—km			Mean Distances		Load Factors			
Railways	Country	Labor (10^3)	Passenger (10^6)	Freight (10^6)	Lines (km)	Passenger (km)	Freight (km)	Passenger (per train)	Freight (tons per train)	Electrification %	Autonomy %[2]
BLS	Switzerland	1.9	4.9	1.1	237	19.8	44.9	61.4	220.9	100.0	100.0
BR	United-Kingdom	229.0	343.6	104.2	19439	40.2	118.4	89.4	204.2	17.4	76.3
CFF	Switzerland	38.5	64.1	28.0	2934	38.2	150.3	131.9	218.1	99.4	66.0
CFL	Luxembourg	4.0	2.9	1.5	292	21.2	37.7	75.4	412.3	49.1	63.5
CH	Greece	11.6	12.8	3.2	2534	133.3	217.2	107.7	198.4	0.0	47.3
CIE	Ireland	8.5	7.6	4.3	2213	58.4	165.8	100.6	123.2	0.0	58.3
CP	Portugal	24.5	24.5	6.2	3595	27.1	217.6	151.3	146.6	11.0	64.0
DB	Germany	351.8	384.7	196.3	28949	38.2	199.8	100.7	304.6	30.4	61.0
DSB	Denmark	19.5	35.7	8.3	2256	30.9	235.3	99.7	200.1	4.5	41.5
FS	Italy	200.1	210.3	60.3	16366	98.3	324.1	164.9	279.8	50.9	67.0
NS	Netherlands	27.3	82.6	15.3	2984	44.1	146.3	101.1	211.6	57.6	70.3
NSB	Norway	16.8	22.9	10.2	4253	57.7	99.4	83.5	240.5	53.9	45.3
OBB	Austria	70.8	56.4	33.6	5834	41.1	201.2	118.9	285.2	44.5	41.8
RENFE	Spain	78.5	85.0	44.3	13162	80.9	316.1	162.0	209.6	30.0	52.3
SJ	Sweden	37.9	64.1	40.7	11837	82.2	284.3	84.6	354.3	59.3	80.0
SNCB	Belgium	54.6	64.4	21.9	4344	40.1	108.3	112.9	331.0	31.4	64.5
SNCF	France	270.7	261.3	204.1	36305	73.7	303.3	179.4	309.4	26.3	69.8
TCDD	Turkey	58.4	20.7	18.2	8089	49.4	449.5	247.2	316.7	1.2	60.0
VR	Finland	24.7	25.2	18.4	5811	86.0	269.3	106.2	353.2	0.6	40.0

[1]The variables are defined in the Appendix (Source: UIC [1961–1988]).

[2]Values obtained on the basis of a survey conducted in 1988–89 (Gathon [1991]).

The use of the labor function as a valid representation of the productive process of the railroads requires an assumption of complementarity (fixed proportions) between all the main inputs (labor, capital and fuel) needed to supply the rail transportation. This assumption can be considered as plausible not only from a technical but also from an empirical viewpoint.[7] Furthermore, for our sample, labor expenses account for about 90% of the variable cost[8] throughout the whole period and for all the railways, that allow us to assume that the substitution possibilities between labor and energy are highly limited.

3.1. The factor requirement function

The function we estimate is log-linear in outputs. It can be represented by equation (2), except that we include only one time-invariant variable z_i:

$$y_{it} = \alpha_i + X_{it}' \beta + r_t \tau + z_i \gamma + \nu_{it}, \quad (i = 1, \ldots, 19; t = 1, \ldots, 28), \tag{9}$$

where

y_{it}	:	labor
X_{it}	:	8 time- and firm-varying variables
$x_{1,it}$	:	train-km (passengers)
$x_{2,it}$	:	train-km (freight)
$x_{3,it}$	:	km of lines
$x_{4,it}$	:	mean distance (passengers)
$x_{5,it}$	:	mean distance (freight)
$x_{6,it}$	:	load factor (passengers)
$x_{7,it}$	:	load factor (freight)
$x_{8,it}$	:	electrification
r_t	:	the trend (firm-invariant)
z_i	:	autonomy (time-invariant).

All these variables, but the trend, are expressed in natural logarithms.[9]

The first two variables in X_{it} are the main outputs of the railways, i.e., the transportation of passengers and freight, evaluated in train-kilometers (train runs performed during one year). The third variable is the length of the network which is here assumed to be an output since an important part of the railroad staff is assigned to the maintenance of tracks and stations independently of the rail traffic intensity.

Variables $x_{4,it}$ to $x_{7,it}$ are output characteristics that allow us to take into account the nature of the demand side in the analysis. We comply here to a tradition[10] that consists in the consideration of some output characteristics as factors determining the production technology. Variables $x_{4,it}$ and $x_{5,it}$ are two indirect indicators of the density of the network, as postulated by Caves et al. [1981]. The load factors $x_{6,it}$ and $x_{7,it}$ (passengers and tons by trains) are used as proxies for the intensity of passengers and freight services demand.

The electrification variable $x_{8,it}$ (% of the electrified network) is assumed to be a good indicator of the technology chosen by the railways. The trend variable, r_t, is included in order to catch the general improvement in productivity not controlled by the other variables in the model. In accordance with Nishimizu and Page [1982], we assume here that productivity gains have two different sources: the results of progress in technology and in technical efficiency. As we will see hereafter, this is a way of relaxing the assumption of constancy of the general level of performance overtime.

Finally, the variable *autonomy*, which is an index of the regulatory and institutional environment that the companies have to face, has been constructed from a survey we conducted among these companies in 1988–1989 (Gathon [1991]). This survey aims at evaluating the autonomy enjoyed by the railways management with respect to public authorities. The numerical value of this index ranges between 40 and 100. The more autonomous the management, the higher is the value of this index.

A difficulty with this variable is the fact that it was observed at the end of the analyzed period. In spite of this, we include this autonomy index in equation (9), next to the other variables, assuming that the institutional environment of the national railways moves little and very slowly.[11]

3.2. *The panel*

On table 1, we reproduce the mean individual values of these variables for all the companies. As it can be seen, the sample includes the Turkish company, partially outside Europe and two companies for Switzerland, one of them (BLS) being private. This aside, the panel consists of European national railways that are for a large part interconnected. The length of the observed period (1961–1988) gives us an excellent basis for comparison and allows us to obtain more confident statistical results.

Some interesting facts can be outlined from table 1.

First, the large scale variations across railroads. The largest firms, BR, DB, and SNCF are more than one hundred times bigger, in terms of lines, labor or outputs, than the smallest companies, BLS and CFL.

Second, we also observe some important differences across firms, in the output composition. Some companies such as SNCF, VR and TCDD, display a fair balance between passengers and freight transportation. Other railroads, such as NS and DSB, are specialized in passenger services, leaving freight traffic to other transportation modes.

Third, mean distances and load factors vary substantially across countries. These variables seem to be partially correlated with the size of the network, but, at the same time, with its density and structure. Concerning the electrification process, we observe that both Swiss companies reach a 100 percent level, while on the opposite, some companies continue to operate a network with fuel traction only.

Note that these exogeneous variables, together with the index of regulation, can be at the same time factors of the production process and factors influencing the performance. However, we do not introduce a priori information about which variables should influence the technical efficiency, except for *autonomy* which is, by construction, expected to be correlated with performance.

4. Estimation and main results

As stated in section 2, we proceed first with the estimation of the Within and GLS models for the labor constrained function. The results of these estimations are presented in columns (a) and (b) of table 2.

Table 2. Estimated parameters for alternative models.[1]

Dependent variable: labor; number of observations: 532					
Variables	Parameters	(a) Within	(b) GLS	(c) GLS-IV	(d) ML
Train-km:					
passengers	β_1	0.223 (0.052)	0.380 (0.041)	0.254 (0.045)	0.269 (0.048)
freight	β_2	0.128 (0.041)	0.149 (0.039)	0.159 (0.062)	0.136 (0.039)
Km of lines	β_3	0.493 (0.074)	0.553 (0.054)	[2] 0.610 (0.060)	0.515 (0.057)
Mean distance:					
passengers	β_4	0.089 (0.089)	-0.142 (0.062)	0.185 (0.055)	-0.070 (0.075)
freight	β_5	-0.210 (0.062)	-0.200 (0.052)	[2] -0.183 (0.059)	-0.192 (0.055)
Load factor:					
passengers	β_6	0.015 (0.040)	0.131 (0.040)	0.019 (0.072)	0.041 (0.041)
freight	β_7	0.067 (0.040)	0.097 (0.042)	0.071 (0.068)	0.063 (0.041)
Electrification	β_8	-0.015 (0.005)	-0.020 (0.004)	-0.013 (0.008)	-0.016 (0.005)
Trend	τ	-0.010 (0.001)	-0.011 (0.001)	-0.010 (0.002)	-0.011 (0.001)
Autonomy	γ	—	-0.175 (0.135)	0.359 (0.081)	-0.054 (0.089)
Intercept	α_0	—	1.66 (0.69)	-0.471 (0.59)	1.94 (0.44)
χ^2(d.f. = 1)		—	105.7	6.63	—

[1]Standard errors are presented in brackets.
[2]Instrumental variable.

As can be observed, the sum of the estimators corresponding to the three outputs (passengers and freight train-km and km of lines) indicates some economies of scale[12] in the Within model ($\hat{\beta}_{W,1} + \hat{\beta}_{W,2} + \hat{\beta}_{W,3} = 0.844$) and diseconomies of scale in the GLS model ($\hat{\beta}_{GLS,1} + \hat{\beta}_{GLS,2} + \hat{\beta}_{GLS,3} = 1.082$). Note that the Within estimators can be interpreted as short-run estimators, since they are performed on variables expressed in deviations from individual means.

Furthermore, concerning the variables controlling for the output characteristics, we observe that overall they present the expected signs. On one hand, average passengers and freight distances appear, in all cases but one, as labor saving factors. On the other hand, the two load factors variables are associated with positive coefficients. Given that the railway output is measured in terms of train-km, a higher loading of the trains is related to a higher demand for the supplied transportation capacity and probably implies more labor consumption. It is important to note, the two coefficients are only statistically significant under the GLS model.

The coefficients associated with the electrification variable (a proxy for the technology chosen by the railways) and with the trend, unambiguously indicate on the one hand that the electrification of the network is labor saving and on the other hand that the sector experienced productivity growth at a rate of about 1 percent each year. Recall that we will interpret the effect of the trend variable as reflecting a technological progress that also includes an overtime general technical efficiency improvement within the sector.[13]

Finally, under the GLS model, the autonomy variable, which is the only time-invariant variable of the model, behaves as a shift factor of the estimated function, influencing labor use favorably, i.e., negatively, but not in a significatively way.

However, as indicated in section 2, the Within and GLS estimators correspond to two extreme models, characterized by general or zero correlation between latent individual effects and explanatory variables, respectively. In order to choose between these models we test the null hypothesis of zero correlation as proposed by H&T [1981].

We proceed to the estimation of the statistic $\hat{m}$ (equation (6)) using the Within and GLS estimators presented before. On the basis of a χ^2 test (df = 1) and the value of $\hat{m}$ ($\hat{m}$ = 105.7), we reject the null hypothesis of zero correlation. Therefore, in order to obtain unbiased and efficient estimators we use the GLS-IV procedure presented in section 1. Note that this procedure has the particularity that the instrumental variables will be chosen between the explanatory variables present in the model. Consequently, we select three of them—km of lines, mean freight distance, and the trend—as instruments following a search path aiming at minimizing the value of the statistic $\hat{m}$ obtained from GLS-IV and Within estimators comparisons.

The results of this estimation are reported in column (c) of table 2. Given that we retain only three instrumental variables the results are, not surprisingly, very close with those corresponding to the Within model. Only two differences may be outlined. On one hand, the coefficient associated with the size of the network is higher (0.609) and thus the labor requirement function is now characterized by nearly constant economies of scale ($\hat{\beta}_{IV,1} + \hat{\beta}_{IV,2} + \hat{\beta}_{IV,3} = 1.023$). On the other hand, the *autonomy* variable, missing under the Within model, presents a positive coefficient.

Nevertheless, these results are not cautioned by the H&T test. When we compare the GLS-IV estimators versus the Within estimators, the value of $\hat{m}$ is now equal to 6.63 and has a weale probability of 1 percent to be accepted on the basis of a χ^2 test (df = 1). That means that some correlation between the individual effects and the explanatory variables subsist in the GLS-IV results. Given this fact, we are inclined to consider the estimations obtained under the Within model as very probable too.[14]

In the last column of table 2 we report the estimated coefficients corresponding to the maximum likelihood (ML) model developed by Battese and Coelli [1988]. Recall that this model was estimated, like the GLS model, under the hypothesis of absence of correlation between the efficiency indicators and the explanatory variables. The coefficients obtained are, unexpectedly, very closed with those corresponding to the fixed effects model.

On table 3, we report the levels of technical efficiency corresponding to the four alternative models (Within, GLS, GLS-IV, and ML) and the 19 railway companies in the sample. These measures were calculated as indicated in section 1. In all the cases, except for the ML model, we obtain these indicators by normalizing the specific individual effects to the most performant company, as it was first suggested by Greene [1980]. Moreover,

Table 3. Labor technical inefficiency of railway companies (period 1961–1988).[1]

										Net measures of efficiency			
		(a) Within		(b) GLS		(c) GLS-IV		(d) ML		(e) Within		(f) GLS-IV	
Railways	Country	Rank	$\hat{\mu}_{W,i}$	Rank	$\hat{\mu}_{GLS,i}$	Rank	$\hat{\mu}_{IV,i}$	Rank	$\hat{\mu}_{ML,i}$	Rank	$\hat{\mu}_{W,i}$	Rank	$\hat{\mu}_{IV,i}$
BLS	Switzerland	1	1.00	4	1.28	4	1.65	3	1.04	8	1.24	9	1.15
BR	United-Kingdom	15	3.33	11	1.62	10	2.54	15	2.41	15	1.39	15	1.36
CFF	Switzerland	12	2.62	12	1.77	11	2.85	12	2.12	7	1.23	14	1.33
CFL	Luxembourg	8	1.86	17	2.28	17	3.52	10	1.92	17	1.48	17	1.54
CH	Greece	5	1.32	7	1.47	5	1.67	5	1.17	11	1.29	12	1.28
CIE	Ireland	3	1.21	5	1.29	3	1.57	4	1.09	15	1.39	16	1.37
CP	Portugal	11	2.51	14	1.81	12	2.99	11	2.09	10	1.26	6	1.06
DB	Germany	18	4.14	12	1.77	15	3.16	17	2.89	14	1.36	11	1.23
DSB	Denmark	9	2.18	8	1.50	14	3.09	8	1.78	6	1.21	4	1.02
FS	Italy	19	4.26	18	2.53	16	3.19	19	3.12	19	1.77	19	1.71
NS	Netherlands	7	1.84	6	1.30	7	1.96	7	1.50	2	1.06	2	1.01
NSB	Norway	2	1.19	2	1.03	2	1.48	1	1.03	4	1.12	7	1.09
OBB	Austria	16	3.54	16	2.18	19	4.13	16	2.77	18	1.64	18	1.58
RENFE	Spain	10	2.42	10	1.56	9	2.15	9	1.83	12	1.32	13	1.29
SJ	Sweden	4	1.28	1	1.00	1	1.00	1	1.03	13	1.33	5	1.03
SNCB	Belgium	13	2.81	15	1.88	12	2.99	14	2.29	5	1.13	9	1.15
SNCF	France	14	3.15	9	1.56	8	2.09	13	2.22	1	1.00	2	1.01
TCDD	Turkey	17	3.65	19	2.59	18	3.65	18	2.94	9	1.25	7	1.09
VR	Finland	6	1.48	3	1.21	6	1.70	6	1.21	3	1.09	1	1.00
Mean			2.41		1.67		2.49		1.92		1.29		1.23
Std. dev.			1.05		0.47		0.87		0.71		0.19		0.21
Table of correlation[2]	Within		1.0		0.812		0.807		0.982		0.289		0.328
	GLS				1.0		0.918		0.879		0.416		0.539
	GLS-IV						1.0		0.851		0.372		0.396
	ML								1.0		0.319		0.394
	Net Within										1.0		0.835
	Net GLS-IV												1.0

[1]The values are normalized; the value of the most efficient firm equals to 1.
[2]Spearman rank correlation coefficients, except for columns (d).

given the reduced number of firms, the estimated levels of inefficiency are consistent for relative comparative analysis but not reliable as indicators of absolute levels of inefficiency.[15] Finally, note that in the context of the labor requirement function we estimate here, technical efficiency corresponds to level 1.0, otherwise, the degree of labor over-utilization is indicated by values greater than 1.0.

A first lecture of table 3 shows an extremely wide dispersion in the Within estimators of performance ($\hat{\mu}_{W,i}$) that in addition appear also highly correlated with the scale. The most and least efficient firms are the smallest (BLS) and two out of the biggest (DB and FS) of the panel, respectively. These results confirm the fact that individual fixed effects are not reliable as indicators of efficiency. They tend to catch differences between firms, other than efficiency, existing at the cross-section level. That is also the case of measures obtained under the ML procedure ($\hat{\mu}_{ML,i}$), presented in column (d) of table 3.

At the opposite, under the random effects model, the efficiency scores ($\hat{\mu}_{GLS,i}$) seem to be free of scale influence, and the variance seems to be more reliable. Moreover, let's remember that these results were obtained under the hypothesis that $E(\mu_i \mid X_{it}, Z_{it}) = 0$, an hypothesis that was severely rejected by the H&T test.

The table of rank correlation coefficients reproduced at the bottom of table 3 shows the degree of convergence between these measures of technical efficiency. Unexpectedly, we obtain high correlation coefficients between the Within, GLS and ML measures. Nevertheless, one can see some noteworthy changes in efficiency measures, from column (a) to column (b), for large railways such as BR and SNCF on the one hand, and for small companies such as BLS and CIE, on the other hand.

Then, we turn to the efficiency estimators obtained using the GLS-IV procedure presented in section 2.2. These indicators, indicated as $\hat{\mu}_{IV,i}$, are reported on column (c) of table 3. It can be noted that the measures of technical efficiency derived from the instrumental variables procedure present high mean and dispersion levels as under the Within model but appear as highly correlated (0.918) with the GLS ranks.

However, as we explained in section 2.3, the indicators of efficiency corresponding to the Within and GLS-IV models cannot be considered as definitive if they are not purged from the influence of the explanatory variables. In order to do that we estimate the auxiliary functions (5) and (8) corresponding to the Within and GLS-IV models, respectively. The results are presented on table 4.

What can we learn from these results? As argued before, the estimated $\hat{\pi}_k$ and $\hat{\xi}$ coefficients can be interpreted as the effect of explanatory variables on the unpurged technical inefficiency indicators. Then, if we adopt this point of view and consider the two main outputs, we can note that more passengers transportation leads to increased inefficiency and vice-versa for freight transportation but with a hardly significant coefficient. Note that, apart from some cases that we will indicate, the coefficients presented in columns (a) and (b) of table 4 are closed each together and that the coefficients corresponding to the two selected instruments (km of lines and mean freight distance) have no significant influence on efficiency under the Within model.

The density factor (mean trip) appears as an exogeneous factor improving efficiency. In other words, long passengers trips or, equivalently, a low density of the network, facilitates the achievement of the efficiency goal. At the opposite, the load factors (defined as the number of passengers or tons by train) reduces efficiency. As expected, for a given

Table 4. The auxiliary function: effect of exogeneous variables on technical inefficiency[1]

Variables	Parameters	(a) Within	(b) GLS-IV
Train-km:			
passengers	π_1	0.362 (0.138)	0.332 (0.144)
freight	π_2	-0.087 (0.197)	-0.244 (0.141)
Km of lines	π_3	-0.005 (0.181)	2
Mean distance:			
passengers	π_4	-0.477 (0.159)	-0.708 (0.142)
freight	π_5	-0.206 (0.180)	2
Load factor:			
passengers	π_6	1.029 (0.237)	0.760 (0.181)
freight	π_7	0.467 (0.223)	0.548 (0.225)
Electrification	π_8	-0.043 (0.025)	-0.037 (0.026)
Autonomy	ξ	-0.265 (0.228)	-0.524 (0.230)
Intercept		-5.53 (1.85)	-1.94 (1.94)
R^2		0.904	0.810
n		19	19

[1]Standard errors are presented in brackets.
[2]Instrumental variable.

production—evaluated by the number of train-km and the length of the network—higher demand implies more input requirements as it was confirmed by the estimation of the labor requirement function (see table 2). Moreover, it appears that this phenomenon is also partially caught by the efficiency indicator and this fact justifies the computation of an indicator free of this influence.

The electrification rate, that we interpreted as an indicator of technology, here again appears as an element in favor of efficiency. Finally, the autonomy variable has, as expected, a negative impact on technical inefficiency (less significant under the Within model). To some extent, this confirms the existence of a positive correlation between the autonomy enjoyed by a firm and its performance.

Finally, in columns (e) and (f) of table 3, we present the net measures of inefficiency estimated on the basis of the residuals ($\hat{\omega}_i$) of the auxiliary functions. Some notable cases aside—CP, DSB, SJ, and TCDD—most of the companies present similar ranks and levels of inefficiency under the two models. Otherwise, as expected, these indicators show a lower dispersion than those obtained before and dramatic changes in evaluation and reclassification of railway performances that confirms the need and rectitude of net measures of efficiency to take into account the environment in which these firms operate.

5. Conclusions

In this article we have presented a method in order to evaluate the technical efficiency of regulated firms such as the European railroads companies. We have stressed and illustrated the fact that, dealing with panel data, the correlation between efficiency and explanatory variables must be taken into account and alternative net measures of efficiency are needed. We believe that research in the field of firms' performance and frontier analysis should be more oriented in this way.

Furthermore, the factor requirements function used in our analysis appears as a simple and convenient way of modelling the productive activity of firms such as the railways, that are highly regulated and do not display strong substitutability possibilities between inputs.

Finally, we observed a negative correlation between institutional managerial autonomy and technical inefficiency. Of course this result requires additional confirmation but it shows at least that when this factor, and other variables affecting the performance, are taken into account the spectrum of inefficiency across firms narrows and becomes more reliable.

Acknowledgments

We are grateful to P. Barla, G.E. Battese, C.A.K. Lovell, G. N'Gbo, P. Pestieau, B. Sak, B. Thiry, and J.P. Urbain for helpful discussions. D.H. Good, P. Schmidt, R. Sickles and the participants at the Third Conference on Panel Data, ENSAE, Paris, June 11–12, 1990 provided constructive comments on an earlier draft.

Appendix. Variables definition and sources

Variable	Description
Labor	Annual mean railway staff (total number of workers assigned to the rail operation)
Mean distance:	
passengers	Average length of passenger journey
freight	Average length of haul of one ton of freight
Train-km:	
passengers	Train kilometers by passenger trains
freight	Train kilometers by freight trains
Load factor:	
passengers	Number of passengers per train
freight	Number of freight tons per train
Km of lines	Length of rail lines operated at the end of year
Electrification	Percentage of electrified lines
Trend	Trend: 1, ...,28 (= 1 in 1961; ...; = 28 in 1988)
Autonomy	Autonomy enjoyed by the railway management with respect to public authorities, index of regulatory and institutional environment

All the data (except *autonomy* are from the International Railways Statistics yearbook (UIC [1961–1988]) published form 1961 to 1988 by the International Railway Union (UIC). Our sample of observations is of cross-section-time-series nature: 19 European railroads over the 1961–1988 period. These railroad companies were selected on two grounds: availability of data and comparability. When gathering data from each individual company, the UIC tries to insure the highest homogeneity and comparability in the definition and the measurement of both inputs and outputs. The variable *autonomy* has been constructed from a survey, as indicated in the text (section 2).

Notes

1. The introduction of environment factors affecting efficiency and the estimation of net efficiency measures were previously analyzed by Perelman and Pestieau [1988] and by Deprins and Simar [1988], in the context of deterministic production frontier analysis.
2. This model was first introduced in frontier analysis by Schmidt and Sickles [1984]. Note that the GLS-IV estimators must be checked against the Within estimators by the H&T test in order to verify the choice of the instrumental variables (Hausman and Taylor [1981] pp. 1388–89).
3. In order to simplify the presentation, the time-varying regressor r, that by definition is an exogeneous variable, is included here in vector X1.
4. Note that in this case, the parameters on the auxiliary function (5) can be also obtained by $\hat{\pi}_W = \hat{\beta}_B - \hat{\beta}_W$ and $\hat{\xi}_W \equiv \hat{\gamma}_B$, where the suffix *B* indicates the *Between* estimators obtained by performing OLS on equation (2) with all the variables expressed in individual means (Mundlak [1978]).
5. Note that we assume here a half-normal distribution for α_i; this is a particular case of the more general model suggested by Battese and Coelli [1988] that considers also normal distributions truncated at points different from the mean. The program we use has been developed by T. Coelli who kindly transmitted it to us (see Coelli [1989]).
6. For an application of this type of function, also called *inverse production function* in the case of single input-multiple output technology, see for instance Bjurek et al. [1990].
7. Perelman and Pestieau [1987] estimated a production frontier for the European railways using capital and labor as the only inputs. They found little evidence of substitutability between capital and labor.
8. Labor and energy costs.
9. Details about the definition and the source of the variables are given in the Appendix.
10. See, for instance, Wang Chiang and Friedlander [1984].
11. One could, of course, argue about this point. From our survey among the railways, it appears that this institutional environment did vary frequently over the analyzed period for companies such as BR, CFF, and DSB. Nevertheless, for a vast majority of the railways, this environment was about the same in the early sixties as in the late eighties.
12. We estimate a labor requirement function under the hypothesis of strict complementarity of inputs. Therefore, the term *economies of scale* has the usual meaning.
13. Alternative treatments with time-varying individual efficiency effects has been proposed by Kumbhakar [1988], Cornwell et al. [1990], and Battese and Coelli [1991].
14. We perform also alternative GLS-IV models as suggested by Amemiya and MaCurdy [1986] and Breusch et al. [1989]. The results obtained confirm the case of severe correlation between technical efficiency and all the explanatory variables in the model.
15. Note that Schmidt and Sickles [1984] stated the conditions for the consistency of estimators (other than the efficiency indicator). They are met by our sample that is composed by nearly 30 years.

References

Aigner, D.J., C.A.K. Lovell, and P. Schmidt. (1977). "Formulation and estimation of stochastic frontier production function models." *Journal of Econometrics* 6, pp. 21–37.

Amemiya, T. and T.E. MaCurdy. (1986). "Instrumental-variable estimation of an error-components model." *Econometrica* 54, pp. 869–880.

Battese, G.E. and T.J. Coelli (1988). "Prediction of firm-level technical efficiencies with a generalized frontier production function and panel data." *Journal of Econometrics* 38, pp. 387–399.

Battese, G.E. and T.J. Coelli. (1991). "Frontier production functions, technical efficiency and panel data: with application to paddy farmers in India." Department of Econometrics, University of New England, Australia.

Bjurek, H., L. Hjalmarsson, and F.R. Forsund. (1990). "Parametric and nonparametric estimation of efficiency in service production: a comparison." Frontier analysis, parametric and non parametric approaches, edited by A.Y. Lewin and C.A. Knox Lovell in *Journal of Econometrics* Annals 1990-4, 46-1/2, pp. 213–228.

Breusch, T.S., G.E. Mizon, and P. Schmidt. (1989). "Efficient estimation using panel data." *Econometrica* 57, pp. 695–700.

Caves, D.W., L.R. Christensen, and J.A. Swanson. (1981). "Productivity growth, scale economies and capacity utilization in U.S. railroads, 1955–1974." *The American Economic Review* 71, pp. 994–1002.

Coelli, T.J. (1989). "Estimation of frontier production functions: A guide to the computer program "Frontier"." Working Papers in Econometrics and Applied Statistics, University of New England, Australia, 34..

Cornwell, C.P., P. Schmidt, and R.C. Sickles. (1990). "Production Frontiers with Cross-Sectional and Time-Series Variation in Efficiency Levels." Frontier analysis, parametric and non parametric approaches, edited by A.Y. Lewin and C.A. Knox Lovell in *Journal of Econometrics* Annals 1990-4, 46-1/2, pp. 185–200.

Deprins, D. and L. Simar. (1988). "Mesure d'efficacité des résaux de chemins de fer." In CORE (ed.) *Gestion de l'économie* et de l'entreprise: l'approche quantitative, Bruxelles, DeBoek-Wesmael, pp. 321–344.

Diewert, W.E. (1973). "Functional forms for profit and transformation functions." *Journal of Economic Theory* 6, pp. 284–316.

Diewert, W.E. (1974). "Functional forms for revenue and factor requirements functions." *International Economic Review* 15-1, pp. 119–130.

Gathon, H.J. (1991). "La performance des chemins de fer européens: Gestion et autonomie." Ph.D. thesis, Department of Economics, University of Liège.

Greene, W.H. (1980). "Maximum likelihood estimation of econometric frontier functions." *Journal of Econometrics* 13, pp. 27–56.

Hausman, J.A. and W.E. Taylor. (1981). "Panel data and unobservable individual effects." *Econometrica* 49, pp. 1377–1398.

Jondrow, J., C.A.K. Lovell, I.S. Materov, and P. Schmidt. (1982). "On the estimation of technical inefficiency in the stochastic frontier production function model." *Journal of Econometrics* 19, pp. 233–238.

Klein, L.R. (1953). *A textbook of econometrics.* New York: Row Peterson.

Kumbhakar, S.C. (1988). "Production frontiers, panel data and time-varying technical inefficiency." Frontier analysis, parametric and non parametric approaches, edited by A.Y. Lewin and C.A. Knox Lovell in *Journal of Econometrics* Annals 1990-4, 46-1/2, pp. 201–212.

Meeusen, W. and J. van den Broeck (1977). "Efficiency estimation from Cobb-Douglas production functions with composed error." *International Economic Review* 18, pp. 435–44.

Mundlak, Y. (1961). "Empirical production function free of management bias." *Journal of Farm Economics* 43, pp. 44–56.

Mundlak, Y. (1978). "On the pooling of time-series and cross-section data." *Econometrica* 49, pp. 69–86.

Nash, C. (1985). "European railways comparisons—What can we learn?" In K.J. Bulton and D.E. Pitfield (eds.) *International Railway Economics.* London: Gower House.

Nishimizu, M. and J.M. Page. (1982). "Total factor productivity growth, technological progress, and technical efficiency change: dimensions of productivity change in Yugoslavia, 1967–1978." *Economic Journal* 92, pp. 920–936.

Perelman, S. and P. Pestieau. (1988). "Technical performance in public enterprises, a comparative study of railways and postal services." *European Economic Review* 32, pp. 432–441.

Schmidt, P. and R.C. Sickles. (1984). "Production frontiers and panel data." *Journal of Business and Economics Statistics* 2, pp. 367–374.

UIC (1961–1988). *International Railway Statistics.* Statistics of individual railways, Paris.

Wallace, T.D. and A. Hussein. (1969). "The use of error components models in combining cross-section with time-series data." *Econometrica* 37, pp. 55–72.

Wang Chiang, S.J. and A.F. Friedlander. (1984). "Output aggregation, network effects, and the measurement of trucking technology." *Review of Economics and Statistics* 20, pp. 267–276.

The Journal of Productivity Analysis, 3, 153–169 (1992)

Frontier Production Functions, Technical Efficiency and Panel Data: With Application to Paddy Farmers in India*

G.E. BATTESE AND T.J. COELLI
Department of Econometrics, University of New England, Armidale, NSW 2351, Australia

Abstract

Frontier production functions are important for the prediction of technical efficiencies of individual firms in an industry. A stochastic frontier production function model for panel data is presented, for which the firm effects are an exponential function of time. The best predictor for the technical efficiency of an individual firm at a particular time period is presented for this time-varying model. An empirical example is presented using agricultural data for paddy farmers in a village in India.

1. Introduction

The stochastic frontier production function, which was independently proposed by Aigner, Lovell, and Schmidt [1977] and Meeusen and van den Broeck [1977], has been a significant contribution to the econometric modeling of production and the estimation of technical efficiency of firms. The stochastic frontier involved two random components, one associated with the presence of technical inefficiency and the other being a traditional random error. Prior to the introduction of this model, Aigner and Chu [1968], Timmer [1971], Afriat [1972], Richmond [1974], and Schmidt [1976] considered the estimation of deterministic frontier models whose values were defined to be greater than or equal to observed values of production for different levels of inputs in the production process.

Applications of frontier functions have involved both cross-sectional and panel data. These studies have made a number of distributional assumptions for the random variables involved and have considered various estimators for the parameters of these models. Survey papers on frontier functions have been presented by Førsund, Lovell, and Schmidt [1980], Schmidt [1986], Bauer [1990] and Battese [1992], the latter article giving particular attention to applications in agricultural economics. Beck [1991] and Ley [1990] have compiled extensive bibliographies on empirical applications of frontier functions and efficiency analysis.

The concept of the technical efficiency of firms has been pivotal for the development and application of econometric models of frontier functions. Although technical efficiency may be defined in different ways (see, e.g., Färe, Grosskopf, and Lovell [1985]), we consider

*This article is a revision of the Invited Paper presented by the senior author in the "Productivity and Efficiency Analysis" sessions at the ORSA/TIMS 30th Joint National Meeting, Philadelphia, Pennsylvania, 29–31 October 1990. We have appreciated comments from Martin Beck, Phil Dawson, Knox Lovell and three anonymous referees. We gratefully acknowledge the International Crops Research Institute for the Semi-Arid Tropics (ICRISAT) for making available to us the data obtained from the Village Level Studies in India.

the definition of the technical efficiency of a given firm (at a given time period) as the ratio of its mean production (conditional on its levels of factor inputs and firm effects) to the corresponding mean production if the firm utilized its levels of inputs most efficiently, (see Battese and Coelli [1988]). We do not consider allocative efficiency of firms in this article. Allocative and economic efficiencies have been investigated in a number of papers, including Schmidt and Lovell [1979, 1980], Kalirajan [1985], Kumbhakar [1988], Kumbhakar, Biswas, and Bailey [1989] and Bailey, et al. [1989]. We define a stochastic frontier production function model for panel data, in which technical efficiencies of firms may vary over time.

2. Time-varying model for unbalanced panel data

We consider a stochastic frontier production function with a simple exponential specification of time-varying firm effects which incorporates unbalanced panel data associated with observations on a sample of N firms over T time periods. The model is defined by

$$Y_{it} = f(x_{it}; \beta)\exp(V_{it} - U_{it}) \tag{1}$$

and

$$U_{it} = \eta_{it} U_i = \{\exp[-\eta(t - T)]\}U_i, \qquad t \in \mathcal{J}(i);\ i = 1, 2, \ldots, N; \tag{2}$$

where Y_{it} represents the production for the ith firm at the tth period of observation;
$f(x_{it}; \beta)$ is a suitable function of a vector, x_{it}, of factor inputs (and firm-specific variables), associated with the production of the ith firm in the tth period of observation, and a vector, β, of unknown parameters;
the V_{it}'s are assumed to be independent and identically distributed $N(0, \sigma_V^2)$ random errors;
the U_i's are assumed to be independent and identically distributed non-negative truncations of the $N(\mu, \sigma^2)$ distribution;
η is an unknown scalar parameter;
and $\mathcal{J}(i)$ represents the set of T_i time periods among the T periods involved for which observations for the ith firm are obtained.[1]

This model is such that the non-negative firm effects, U_{it}, decrease, remain constant or increase as t increases, if $\eta > 0$, $\eta = 0$ or $\eta < 0$, respectively. The case in which η is positive is likely to be appropriate when firms tend to improve their level of technical efficiency over time. Further, if the Tth time period is observed for the ith firm then $U_{iT} = U_i$, $i = 1, 2, \ldots, N$. Thus the parameters, μ and σ^2, define the statistical properties of the firm effects associated with the last period for which observations are obtained. The model assumed for the firm effects, U_i, was originally proposed by Stevenson [1980] and is a generalization of the half-normal distribution which has been frequently applied in empirical studies.

The exponential specification of the behavior of the firm effects over time (equation (2)) is a rigid parameterization in that technical efficiency must either increase at a decreasing rate ($\eta > 0$), decrease at an increasing rate ($\eta < 0$) or remain constant ($\eta = 0$). In order to permmit greater flexibility in the nature of technical efficiency, a two-parameter specification would be required. An alternative two-parameter specification, which is being investigated, is defined by

$$\eta_{it} = 1 + \eta_1(t - T) + \eta_2(t - T)^2,$$

where η_1 and η_2 are unknown parameters. This model permits firm effects to be convex or concave, but the time-invariant model is the special case in which $\eta_1 = \eta_2 = 0$.

Alternative time-varying models for firm effects have been proposed by Cornwell, Schmidt, and Sickles [1990] and Kumbhakar [1990]. Cornwell, Schmidt, and Sickles [1990] assumed that the firm effects were a quadratic function of time, in which the coefficients varied over firms according to the specifications of a multivariate distribution. Kumbhakar [1990] assumed that the non-negative firm effects, U_{it}, were the product of deterministic function of time, $\gamma(t)$, and non-negative time-invariant firm effects, U_i. The time function, $\gamma(t)$, was assumed to be defined by,

$$\gamma(t) = [1 + \exp(bt + ct^2)]^{-1}, \qquad t = 1, 2, \ldots, T.$$

This model has values for $\gamma(t)$ between zero and one and could be monotone decreasing (or increasing) or convex (or concave) depending on the values of the parameters, b and c. Kumbhakar [1990] noted that, if $b + ct$ was negative (or positive), the simpler function, $\gamma(t) = (1 + e^{bt})^{-1}$, may be appropriate.[2] The more general model of Kumbhakar [1990] would be considerably more difficult to estimate than that of the simpler exponential model of equation (2).

Given the model (1)–(2), it can be shown [see the Appendix] that the minimum-mean-squared-error predictor of the technical efficiency of the *i*th firm at the *t*th time period, $TE_{it} = \exp(-U_{it})$ is

$$E[\exp(-U_{it})|E_i] = \left\{ \frac{1 - \Phi[\eta_{it}\sigma_i^* - (\mu_i^*/\sigma_i^*)]}{1 - \Phi(-\mu_i^*/\sigma_i^*)} \right\} \exp\left[-\eta_{it}\mu_i^* + \frac{1}{2}\eta_{it}^2\sigma_i^{*2} \right] \tag{3}$$

where E_i represents the $(T_i \times 1)$ vector of E_{it}'s associated with the time periods observed for the *i*th firm, where $E_{it} \equiv V_{it} - U_{it}$;

$$\mu_i^* = \frac{\mu\sigma_V^2 - \eta_i'E_i\sigma^2}{\sigma_V^2 + \eta_i'\eta_i\sigma^2} \tag{4}$$

$$\sigma_i^{*2} = \frac{\sigma_V^2\sigma^2}{\sigma_V^2 + \eta_i'\eta_i\sigma^2} \tag{5}$$

where η_i represents the $(T_i \times 1)$ vector of η_{it}'s associated with the time periods observed for the *i*th firm; and

$\Phi(\cdot)$ represents the distribution function for the standard normal random variable.

If the stochastic frontier production function (1) is of Cobb–Douglas or transcendental logarithmic type, then E_{it} is a linear function of the vector, β.

The result of equation (3) yields the special cases given in the literature. Although Jondrow, Lovell, Materov, and Schmidt [1982] only derived $E[U_i|V_i - U_i]$, the more appropriate result for cross-sectional data, $E[\exp(-U_i)|V_i - U_i]$, is obtained from equations (3)–(5) by substituting $\eta_{it} = 1 = \eta_i$ and $\mu = 0$. The special cases given in Battese and Coelli [1988] and Battese, Coelli, and Colby [1989] are obtained by substituting $\eta_i'\eta_i = T$ and $\eta_i'\eta_i = T_i$, respectively, where $\eta_{it} = 1$ (i.e., $\eta = 0$) in both cases.

Kumbhakar [1990] derived the conditional expectation of U_i, given the value of the random variables, $E_{it} \equiv V_{it} - \gamma(t)U_i$, $t = 1, 2, \ldots, T$, under the assumptions that the U_i's had half-normal distribution. Kumbhakar's [1990] model also accounted for the presence of allocative inefficiency, but gave no empirical application.

The mean technical efficiency of firms at the tth time period,

$$TE_t \equiv E[\exp(-\eta_t U_i)], \qquad \text{where } \eta_t = \exp[-\eta(t - T)],$$

obtained by straightforward integration with the density function of U_i, is

$$TE_t = \left\{\frac{1 - \Phi[\eta_t\sigma - (\mu/\sigma)]}{[1 - \Phi(-\mu/\sigma)]}\right\}\exp\left[-\eta_t\mu + \frac{1}{2}\eta_t^2\sigma^2\right]. \tag{6}$$

If the firm effects are time invariant, then the mean technical efficiency of firms in the industry is obtained from equation (6) by substitution of $\eta_t = 1$. This gives the result presented in equation (8) of Battese and Coelli [1988].

Operational predictors for equations (3) and (6) may be obtained by substituting the relevant parameters by their maximum-likelihood estimators. The maximum-likelihood estimates for the parameters of the model and the predictors for the technical efficiencies of firms can be approximated by the use of the computer program, FRONTIER, which was written by Tim Coelli.[3] The likelihood function for the sample observations, given the parameterization of the model (1)–(2) used in FRONTIER, is presented in the Appendix.

3. Empirical example

Battese, Coelli, and Colby [1989] used a set of panel data on 38 farmers from an Indian village to estimate the parameters of a stochastic frontier production function for which the technical efficiencies of individual farmers were assumed to be time invariant. We consider a subset of these data for those farmers, who had access to irrigation and grew paddy, to estimate a stochastic frontier production frontier with time-varying firm effects, as specified by equations (1)–(2) in Section 2. The data were collected by the International Crops Research Institute for the Semi-Arid Tropics (ICRISAT) from farmers in the village of Aurepalle. We consider the data for fifteen farmers who engaged in growing paddy for between four and ten years during the period, 1975–1976 through 1984–1985. Nine of the fifteen farmers were observed for all the ten years involved. A total of 129 observations were used, so 21 observations were missing from the panel.

The stochastic frontier production function for the panel data on the paddy farmers in Aurepalle which we estimate is defined by

$$\log(Y_{it}) = \beta_0 + \beta_1 \log(\text{Land}_{it}) + \beta_2(\text{IL}_{it}/\text{Land}_{it}) + \beta_3 \log(\text{Labor}_{it}) + \beta_4 \log(\text{Bullock}_{it}) + \beta_5 \log(\text{Costs}_{it}) + V_{it} - U_{it}, \quad (7)$$

where the subscripts i and t refer to the ith farmer and the tth observation, respectively;

Y represents the total value of output (in Rupees) from paddy and any other crops which might be grown;

Land represents the total area (in hectares) of irrigated and unirrigated land, denoted by IL_{it} and UL_{it}, respectively;

Labor represents the total number of hours of human labor (in male equivalent units)[4] for family members and hired laborers;

Bullock represents the total number of hours of bullock labor for owned or hired bullocks (in pairs);

Costs represents the total value of input costs involved (fertilizer, manure, pesticides, machinery, etc.); and

V_{it} and U_{it} are the random variables whose distributional properties are defined in Section 2.

A summary of the data on the different variables in the frontier production function is given in table 1. It is noted that about 30 percent of the total land operated by the paddy farmers in Aurepalle was irrigated. Thus the farmers involved were generally also engaged in dryland farming. The minimum value of irrigated land was zero because not all the farmers involved grew paddy (irrigated rice) in all the years involved.

The production function, defined by equation (7), is related to the function which was estimated in Battese, Coelli, and Colby [1989, p. 333], but family and hired labor are aggregated (i.e., added).[5] The justification for the functional form considered in Battese, Coelli, and Colby [1989] is based on the work of Bardhan [1973] and Deolalikar and Vijverberg

Table 1. Summary statistics for variables in the stochastic frontier production function for paddy farmers in Aurepalle.[1]

Variable	Sample Mean	Sample Standard Deviation	Minimum Value	Maximum Value
Value of Output (Rupees)	6939	4802	36	18094
Total Land (hectares)	6.70	4.24	0.30	20.97
Irrigated Land (hectares)	1.99	1.47	0.00	7.09
Human Labor (hours)	4126	2947	92	6205
Bullock Labor (hours)	900.4	678.2	56	4316
Input Costs (Rupees)	1273	1131	0.7	6205

[1]The data, consisting of 129 observations for each variable, collected from 15 paddy farmers in Aurepalle over the ten-year period, 1975–1976 to 1984–1985, were collected by the International Crops Research Institute for the Semi-Arid Tropics (ICRISAT) as part of its Village Level Studies (see Binswanger and Jodha [1978]).

[1983] with Indian data on hired and family labor and irrigated and unirrigated land. The production function of equation (7) is a linearized version of that which was directly estimated in Battese, Coelli, and Colby [1989][6] (see the model in Defourny, Lovell, and N'gbo [1990]).

The original values of output and input costs used in Batese, Coelli, and Colby [1989] are deflated by a price index for the analyses in this article. The price index used was constructed using data, supplied by ICRISAT, on prices and quantities of crops grown in Aurepalle.

The stochastic frontier model, defined by equation (7), contains six β-parameters and the four additional parameters associated with the distributions of the V_{it}- and U_{it}-random variables. Maximum-likelihood estimates for these parameters were obtained by using the computer program, FRONTIER. The frontier function (7) is estimated for five basic models:

Model 1.0 involves all parameters being estimated;
Model 1.1 assumes that $\mu = 0$;
Model 1.2 assumes that $\eta = 0$;
Model 1.3 assumes that $\mu = \eta = 0$; and
Model 1.4 assumes that $\gamma = \mu = \eta = 0$.

Model 1.0 is the stochastic frontier production function (7) in which the farm effects, U_{it}, have the time-varying structure defined in Section 2 (i.e., η is an unknown parameter and the U_i's of equation (2) are non-negative truncations of the $N(\mu, \sigma^2)$ distribution). Model 1.1 is the special case of Model 1.0 in which the U_i's have half-normal distribution (i.e., μ is assumed to be zero). Model 1.2 is the time-invariant model considered by Battese, Coelli, and Colby [1989]. Model 1.3 is the time-invariant model in which the farm effects, U_i, have half-normal distribution. Finally, Model 1.4 is the traditional average response function in which farms are assumed to be fully technically efficient (i.e., the farm effects, U_{it}, are absent from the model).

Empirical results for these five models are presented in table 2. Tests of hypotheses involving the parameters of the distributions of the U_{it}-random variables (farm effects) are obtained by using the generalized likelihood-ratio statistic. Several hypotheses are considered for different distributional assumptions and the relevant statistics are presented in table 3.

Given the specifications of the stochastic frontier with time-varying farm effects (Model 1.0), it is evident that the traditional average production function is not an adequate representation of the data (i.e., the null hypothesis, H_0: $\gamma = \mu = \eta = 0$, is rejected). Further, the hypotheses that time-invariant models for farm effects apply are also rejected (i.e., both H_0: $\mu = \eta = 0$ and H_0: $\eta = 0$ would be rejected). However, the hypothesis that the half-normal distribution is an adequate representation for the distribution of the farm effects is not rejected using these data. Given that the half-normal distribution is assumed appropriate to define the distribution of the farm effects, the hypothesis that the yearly farm effects are time invariant is also rejected by the data.

On the basis of these results it is evident that the hypothesis of time-invariant technical efficiencies of paddy farmers in Aurepalle would be rejected. Given the specifications of Model 1.1 (involving the half-normal distribution), the technical efficiencies of the individual paddy farmers are calculated using the predictor, defined by equation (3). The values obtained, together with the estimated mean technical efficiencies (obtained using equation (6)) in the ten years involved, are presented in table 4.

Table 2. Maximum-likelihood estimates for parameters of stochastic frontier production functions for Aurepalle paddy farmers.[1]

		MLE Estimates for Models				
Variable	Parameter	Model 1.0	Model 1.1	Model 1.2	Model 1.3	Model 1.4
Constant	β_0	3.74 (0.96)	3.86 (0.94)	3.90 (0.73)	3.87 (0.68)	3.71 (0.66)
log(Land)	β_1	0.61 (0.23)	0.63 (0.20)	0.63 (0.15)	0.63 (0.15)	0.62 (0.15)
IL/Land	β_2	0.81 (0.43)	1.05 (0.33)	0.90 (0.30)	0.89 (0.29)	0.80 (0.27)
log(Labor)	β_3	0.76 (0.21)	0.74 (0.18)	0.74 (0.15)	0.74 (0.14)	0.74 (0.14)
log(Bullocks)	β_4	−0.45 (0.16)	−0.43 (0.11)	−0.44 (0.11)	−0.44 (0.11)	−0.43 (0.12)
log(Costs)	β_5	0.079 (0.048)	0.058 (0.038)	0.052 (0.042)	0.052 (0.042)	0.053 (0.043)
	$\sigma_S^2 \equiv \sigma_V^2 + \sigma^2$	0.129 (0.048)	0.104 (0.010)	0.136 (0.040)	0.142 (0.028)	0.135 (0.019)
	$\gamma \equiv \sigma^2/\sigma_S^2$	0.22 (0.21)	0.056 (0.012)	0.11 (0.26)	0.14 (0.17)	0
	μ	−0.77 (1.79)	0	−0.07 (0.43)	0	0
	η	0.27 (0.97)	0.138 (0.047)	0	0	0
	Log (likelihood)	−40.788	−40.798	−50.408	−50.416	−50.806

[1]The estimated standard errors for the parameter estimators are presented below the corresponding estimates. These values are generated by the computer program, FRONTIER.

Table 3. Tests of hypotheses for parameters of the distribution of the farm effects, U_{it}.

Assumptions	Null Hypothesis H_0	χ^2-statistic	$\chi^2_{0.95}$-value	Decision
Model 1.0	$\gamma = \mu = \eta = 0$	20.04	7.81	Reject H_0
Model 1.0	$\mu = \eta = 0$	19.26	5.99	Reject H_0
Model 1.0	$\mu = 0$	0.02	3.84	Accept H_0
Model 1.0	$\eta = 0$	19.24	3.84	Reject H_0
Model 1.1 ($\mu = 0$)	$\gamma = \eta = 0$	20.02	5.99	Reject H_0
Model 1.1 ($\mu = 0$)	$\eta = 0$	19.24	3.84	Reject H_0

Table 4. Predicted technical efficiencies of paddy farmers in Aurepalle for the years 1975–1976 through 1984–1985.[1]

Farmer Number	75–76	76–77	77–78	78–79	79–80	80–81	81–82	82–83	83–84	84–85
1	.861	.878	.892	.905	.916	.927	.936	.944	.951	.957
2	.841	.859	.876	.891	.904	.915	.926	.935	.943	.950
3	.569	.611	.651	.687	.721	.752	—	—	—	—
4	.549	.593	.633	.671	.706	.738	.767	.794	.818	.839
5	.711	.743	.771	.797	.820	.841	.860	.876	.891	.904
6	.798	.821	.842	.860	.877	.891	.905	.916	.926	.935
7	.576	.618	.657	.693	.726	.756	.784	.808	.831	—
8	.776	.801	.823	—	.862	.878	.893	.906	.917	.927
9	.575	.617	.656	.692	.725	.756	.783	.808	.830	.850
10	.862	.878	.892	.905	.917	.927	.936	.944	.951	.957
11	.778	.803	.825	.846	.864	.880	.894	.907	.918	.928
12	.712	.743	.771	.797	.820	.841	.860	.876	.891	.904
13	.601	.678	.712	.743	.772	.798	.821	—	—	—
14	—	.789	.813	.834	.853	—	—	—	—	—
15	—	—	—	—	—	—	.908	.919	.929	.938
Mean	.821	.841	.859	.875	.890	.903	.915	.925	.934	.942

[1]In years when particular farmers were not observed, no values of technical efficiencies are calculated.

The technical efficiencies range between 0.549 and 0.862 in 1975–1976 and, between 0.839 and 0.957 in 1984–1985. Because the estimate for the parameter, η, is positive ($\hat{\eta} = 0.138$) the technical efficiencies increase over time, according to the assumed exponential model, defined by equation (2). These predicted technical efficiencies of the 15 paddy farmers are graphed against year of observation in figure 1. These data indicate that there exist considerable variation in the efficiencies of the paddy farmers, particularly at the beginning of the sample period. Given the assumption that the farm effects change exponentially over time, it is expected that the predicted efficiencies converge over a period of generally increasing levels of technical efficiency.

The above results are, however, based on the stochastic frontier production function (7), which assumes that the parameters are time invariant. In particular, the presence of technical progress is not accounted for in the model. Given that year of observation is included as an additional explanatory variable, then the estimated stochastic frontier production function is

$$\begin{aligned} \log Y = {} & \underset{(1.75)}{2.80} + \underset{(0.37)}{0.50} \log(\text{Land}) + \underset{(0.47)}{0.53} (\text{IL/Land}) + \underset{(0.32)}{0..91} \log(\text{Labor}) \\ & - \underset{(0.098)}{0.489} \log(\text{Bullocks}) + \underset{(0.040)}{0.051} \log(\text{Costs}) + \underset{(0.019)}{0.050} \text{ Year} \end{aligned} \tag{8}$$

where $\underset{(0.084)}{\hat{\sigma}_S^2 = 0.130}$, $\underset{(0.44)}{\hat{\gamma} = 0.21}$, $\underset{(0.98)}{\hat{\mu} = -0.69}$, $\underset{(0.65)}{\hat{\eta} = 0.11}$

and log (likelihood) = − 38.504.

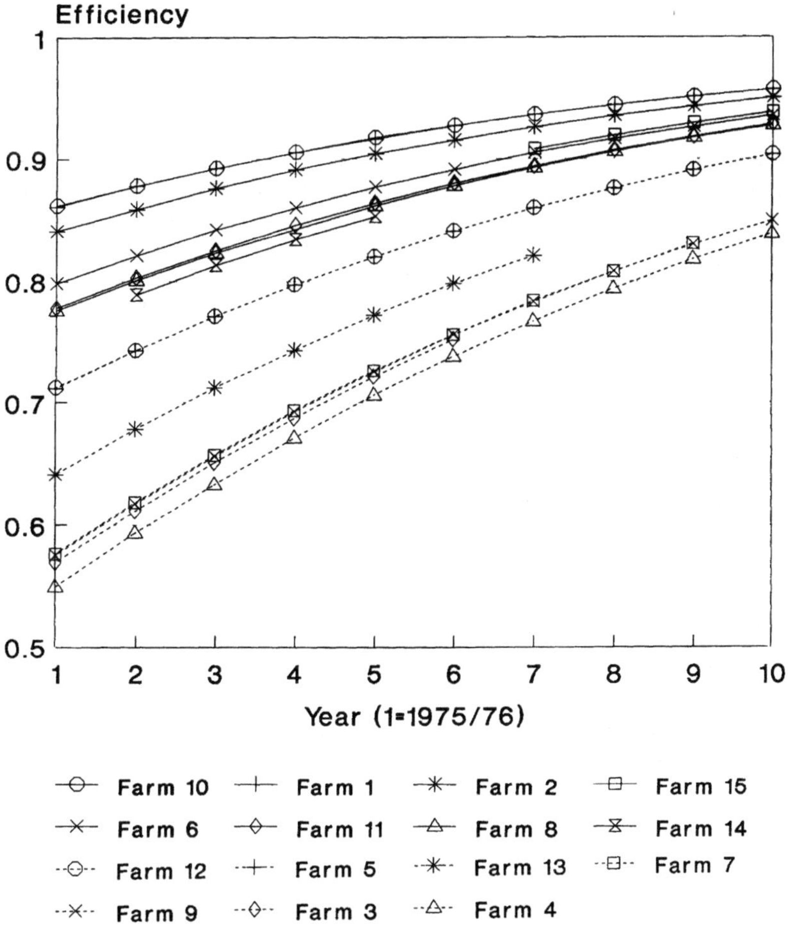

Figure 1. Predicted technical efficiencies.

Generalized likelihood-ratio tests of the hypotheses that the parameters, μ, η and γ, are zero (individually or jointly) yield insignificant results. Thus the inclusion of the year of observation in the model (i.e., Hicksian neutral technological change), leads not only to the conclusion that technical efficiency of the paddy farmers is time invariant, but that the stochastic frontier production function is not significantly different from the traditional average response model. This response function is estimated by

$$\begin{aligned}\log Y = {} & \underset{(0.63)}{2.73} + \underset{(0.13)}{0.51}\log(\text{Land}) + \underset{(0.26)}{0.50}(\text{IL/Land}) + \underset{(0.14)}{0.91}\log(\text{Labor}) \\ & - \underset{(0.11)}{0.48}\log(\text{Bullocks}) + \underset{(0.040)}{0.048}\log(\text{Costs}) + \underset{(0.011)}{0.054}\,\text{Year}\end{aligned} \tag{9}$$

where $\hat{\sigma}_V^2 = 0.113$ and log (likelihood) $= -38.719$.

The estimated response function in equation (9) is such that the returns-to-scale parameter is estimated by 0.990 which is not significantly different from one, because the estimated standard error of the estimator is 0.065. Thus, the hypothesis of constant returns to scale for the paddy farmers would not be rejected using these data.

The coefficient of the ratio of irrigated land to total land operated, IL/Land, is significantly different from zero. Using the estimates for the elasticity of land and the coefficient of the land ratio, one hectare of irrigated land is estimated to be equivalent to about 1.98 hectares of unirrigated land for Aurepalle farmers who grow paddy and other crops.[7] This compares with 3.50 hectares obtained by Battese, Coelli, and Colby [1989] using data on all 38 farmers in Aurepalle. The smaller value obtained using only data on paddy farmers is probably due to the smaller number of unirrigated hectares in this study than in the earlier study involving all farmers in the village.

The estimated elasticity for bullock labor on paddy farms is negative. This result was also observed in Saini [1979] and Battese, Coelli, and Colby [1989]. A plausible argument for this result is that paddy farmers may use bullocks more in years of poor production (associated with low rainfall) for the purpose of weed control, levy bank maintenance, etc., which are difficult to conduct in years of higher rainfall and higher output. Hence, the bullock-labor variable may be acting as an inverse proxy for rainfall.

The coefficient, 0.054, of the variable, year of observation, in the estimated response function, given by equation (9), implies that value of output (in real terms) is estimated to have increased by about 5.4 percent over the ten-year period for the paddy farmers in Aurepalle.

4. Conclusions

The empirical application of the stochastic frontier production function model with time-varying firm effects (1)–(2), in the analysis of data from paddy farmers in an Indian village, revealed that the technical efficiencies of the farmers were not time invariant when year of observation was excluded from the stochastic frontier. However, the inclusion of year of observation in the frontier model led to the finding that the corresponding technical efficiencies were time invariant. In addition, the stochastic frontier was not significantly different from the traditional average response function. This implies that, given the state of technology among paddy farmers in the Indian village involved, technical inefficiency is not an issue of significance provided technical change is accounted for in the empirical analysis. However, in other empirical applications of the time-varying model which we have conducted (see Battese and Tessema [1992]), the inclusion of time-varying parameters in the stochastic frontier has not necessarily resulted in time-invariant technical efficiencies or the conclusion that technical inefficiency does not exist.

The stochastic frontier production function estimated in Section 3 did not involve farmer-specific variables. To the extent that farmer- (and farm-) specific variables influence technical efficiencies, the empirical analysis presented in Section 3 does not appropriately predict technical efficiencies. More detailed modeling of the variables influencing production and the statistical distribution of the random variables involved will lead to improved analysis of production and better policy decisions concerning productive activity. We are confident that further theoretical developments in stochastic frontier modeling and the prediction of technical efficiencies of firms will assist such practical decision making.

Appendix

Consider the frontier production function[8]

$$Y_{it} = x_{it}\beta + E_{it} \tag{A.1}$$

where

$$E_{it} = V_{it} - \eta_{it} U_i \tag{A.2}$$

and

$$\eta_{it} = e^{-\eta(t-T)}, \quad t \in \mathcal{G}(i);\ i = 1, 2, \ldots, N. \tag{A.3}$$

It is assumed that the V_{it}'s are iid $N(0, \sigma_V^2)$ random variables, independent of the U_i's, which are assumed to be non-negative truncations of the $N(\mu, \sigma^2)$ distribution.

The density function for U_i is

$$f_{U_i}(u_i) = \frac{\exp\left[-\frac{1}{2}(u_i - \mu)^2/\sigma^2\right]}{(2\pi)^{1/2}\sigma[1 - \phi(-\mu/\sigma)]}, \quad u_i \geq 0, \tag{A.4}$$

where $\Phi(\cdot)$ represents the distribution function for the standard normal random variable.

It can be shown that the mean and variance of U_i are[9]

$$E(U_i) = \mu + \sigma\{\phi(-\mu/\sigma)/[1 - \Phi(-\mu/\sigma)]\} \tag{A.5}$$

and

$$\mathrm{Var}(U_i) = \sigma^2\left\{1 - \frac{\phi(-\mu/\sigma)}{1 - \Phi(-\mu/\sigma)}\left[\frac{\mu}{\sigma} + \frac{\phi(-\mu/\sigma)}{1 - \Phi(-\mu/\sigma)}\right]\right\}, \tag{A.6}$$

where $\phi(\cdot)$ represents the density function for the standard normal distribution.

From the joint density function for U_i and V_i, where V_i represents the $(T_i \times 1)$ vector of the V_{it}'s associated with the T_i observations for the ith firm, it follows readily that the joint density function for U_i and E_i, where E_i is the $(T_i \times 1)$ vector of the values of $E_{it} \equiv V_{it} - \eta_{it} U_i$, is

$$f_{U_i,E_i}(u_i, e_i) = \frac{\exp - \frac{1}{2} \{[(u_i - \mu)^2/\sigma^2] + [(e_i + \eta_i u_i)'(e_i + \eta_i u_i)/\sigma_V^2]\}}{(2\pi)^{(T_i+1)/2} \sigma \, \sigma_V^{T_i}[1 - \Phi(-\mu/\sigma)]} \tag{A.7}$$

where e_i is a possible value for the random vector, E_i.

The density function for E_i, obtained by integrating $f_{U_i,E_i}(u_i, e_i)$ with respect to the range for U_i, namely $u_i \geq 0$, is

$$f_{E_i}(e_i) = \frac{[1 - \Phi(-\mu_i^*/\sigma_i^*)] \exp - \frac{1}{2} \{(e_i'e_i/\sigma_V^2) + (\mu/\sigma)^2 - (\mu_i^*/\sigma_i^*)^2\}}{(2\pi)^{T_i/2}\sigma_V^{(T_i-1)}[\sigma_V^2 + \eta_i'\eta_i\sigma^2]^{1/2}[1 - \Phi(-\mu/\sigma)]} \tag{A.8}$$

where

$$\mu_i^* \equiv \frac{\mu\sigma_V^2 - \eta_i'e_i\sigma^2}{\sigma_V^2 + \eta_i'\eta_i\sigma^2} \tag{A.9}$$

and

$$\sigma_i^{*2} \equiv \frac{\sigma^2\sigma_V^2}{\sigma_V^2 + \eta_i'\eta_i\sigma^2}. \tag{A.10}$$

From the above results, it follows that the conditional density function of U_i, given that the random vector, E_i, has value, e_i, is

$$f_{U_i|E_i=e_i}(u_i) = \frac{\exp - \frac{1}{2} [(u_i - \mu_i^*)/\sigma_i^*]^2}{(2\pi)^{1/2}\sigma_i^*[1 - \Phi(-\mu_i^*/\sigma_i^*)]}, \quad u_i \geq 0. \tag{A.11}$$

This is the density function of the positive truncation of the $N(\mu_i^*, \sigma_i^{*2})$ distribution. Since the conditional expectation of $\exp(-\eta_{it}U_i)$, given $E_i = e_i$, is defined by

$$E\{\exp(-\eta_{it}U_i|E_i = e_i)\} = \int_0^\infty \exp(-\eta_{it}u_i) f_{U_i|E_i=e_i}(u_i)du_i,$$

the result of equation (3) of the text of this article is obtained by straightforward integral calculus.

If the frontier production function (A.1)–(A.3) is appropriate for production, expressed in the original units of output, then the prediction of the technical efficiency of the ith firm at the time of the tth observation, $TE_{it} = 1 - (\eta_{it} U_i / x_{it}\beta)$, requires the conditional expectation of U_i, given $E_i = e_i$. This can be shown to be

$$E(U_i|E_i = e_i) = \mu_i^* + \sigma_i^* \{\phi(-\mu_i^*/\sigma_i^*)/[1 - \Phi(-\mu_i^*/\sigma_i^*)]\} \tag{A.12}$$

where μ_i^* and σ_i^{*2} are defined by equations (A.9) and (A.10), respectively.

The density function for Y_i, the $(T_i \times 1)$ random vector of Y_{it}'s for the ith firm, is obtained from (A.8) by substituting $(y_i - x_i\beta)$ for e_i, where x_i is the $(T_i \times k)$ matrix of x_{it}'s for the ith firm, where k is the dimension of the vector, β. The logarithm of the likelihood function for the sample observations, $y \equiv (y_1', y_2', \ldots, y_N')'$, is thus

$$\begin{aligned} L^*(\theta^*; y) = & -\frac{1}{2}\left(\sum_{i=1}^{N} T_i\right) \ell n(2\pi) - \frac{1}{2}\sum_{i=1}^{N} (T_i - 1)\ell n(\sigma_V^2) - \frac{1}{2}\sum_{i=1}^{N} \ell n(\sigma_V^2 + \eta_i'\eta_i\sigma^2) \\ & - N\,\ell n[1 - \Phi(-\mu/\sigma)] + \sum_{i=1}^{N} \ell n[1 - \Phi(-\mu_i^*/\sigma_i^*)] \\ & - \frac{1}{2}\sum_{i=1}^{N} [(y_i - x_i\beta)'(y_i - x_i\beta)/\sigma_V^2] - \frac{1}{2} N(\mu/\sigma)^2 + \frac{1}{2}\sum_{i=1}^{N} (\mu_i^*/\sigma_i^*)^2, \end{aligned} \tag{A.13}$$

where $\theta^* \equiv (\beta', \sigma_V^2, \sigma^2, \mu, \eta)'$.

Using the reparameterization of the model, suggested by Battese and Corra [1977], where $\sigma_V^2 + \sigma^2 = \sigma_S^2$ and $\gamma = \sigma^2/\sigma_S^2$, the logarithm of the likelihood function is expressed by

$$\begin{aligned} L^*(\theta; y) = & -\frac{1}{2}\left(\sum_{i=1}^{N} T_i\right) \{\ell n(2\pi) + \ell n(\sigma_S^2)\} - \frac{1}{2}\sum_{i=1}^{N} (T_i - 1)\ell n(1 - \gamma) \\ & - \frac{1}{2}\sum_{i=1}^{N} \ell n[1 + (\eta_i'\eta_i - 1)\gamma] - N\ell n[1 - \Phi(-z)] - \frac{1}{2} Nz^2 \\ & + \sum_{i=1}^{N} \ell n[1 - \Phi(-z_i^*)] + \frac{1}{2}\sum_{i=1}^{N} z_i^{*2} \\ & - \frac{1}{2}\sum_{i=1}^{N} (y_i - x_i\beta)'(y_i - x_i\beta)/(1 - \gamma)\sigma_S^2, \end{aligned} \tag{A.14}$$

where $\theta \equiv (\beta', \sigma_S^2, \gamma, \mu, \eta)'$, $z \equiv \mu/(\gamma\sigma_S^2)^{1/2}$ and

$$z_i^* = \frac{\mu(1 - \gamma) - \gamma\eta_i'(y_i - x_i\beta)}{\{\gamma(1 - \gamma)\sigma_S^2[1 + (\eta_i'\eta_i - 1)\gamma]\}^{1/2}}.$$

The partial derivations of the loglikelihood function (A.14) with respect to the parameters, β, σ_S^2, γ, μ and η, are given by

$$\frac{\partial L^*}{\partial \beta} = \sum_{i=1}^{N} x'_i(y_i - x_i\beta)[(1-\gamma)\sigma_S^2]^{-1}$$

$$+\sum_{i=1}^{N}\left[\frac{\phi(-z_i^*)}{1-\Phi(-z_i^*)} + z_i^*\right]\gamma\, x_i'\eta_i\{\gamma(1-\gamma)\sigma_S^2[1+(\eta_i'\eta_i-1)\gamma]\}^{-1/2}$$

$$\frac{\partial L^*}{\partial \sigma_S^2} = -\frac{1}{2\sigma_S^2}\left\{\sum_{i=1}^{N} T_i - N\left[\frac{\phi(-z)}{1-\Phi(-z)} + z_3\right]z + \sum_{i=1}^{N}\left[\frac{\phi(-z_i^*)}{1-\Phi(-z_i^*)} + z_i^*\right]z_i^*\right.$$

$$\left.-\sum_{i=1}^{N}(y_i - x_i\beta)'(y_i - x_i\beta)[(1-\gamma)\sigma_S^2]^{-1}\right\}$$

$$\frac{\partial L^*}{\partial \gamma} = \frac{(1-\gamma)^{-1}}{2}\sum_{i=1}^{N}(T_i - 1) - \frac{1}{2}\sum_{i=1}^{N}(\eta_i'\eta_i - 1)[1+(\eta_i'\eta_i-1)\gamma]^{-1}$$

$$+\frac{N}{2}\left[\frac{\phi(-z)}{1-\Phi(-z)} + z\right]z\gamma^{-1} + \sum_{i=1}^{N}\left[\frac{\phi(-z_i^*)}{1-\Phi(-z_i^*)} + z_i^*\right]\frac{\partial z_i^*}{\partial \gamma}$$

$$-\frac{1}{2}\sum_{i=1}^{N}(y_i - x_i\beta)'(y_i - x_i\beta)[(1-\gamma)\sigma_S]^{-2}$$

$$\frac{\partial L^*}{\partial \mu} = -\frac{N}{(\gamma\sigma_S^2)^{1/2}}\left[\frac{\phi(-z)}{1-\Phi(-z)} + z\right] + \sum_{i=1}^{N}\left[\frac{\phi(-z_i^*)}{1-\Phi(-z_i^*)} + z_i^*\right]$$

$$\times\frac{(1-\gamma)}{\{\gamma(1-\gamma)\sigma_S^2[1+(\eta_i'\eta_i-1)\gamma\}^{1/2}}$$

$$\frac{\partial L^*}{\partial \eta} = \sum_{i=1}^{N}\left[\frac{\phi(-z_i^*)}{1-\Phi(-z_i^*)} + z_i^*\right]\frac{\partial z_i^*}{\partial \eta} - \frac{\gamma}{2}\sum_{i=1}^{N}\frac{\partial \eta_i'\eta_i}{\partial \eta}[1+(\eta_i'\eta_i-1)\gamma]^{-1}$$

where

$$\frac{\partial z_i^*}{\partial \gamma} = -\frac{[\mu + \eta_i'(y_i - x_i\beta)]}{\sigma_S\{\gamma(1-\gamma)[1+(\eta_i'\eta_i-1)\gamma]\}^{1/2}}$$

$$-\frac{1}{2}\frac{[\mu(1-\gamma) - \gamma\eta_i'(y_i - x_i\beta)][(1-2\gamma)+(\eta_i'\eta_i-1)\gamma(2-3\gamma)]}{\sigma_S\{\gamma(1-\gamma)[1+(\eta_i'\eta_i-1)\gamma]\}^{3/2}}$$

$$\frac{\partial z_i^*}{\partial \eta} = \frac{\gamma \sum_{t \in \mathcal{J}(i)} (t - T)e^{-\eta(t-T)}(y_{it} - x_{it}\beta)}{\{\gamma(1 - \gamma)\sigma_S^2[1 + (\eta_i'\eta_i - 1)\gamma]\}^{1/2}}$$

$$- \frac{[\mu(1 - \gamma) - \gamma\eta_i'(y_i - x_i\beta)]\,\frac{1}{2}\,\gamma^2(1 - \gamma)\sigma_S^2\,\frac{\partial \eta_i'\eta_i}{\partial \eta}}{\{\gamma(1 - \gamma)\sigma_S^2[1 + (\eta_i'\eta_i - 1)\gamma]\}^{3/2}}$$

and

$$\frac{\partial \eta_i'\eta_i}{\partial \eta} = -2 \sum_{t \in \mathcal{J}(i)} (t - T)e^{-2\eta(t-T)} \qquad \text{if } \eta \neq 0.$$

Notes

1. If the *i*th firm is observed in all the T time periods involved, then $\mathcal{J}(i) = \{1, 2, \ldots, T\}$. However, if the *i*th firm was continuously involved in production, but observations were only obtained at discrete intervals, then $\mathcal{J}(i)$ would consist of a subset of the integers, 1, 2, ..., T, representing the periods of observations involved.
2. It is somewhat unusual that the value of $\gamma(t)$ for the period before the first observation, $t = 0$, is 0.5.
3. The original version of FRONTIER (see Coelli [1989]) was written to estimate the time-invariant panel data model presented in Battese and Coelli [1988]. It was amended to account for unbalanced panel data and applied in Battese, Coelli, and Colby [1989]. Recently, FRONTIER was updated to estimate the time-varying model defined by equations (1) and (2), (see Coelli [1991, 1992]). FRONTIER Version 2.0 is written in Fortran 77 for use on IBM compatible PC's. The source code and executable program are available from Tim Coelli on a 5.25 inch disk.
4. Labor hours were converted to male equivalent units according to the rule that female and child hours were considered equivalent to 0.75 and 0.50 male hours, respectively. These ratios were obtained from ICRISAT.
5. The hypothesis that family and hired labor were equally productive was tested and accepted in Battese, Coelli, and Colby [1989]. Hence only total labor hours are considered in this paper.
6. The deterministic component of the stochastic frontier production function estimated in Battese, Coelli, and Colby [1989], considering only the land variable (consisting of a weighted average of unirrigated land and irrigated land), is defined by,

   $$Y = a_0[a_1UL + (1 - a_1)IL]^{\beta_1}.$$

   This model is expressed in terms of Land $\equiv$ UL + IL and IL/Land, as follows

   $$Y = a_0 \times a_1^{\beta_1} (\text{Land})^{\beta_1}[1 + (b_1 - 1)(\text{IL/Land})]^{\beta_1}, \text{ where } b_1 = (1 - a_1)/a_1.$$

   By taking logarithms of both sides and considering only the first term of the infinite series expansions of the function involving the land ratio, IL/Land, we obtain

   $$\log Y \doteq \text{constant} + \beta_1 \log(\text{Land}) + \beta_2 (\text{IL/Land}), \text{ where } \beta_2 = \beta_1(b_1 - 1).$$

7. The calculations involved are: $\hat{\beta}_1 = 0.512$, $\hat{\beta}_2 \equiv \hat{\beta}_1(\hat{b}_1 - 1) = 0.501$ implies $\hat{b}_1 = 1.98$, where b_1 is the value of one hectare of irrigated land in terms of unirrigated land for farmers who grow paddy and other crops.
8. In the frontier model (2), the notation, Y_{it}, represented the actual production at the time of the *t*th observation for the *i*th firm. However, given that (2) involves a Cobb-Douglas or transcendental logarithmic model, then Y_{it} and x_{it} in this Appendix would represent logarithms of output and input values, respectively.

9. We prefer not to use the notation, σ_U^2, for the variance of the normal distribution which is truncated (at zero) to obtain the distribution of the non-negative firm effects, because this variance is *not* the variance of U_i. For the case of the half-normal distribution the variance of U_i is $\sigma^2(\pi - 2)/\pi$. This fact needs to be kept in mind in the interpretation of empirical results for the stochastic frontier model.

References

Afriat, S.N. (1972). "Efficiency Estimation of Production Functions." *International Economic Review* 13, pp. 568–598.

Aigner, D.J. and S.F. Chu. (1968). "On Estimating the Industry Production Function." *American Economic Review* 58, pp. 826–839.

Aigner, D.J., C.A.K. Lovell, and P. Schmidt. (1977). "Formulation and Estimation of Stochastic Frontier Production Function Models." *Journal of Econometrics* 6, pp. 21–37.

Bailey, D.V., B. Biswas, S.C. Kumbhakar, and B.K. Schulthies. (1989). "An Analysis of Technical, Allocative, and Scale Inefficiency: The Case of Ecuadorian Dairy Farms." *Western Journal of Agricultural Economics* 14, pp. 30–37.

Bardhan, P.K. (1973). "Size, Productivity, and Returns to Scale: An Analysis of Farm-Level Data in Indian Agriculture." *Journal of Political Economy* 81, pp. 1370–1386.

Battese, G.E. (1991). "Frontier Production Functions and Technical Efficiency: A Survey of Empirical Applications in Agricultural Economics." *Agricultural Economics* (to appear).

Battese, G.E. and T.J. Coelli. (1988). "Prediction of Firm-Level Technical Efficiencies With a Generalized Frontier Production Function and Panel Data." *Journal of Econometrics* 38, pp. 387–399.

Battese, G.E., T.J. Coelli, and T.C. Colby. (1989). "Estimation of Frontier Production Functions and the Efficiencies of Indian Farms Using Panel Data From ICRISAT's Village Level Studies," *Journal of Quantitative Economics* 5, pp. 327–348.

Battese, G.E. and G.S. Corra. (1977). "Estimation of a Production Frontier Model: With Application to the Pastoral Zone of Eastern Australia." *Australian Journal of Agricultural Economics* 21, pp. 169–179.

Battese, G.E. and G.A. Tessema. (1992). "Estimation of Stochastic Frontier Production Functions with Time-Varying Parameters and Technical Efficiencies Using Panel Data from Indian Villages." Paper presented at the 36th Annual Conference of the Australian Agricultural Economics Society, Canberra, 10–12 February, 1992.

Bauer, P.W. (1990). "Recent Developmens in the Econometric Estimation of Frontiers." *Journal of Econometrics* 46, pp. 39–56.

Beck, M. (1991). "Empirical Applications of Frontier Functions: A Bibliography." mimeo, Joachim-Ringelnatz-Str. 20, W-6200 Wiesbaden, Germany, pp. 9.

Binswanger, H.P. and N.S. Jodha. (1978). *Manual of Instructions for Economic Investigators in ICRISAT's Village Level Studies* Volume II. Village Level Studies Series, Economics Program, International Crops Research Institute for the Semi-Arid Tropics, Patancheru, Andhra Pradesh, India.

Coelli, T.J. (1989). "Estimation of Frontier Production Functions: A Guide to the Computer Program, FRONTIER." *Working Papers in Econometrics and Applied Statistics* no. 34, Department of Econometrics, University of New England, Armidale, p. 31.

Coelli, T.J. (1991). "Maximum-Likelihood Estimation of Stochastic Frontier Production Functions with Time-Varying Technical Efficiency Using the Computer Program, FRONTIER Version 2.0." *Working Papers in Econometrics and Applied Statistics* no. 57, Department of Econometrics, University of New England, Armidale, p. 45.

Coelli, T.J. (1992). "A Computer Program for Frontier Production Function Estimation." *Economics Letters* (to appear).

Cornwell, C., P. Schmidt, and R.C. Sickles. (1990). "Production Frontiers with Cross-Sectional and Time-Series Variation in Efficiency Levels." *Journal of Econometrics* 46, pp. 185–200.

Defourny, J., C.A.K. Lovell, and A.G.M. N'Gbo. (1990). "Variation in Productive Efficiency in French Workers' Cooperatives." *Journal of Productivity Analysis* 3(1/2), pp. 103–117.

Deolalikar, A.B. and W.P.M. Vijverberg. (1983). "The Heterogeneity of Family and Hired Labor in Agricultural Production: A Test Using District-Level Data from India." *Journal of Economic Development* 8(2), pp. 45–69.

Färe, R., S. Grosskopf, and C.A.K. Lovell. (1985). *The Measurement of Efficiency of Production*. Dordrecht: Kluwer-Nijhoff.

Førsund, F.R., C.A.K. Lovell, and P. Schmidt. (1980). "A Survey of Frontier Production Functions and of Their Relationship to Efficiency Measurement." *Journal of Econometrics* 13, pp. 5–25.

Jondrow, J., C.A.K. Lovell, I.S. Materov, and P. Schmidt. (1982). "On the Estimation of Technical Inefficiency in the Stochastic Frontier Production Function Model." *Journal of Econometrics* 19, pp. 233–238.

Kalirajan, K.P. (1985). "On Measuring Absolute Technical and Allocative Efficiencies." *Sankhya: The Indian Journal of Statistics*, Series B, 47, pp. 385–400.

Kumbhakar, S.C. (1988). "On the Estimation of Technical and Allocative Inefficiency Using Stochastic Frontier Functions: The Case of U.S. Class 1 Railroads." *International Economic Review* 29, pp. 727–743.

Kumbhakar, S.C. (1990). "Production Frontiers, Panel Data and Time-Varying Technical Inefficiency." *Journal of Econometrics* 46, pp. 201–211.

Kumbhakar, S.C., B. Biswas, and D.V. Bailey. (1989). "A Study of Economic Efficiency and Utah Dairy Farms: A System Approach." *The Review of Economics and Statistics* 71(4), pp. 595–604.

Ley, E. (1990). "A Bibliography on Production and Efficiency." mimeo, Department of Economics, University of Michigan, Ann Arbor, MI 48109, p. 32.

Meeusen, W. and J. van den Broeck. (1977). "Efficiency Estimation from Cobb-Douglas Production Functions With Composed Error." *International Economic Review* 18, pp. 435–444.

Richmond, J. (1974). "Estimating the Efficiency of Production." *International Economic Review* 15, pp. 515–521.

Saini, G.R. (1979). *Farm Size, Resource-Use Efficiency and Income Distribution*. New Delhi: Allied Publishers.

Schmidt, P. (1976). "On the Statistical Estimation of Parametric Frontier Production Functions." *The Review of Economics and Statistics* 58, pp. 238–239.

Schmidt, P. (1986). "Frontier Production Functions." *Economic Reviews* 4, pp. 289–328.

Schmidt, P. and C.A.K. Lovell. (1979). "Estimating Technical and Allocative Inefficiency Relative to Stochastic Production and Cost Frontiers." *Journal of Econometrics* 9, pp. 343–366.

Schmidt, P. and C.A.K. Lovell. (1980). "Estimating Stochastic Production and Cost Frontiers When Technical and Allocative Inefficiency are Correlated." *Journal of Econometrics* 13, pp. 83–100.

Stevenson, R.E. (1980). "Likelihood Functions for Generalized Stochastic Frontier Estimation." *Journal of Econometrics* 13, pp. 56–66.

Timmer, C.P. (1971). "Using a Probabilistic Frontier Function to Measure Technical Efficiency." *Journal of Political Economy* 79, pp. 776–794.

The Journal of Productivity Analysis, 3, 171–203 (1992)

Estimating Efficiencies from Frontier Models with Panel Data: A Comparison of Parametric, Non-Parametric and Semi-Parametric Methods with Bootstrapping*

LÉOPOLD SIMAR
SMASH, Facultés Universitaires Saint-Louis, Bruxelles, Belgium and CORE, Université Catholique de Louvain, Louvain la Neuve, Belgium

Abstract

The aim of this article is first to review how the standard econometric methods for panel data may be adapted to the problem of estimating frontier models and (in)efficiencies. The aim is to clarify the difference between the fixed and random effect model and to stress the advantages of the latter. Then a semi-parametric method is proposed (using a non-parametric method as a first step), the message being that in order to estimate frontier models and (in)efficiences with panel data, it is an appealing method. Since analytic sampling distributions of efficiencies are not available, a bootstrap method is presented in this framework. This provides a tool allowing to assess the statistical significance of the obtained estimators. All the methods are illustrated in the problem of estimating the inefficiencies of 19 railway companies observed over a period of 14 years (1970–1983).

1. Introduction

The estimation of (technical) efficiencies of production units from frontier models has been extensively used in the literature since the pioneering work of Farell [1957] for a non-parametric approach and of Aigner and Chu [1968] for a parametric approach.

The idea is the following: the efficiency[1] of a production unit is characterized by the distance between the output (production) level attained by this unit and the level it should obtain if it were efficient. The latter is defined as the maximal output attainable for a given combination of inputs (the factors); the geometric locus of the optimal productions may be represented by a production function (or frontier function) which can be modeled by a parametric model (i.e., a particular analytical function with a *a priori* fixed number of parameters) or by a non-parametric model.

From a statistical point of view, in general, the frontier function will be estimated from a set of observations of particular production units. Then the efficiency of each unit is derived from its distance to the estimated frontier.

*Article presented at the ORSA/TIMS joint national meeting, *Productivity and Global Competition*, Philadelphia, October 29–31, 1990. An earlier version of the paper was presented at the European Workshop on *Efficiency and Productivity Measurement in the Service Industries* held at CORE, October 20–21, 1989. Helpful comments of Jacques Mairesse, Benoît Mulkay, Sergio Perelman, Michel Mouchart, Shawna Grosskopf and Rolf Färe, at various stages of the paper, are gratefully acknowledged.

In the parametric approach, there exist *deterministic* frontier models, where all the observations lie on one side (below) of the production function or *stochastic* frontier models allowing for random noise around the production function.

Let y_i and $x_i \in \mathbf{R}^k$ represent the output and the vector of inputs of the ith observation. The frontier model may be written (in its loglinear version):

$$y_i = \beta_o + x_i' \beta + v_i \qquad i = 1, \ldots, n,$$

where for the *stochastic* model,

$$v_i = -\alpha_i + \epsilon_i,$$

with $\alpha_i \geq 0$ is the random component expressing inefficiency, and ϵ_i is the usual random noise; whereas in the *deterministic* case:

$$v_i = -\alpha_i.$$

When an estimator of β_o and of β is obtained, the optimal level of production is estimated by

$$\hat{y}_i = \hat{\beta}_o + x_i' \hat{\beta} \qquad i = 1, \ldots, n.$$

In the deterministic case, an estimation of the (in)efficiency of the ith production unit is then given (for outputs measured in logarithms) by:

$$eff_i = \exp(y_i - \hat{y}_i) = \exp(-\hat{\alpha}_i),$$

whereas in the stochastic case, an estimation of the ϵ_i's is also needed (see e.g., Jondrow et al. [1982]); the (in)efficiency is given by:

$$eff_i = \exp(y_i - \hat{y}_i - \hat{\epsilon}_i) = \exp(-\hat{\alpha}_i)$$

The estimation of the parameters of these models does not raise particular problems (see e.g., Greene [1980] and Aigner et al. [1977]) but the estimation of the efficiencies of each production unit is questionable: how to give statistical meaning to estimation based on one observation. Indeed, the estimation eff_i is based on one observed residual.

In other words, the model says that, conditionally on the x_i, the y_i are generated by the following distribution[2]:

$$y_i | x_i \approx D(\beta_o + x_i' \beta - a, \sigma^2_{v_i}),$$

where a is the mean of α_i and $\exp(-a)$ may be interpreted as an overall measure of efficiency of the sector of activity analyzed. An estimation of a is for instance obtained by averaging over the α_i's. Note that for the model, all the production units have, at the mean, the same efficiency level; the estimation eff_i for each individual observation is in fact derived from the observed deviation of that observation from the mean a.

As far as efficiency measures are concerned, the statistical properties of these estimators are uncertain. In fact several observations of each production unit are needed in order to bring statistical grounds to those measures; this is e.g., the case for time series-cross section data (panel data). Otherwise, only descriptive comments on the efficiencies eff_i obtained above will be allowed.

Note that in this article, the deviations from the production frontier are mainly interpreted in terms of inefficiency. If a part of this distance may be explained by other factors (like environmental conditions, etc...) the model has to be adapted in the spirit e.g., of Deprins and Simar [1989a,b] (introducing those factors through an exponential function). Only the remaining part of the distance is then interpreted in terms of inefficiency.

The aim of the article is first to review how the standard econometric methods for panel data may be adapted to the prolem of estimating frontier models and (in)efficiencies. The aim is to clarify the difference between the fixed and random effects model and to stress the hypotheses needed for both approaches. Then a non-parametric and a semi-parametric method is proposed (using a non-parametric method as a first step), the message being that in order to estimate frontier models and (in)efficiencies with panel data, the latter is appealing.

Since the ranking of all production units are based on the estimated efficiencies, it is important to analyze the sampling distributions of those estimators. In the framework here, no analytical results are generally obtainable; as shown in this article, the bootstrap provides a flexible tool to address this issue. It gives some insight into the precision of the procedures allowing e.g., to assess the statistical significance of the obtained estimators.

Section 2 presents the basic features of the methodology of estimating frontier models with panel data from a pure parametric point of view. This provides a correct treatment of the problem using only simple computational procedures (least-squares). Section 3 and 4 show how non-parametric and semi-parametric methods can be performed. Section 5 presents how the bootstrap can be adapted in each model. Finally, section 6 illustrates the methods in the estimation of the efficiencies of 19 railways observed for a period of 14 years.

2. The use of panel data

The statistical analysis of econometric models with panel data is a well known problem (see Mundlak [1978] and Hausman and Taylor [1981]). Its application to the estimation of frontier models has been analyzed by Schmidt and Sickles [1984] for the basic ideas, and Cornwell, Schmidt, and Sickles [1988] propose further extensions.

In this section, we present the basic principles of the method, pointing out the difference between the fixed effects and the random effects models in a simple case where only a firm effect is present.[3] The methods are also extended to the case of unbalanced samples.

The observations are now indexed by a firm index $i = 1, \ldots, p$ and a time index $t = 1, \ldots, T$.

2.1. *The pure parametric deterministic case*

In the pure parametric deterministic case, the panel structure of the data is not taken into account to estimate the frontier but only in order to give some statistical meaning to the obtained efficiencies.

It is here mentioned in order to facilitate the understanding of the more specific methods presented below. The model may be written as follows:

$$y_{it} = \beta_o + x_{it}' \beta + v_{it} \begin{cases} i = 1, \ldots, p \\ t = 1, \ldots, T, \end{cases} \tag{1}$$

where $v_{it} \leq 0$. The estimation procedure is straightforward (Greene [1980]). OLS leads to a consistent estimator of β. A consistent estimator of β_o is obtained from the OLS estimator shifted in order to obtain negative values for the residuals:

$$\tilde{\beta}_o = \hat{\beta}_o + \max_{i,t} \hat{v}_{it}, \tag{2}$$

where $\hat{v}_{it}$ are the OLS residuals from equation (1). The efficiencies of each observed unit may be obtained by:

$$eff_i = \exp(\hat{v}_{it} - \max_{i,t} \hat{v}_{it}). \tag{3}$$

A two way ANOVA could be performed on these efficiencies in order to detect a firm effect or a time effect. The estimation of the efficiency of the ith firm may be obtained by averaging over time.

The limitation of the deterministic approach rests in the fact that *all* the observations lie on one side of the frontier; the procedure is therefore very sensitive to outliers (super efficient observations) and it does not allow for random shocks around an average production frontier. This will appear in the illustration in Section 6.

2.2. *The panel models*

The model for the frontier, taking the panel structure of the data into account, can be written as follows:

$$y_{it} = \beta_o + x_{it}' \beta - \alpha_i + \epsilon_{it} \begin{cases} i = 1, \ldots, p \\ t = 1, \ldots, T, \end{cases} \tag{4}$$

where the α_i's characterize the (in)efficiency of the ith unit, they are positive and i.i.d. random variables independent of ϵ_{it}:

$$\alpha_i \approx D(a, \sigma_\alpha^2) \qquad i = 1, \ldots, p.$$

It will be useful to denote the overall residual as above by v_{it}:

$$v_{it} = -\alpha_i + \epsilon_{it}.$$

The parameter a is the mean of these variables and represents the latent (average) inefficiency level of the technology. The efficiency measure of a particular unit will now be obtained from the estimation (the prediction) of the random variable α_i based on the sample of observations.

Traditionally, two levels of analysis are proposed in the literature, whether the estimation of the production frontier is performed conditionally on fixed values of the α_i's whatever their realizations may be (this leads to the fixed effects model and the within estimator of the β's) or whether this estimation is performed marginally on the effects (leading to the random effect model and GLS estimation of the parameters). The two approaches are presented below.

2.2.1. The fixed effects model (within estimators). In the fixed effects model, the α_i are thus considered as unknown *fixed parameters* to be estimated from equation (4) above. Clearly the parameter β_o is not identified in the mean.[4] In fact, the model which is indeed specified is the following:

$$y_{it} = x'_{it}\,\beta + \gamma_i + \epsilon_{it} \begin{cases} i = 1, \ldots, p \\ t = 1, \ldots, T \end{cases} \tag{5}$$

where $\gamma_i = \beta_o - \alpha_i$.

Thus each firm has its own production level sharing only the slope with the others.

An estimator of β, referred as the within estimator, may be obtained by regressing the within group deviations of y_{it} on those of x_{it}. The procedure may be summarized as follows.

The within group means are defined as:

$$\bar{y}_{i\cdot} = \frac{1}{T}\sum_t y_{it} \quad \text{and} \quad \bar{x}_{i\cdot} = \frac{1}{T}\sum_t x_{it}$$

the within estimator of β is obtained by OLS on:

$$y_{it} - \bar{y}_{i\cdot} = \beta'(x_{it} - \bar{x}_{i\cdot}) + u_{it}. \tag{6}$$

Finally, we have[5]

$$\hat{\gamma}_i = \bar{y}_{i\cdot} - \hat{\beta}'\bar{x}_{i\cdot}.$$

Now, if estimation of β_o and of the α_i's is wanted, this may be obained by a shift of the $\hat{\gamma}_i$'s. The translation (shift) is indeed needed in order to obtain positive values for $\hat{\alpha}_i$; this allows us to bound the intercept β_o. (This is in fact a translation of the frontier, in the spirit of Greene [1980]).

The procedure is as follows:

$$\hat{\alpha}_i = \max_j \hat{\gamma}_i - \hat{\gamma}_i \qquad i = 1, \ldots, p$$

$$\hat{\beta}_o = \max \hat{\gamma}_j.$$

The efficiency measures are finally given by

$$eff_i = \exp(-\hat{\alpha}_i) \qquad i = 1, \ldots, p.$$

Note that the most efficient unit will have a measure equal to one. Here again, a descriptive analysis of the time effect could be provided through the analysis of the obtained residuals v_{it} (recomputed from equation (4) with the final estimators of β_o and β).

Schmidt and Sickles [1988], following the argument of Greene [1980], show that the estimation is consistent if T grows to infinity. As it is well known in the literature on panel models, the main interest of the approach lies in the fact that the statistical properties of the within estimator of β do not depend on the assumption of uncorrelatedness of the regressors x_{it} with the effects α_i.

The main disadvantage, however, is that the coefficients of time-invariant regressors cannot be estimated in the fixed model approach: the matrix of regressors in this case is singular in equation (5) or equivalently saying, those regressors are eliminated in the within transformation above in equation (6).

It should be noticed that even in this simplest model, the sampling distributions of the efficiencies cannot be analytically derived due the max transformation on non-independent variables (γ_j).

In the particular framework of production frontier estimation, the estimation of β_o (and thus of the efficiencies) may be viewed as being somewhat arbitrary. Indeed, the model makes the assumption that each firm has its own production level (γ_i) and the differences between these levels are solely interpreted in terms of inefficiencies: the inefficiency measures will then typically be sensitive to scale factors and the estimation of the production frontier will solely be based on the temporal variation of the production factors.

Further, in this framework, the regressors, if not time-invariant, are generally not much time-varying leading to almost multicollinear regressors in equation (5). They will produce a poor estimation of the parameters. Note, also that the stochastic nature of the (in)efficiency effects is not really taken into account.

Therefore, depending on the application, this model may not be very attractive. In the railways illustration of Section 6, the fixed effect model will indeed appear as providing a poor estimation of the intercepts and of the slope of the production frontiers and so, unreasonable measures of efficiency.

2.2.2. The random effects model (GLS estimators). In the random effects model, instead of working conditionally on the effects α_i, we take explicitly into account their stochastic nature. This may be particularly appealing in the framework of estimating efficiencies since random elements (not predetermined or not under the control of the firm) may affect the efficiency of each unit. In this approach, there is a unique production frontier but one sided random deviations are allowed in order to characterize inefficiencies. This leads in fact to a stochastic frontier model taking into account the panel structure of the data.

The estimation of such a model is well known, but in order to be complete, these aspects are summarized in the Appendix.

The main problem in this approach is that the GLS estimators are consistent (and unbiased) if the regressors x_{it} are uncorrelated with the effects α_i. Note that in some cases, this may be a too strong assumption (for instance, as pointed by Schmidt and Sickles [1984], if the firms know their level of inefficiency it should affect their level of inputs). If this uncorrelatedness assumption is not realistic, one has to look for instrumental variables methods (see Hausman and Taylor [1981] where also tests for uncorrelatedness are proposed).

The estimation of the efficiencies is straightforward: let

$$\bar{v}_{i\cdot} = \frac{1}{T} \sum_{t=1}^{T} \hat{v}_{it}$$

where $\hat{v}_{it}$ are the obtained residuals (see the Appendix). Define

$$\hat{\alpha}_i = \max_j \bar{v}_{j\cdot} - \bar{v}_{i\cdot}$$

where the maximum is introduced in order to provide positive values of the α_i's. As before, the estimation of the (in)efficiency of the ith production unit is given by

$$eff_i = \exp(-\hat{\alpha}_i),$$

and the overall efficiency level may be obtained by averaging the α_i's.[6] Note that here, the procedure gives an estimation of σ_α^2, too. This allows, for instance to appreciate the statistical significance of the estimated α_i and of the obtained efficiencies.[7] Note that Section 5 provides a general flexible tool to obtain these distributions.

The random effects model seems thus to be very attractive in this framework since it takes into account the random structure of the inefficiencies and does not share the disadvantage of the fixed model approach (the within estimator); the price to pay is the uncorrelatedness assumption between the effects and the regressors.

2.3. *The unbalanced case*

The procedures above can be extended in the case of unbalanced samples i.e., when the number of observations per firm is not a constant. The extension of the fixed effects model is straightforward but the random effects model requires more details.

Suppose there are still p different production units, but we only have T_i observations on the ith firm. The model may be written:

$$y_{it} = \beta_o + x_{it}'\beta - \alpha_i + \epsilon_{it} \quad \begin{cases} i = 1, \ldots, p \\ t = 1, \ldots, T_i \end{cases} \tag{7}$$

The vector of residuals v has now a dimension n:

$$n = \sum_{i=1}^{p} T_i.$$

The covariance matrix of v can be written:

$$\Sigma_v = \begin{pmatrix} A_1 & O & \dots & O \\ O & A_2 & \dots & O \\ \vdots & \vdots & \dots & \vdots \\ O & O & \dots & A_p \end{pmatrix},$$

where each A_i has the same structure as the matrix A in the balanced case but with dimension $(T_i \times T_i)$.

In particular, we have again:

$$A_i^{-1} = \left(\frac{-\sigma_\alpha^2}{\sigma_\epsilon^2(\sigma_\epsilon^2 + T_i\sigma_\alpha^2)}\right) i_{T_i}\, i'_{T_i} + \frac{1}{\sigma_\epsilon^2} I_{T_i}.$$

The same argument applies and the GLS estimtors of β_o and β, can be easily obtained. The only change is to derive a consistent estimator of σ_α^2 and of σ_ϵ^2. This is possible through a corrected decomposition of the variance of the residuals obtained by the OLS estimation of the model:

$$y_{it} = \beta_o + x'_{it}\,\beta + v_{it} \begin{cases} i = 1, \dots, p \\ t = 1, \dots, T_i \end{cases}.$$

It can be shown that the expectation of the within sum of squares is given by

$$E\left[\sum_{i,t} (v_{it} - \bar{v}_{i\cdot})^2\right] = (n - p)\sigma_\epsilon^2, \tag{8a}$$

and that the expected between sum of squares is

$$E\left[\sum_i T_i(\bar{v}_{i\cdot} - \bar{v}_{\cdot\cdot})^2\right] = (p - 1)\left(\sigma_\epsilon^2 + \frac{n}{p}\sigma_\alpha^2\right). \tag{8b}$$

This allows determination of consistent estimators of σ_α^2 and σ_ϵ^2.

Once the GLS estimator of β_o and β is obtained,[8] the estimation of the efficiencies follows easily as above in the balanced case: the residuals $\hat{v}_{it}$ are recomputed with the new values of β and β_o, and we have respectively,

$$\hat{\alpha}_i = \max_j \bar{v}_{j\cdot} - \bar{v}_{i\cdot}$$

$$\tilde{\beta}_o = \hat{\beta}_o + \max_j \bar{v}_j.$$

and,

$$\mathit{eff}_i = \exp(-\hat{\alpha}_i).$$

3. A Non-parametric method

A flexible non-parametric method for estimating efficiencies is the so-called Free Disposal Hull (FDH) method proposed by Deprins, Simar, and Tulkens [1984].

In this approach, the attainable production set is defined as the union of all the positive orthants in the inputs and of the negative orthants in the outputs whose origin coincides with the observed points. More precisely, denoting Y_o the set of observed units, this set is defined (in the case of one output y and k inputs x) as follows:

$$\left\{ \begin{pmatrix} y \\ x \end{pmatrix} \in \mathcal{R}^{k+1} \middle| \begin{pmatrix} y \\ x \end{pmatrix} = \begin{pmatrix} y_i \\ x_i \end{pmatrix} + \sum_{j=1}^{k} \mu_j \begin{pmatrix} 0 \\ e_j^k \end{pmatrix} - \delta \begin{pmatrix} 1 \\ 0_k \end{pmatrix}; \begin{pmatrix} y_i \\ x_i \end{pmatrix} \in Y_o; \mu_j \geq 0; \delta \geq 0 \right\},$$

where e_j^k is the jth column of the identity matrix of order k.

Then for each observed unit (y_i, x_i), the dominating set $D(y_i, x_i)$ is defined as the set of production units which dominates the point in the sense of free disposal, i.e., producing more output with less inputs:

$$D(y_i, x_i) = \left\{ \begin{pmatrix} y_i \\ x_i \end{pmatrix} \right\} \cup \left\{ \begin{pmatrix} y \\ x \end{pmatrix} \in Y_o \middle| \begin{pmatrix} y \\ x \end{pmatrix} = \begin{pmatrix} y_i \\ x_i \end{pmatrix} - \sum_{j=1}^{k} \mu_j \begin{pmatrix} 0 \\ e_j^k \end{pmatrix} + \delta \begin{pmatrix} 1 \\ 0_k \end{pmatrix} \right\}.$$

The measure of (in)efficiency is then simply given by (if the outputs are measured in logarithms):

$$\mathit{eff}_i = \exp(y_i - yd_i),$$

where yd_i is the maximum output level attained by the dominating units

$$yd_i = \max \left\{ y \middle| \begin{pmatrix} y \\ x \end{pmatrix} \in D(y_i, x_i) \right\}.$$

In the case of panel data, the same procedure can be applied, so that for each observation, one obtains eff_{it}. A two way ANOVA could help to detect a firm or a time effect.

If a firm effect is assumed for modeling the (in)efficiencies, this can be formally achieved as follows.

$$y_{it} = yd_{it} - \alpha_i + \epsilon_{it},$$

where ϵ_{it} represents the usual random noise. Defining the residuals as

$$v_{it} = y_{it} - yd_{it}.$$

The firm effects can be estimated in a second step, since we have

$$v_{it} = -\alpha_i + \epsilon_{it},$$

the estimation of the α_i's is simply

$$\hat{\alpha}_i = -\bar{v}_{i\cdot} = -\sum_{t=1}^{T} (y_{it} - yd_{it}).$$

Finally the efficiencies are given by

$$\mathit{eff}_i = \exp(-\hat{\alpha}_i).$$

This non-parametric approach has the advantage of its simplicity (it is easy to compute) and its flexibility (it rests only on free disposal assumptions). Of course, as for other non-parametric approaches and/or for determinic frontiers, the procedure is very sensitive to the presence of super-efficient outliers.

4. A semi-parametric approach

Another way of estimating frontier models and efficiencies is a semi-parametric approach combining both parametric and non-parametric aspects.

The idea may be presented as follows. A frontier model, with panel data, can be written as in equation (4), where a parametric model is chosen for the form of the production function (e.g., $\beta_o + x_{it}' \beta$) and for the random term ϵ_{it} characterizing the usual noise. In contrast, a non-parametric model is chosen to calculate inefficiency α_i. The motivations for a non-parametric treatment of the inefficiency terms are the usual ones (in particular, the robustness w.r.t. the distributional assumptions). On the other hand, a parametric form for the production function allows for a richer economic interpretation of the production process under analysis than a pure non-parameric model (in a parametric model, we can estimate elasticities, etc.).

Semi-parametric models are often estimated in two steps; the procedure of frontier's estimation, which is proposed here, may also be viewed as a two step procedure as follows:

1. the effects of inefficiency are eliminated by a non-parametric method (which is robust w.r.t. the particular form of the frontier and to the distributional assumptions);
2. based on the filtered "efficient" data, the parametric part of the model is estimated by standard parametric methods.

In this article, we use the flexible FDH method to perform the first step and then, in a second step, we use OLS to estimate the (log)linear production frontier based only on the FDH-efficient units.[9]

Note, the first step provides a filter which eliminates the production units which are clearly inefficient (the non-parametric treatment of this step is therefore certainly appealing). The whole procedure may thus be viewed as a trimmed frontier estimate in the spirit of the Huber-type robust estimators. With that point of view, the OLS of the second step is in fact a weighted least squares (with weight equal to one for the FDH-efficient units and weight zero for the others), but the weights are endogenous.

The procedure could clearly be modified by the use of other estimation procedures at each step (e.g., a DEA method for the non-parametric step; but the FDH has the advantage of allowing for a non-convex production set due to the free disposal assumption).

The filtering process may be costly in terms of data reduction (althoug the flexibility of the FDH method allows us to keep a large number of observations for the second step, see the illustration below). If such is the case, one could use, for the inefficient units, the estimated output level on the production frontier (obtained by the non-parametric estimator: e.g., yd_{it} in the FDH method) as a pseudo-observation to keep the whole set of data for the second step. This idea[10] is not pursued in this article.

This idea of filtering the data with the FDH method was introduced by Thiry and Tulkens [1988], the argument being that the procedure allows estimation of a production frontier (which is, by definition, the locus of optimal production situations) with a sample of points initially containing inefficient units. The filtering process should reduce the variance of the estimators and the non-parametric treatment of the filter allows us to consider any distribution for the stochastic inefficiency term.

It is clear that the initial cloud of points should not contain statistical outliers: in particular, super-efficient outliers should be removed from the sample before the analysis. The bootstrap method proposed below could help to analyze sensitivity to those outliers.

Formally, the whole procedure may be written as follows. First determine by the FDH method the FDH-efficient units and note by $T_1, T_2, \ldots, T_p$ the number of observations in the panel which are FDH-efficient.

The estimation of the frontier may be obtained by OLS on the sub-sample of FDH-efficient units:

$$y_{it} = \beta_o + x_{it}' \beta + \epsilon_{it} \begin{cases} i = 1, \ldots, p \\ t = 1, \ldots, T_i \end{cases} . \tag{9}$$

This provides estimators of β_o and β.

In order to estimate the efficiency level of each unit, we need to compute, *for all* observed units, the residuals with respect to the obtained frontier:

$$\hat{v}_{it} = y_{it} - \hat{\beta}'x_{it} - \hat{\beta}_o \begin{cases} i = 1, \ldots, p \\ t = 1, \ldots, T \end{cases}. \tag{10}$$

The estimation of the parameters α_i, is then obtained from equation (4):

$$\hat{v}_{it} = -\alpha_i + \epsilon_{it} \begin{cases} i = 1, \ldots, p \\ t = 1, \ldots, T \end{cases}. \tag{11}$$

And now, as above:

$$\hat{\alpha}_i = \max_j \bar{v}_{j\cdot} - \bar{v}_{i\cdot} \tag{12}$$

so that,

$$eff_i = \exp(-\hat{\alpha}_i).$$

Finally, in this case, the correction of the OLS estimator of β_o, in order to conform to the model (2.4) should be:

$$\tilde{\beta}_o = \hat{\beta}_o + \max_j \bar{v}_{j\cdot}. \tag{13}$$

Note, the random component in equation (11) and the averaging in equation (12) or in equation (13), should reduce extreme sensitivity to any particular super-efficient outlier in the sample.

Remark: since we are in fact in the presence of *panel* data, one could think that a firm effect could be introduced in the second step. In this case, due to the preliminary filter, the model should be written:

$$y_{it} = \beta_o + x_{it}'\beta - \alpha_i + \epsilon_{it} \begin{cases} i = 1, \ldots, p \\ t = 1, \ldots, T_i \end{cases}. \tag{14}$$

The direct estimation of equation (14) could then be achieved using the results of Section 2.4 (unbalanced samples). But this seems to be inappropriate. First, it may happen that some production units are not represented in the remaining sample of FDH-efficient units. But the main argument is that the coefficients α_i in the model capture the inefficiency of the production units. Since the filtered observations are efficient, the estimtion of those coefficients may be viewed as being irrelevant. Therefore, the direct estimation of equation (14), after filtering, is not appropriate. Since the objective of the filtering is to provide a statistically more efficient estimator of the production frontier itself, the estimation of equation (9) is performed as above, providing an average production frontier for efficient units. Further, the model (14) is not consistent with the semi-parametric formulation of model (4) we present here.

The semi-parametric approach, and the estimation procedure which is proposed in this paper, may be viewed as a first exploratory step in this very appealing approach. At this stage of our work, we don't have a proof that the obtained estimators share the usual statistical properties of the estimators obtained in the parametric models (consistency, etc.). One knows the difficulties of analyzing the statistical properties in semi-parametric models: for instance, in the weighted least squares presentation above, remember that the weights are endogenous and stochastic. The motivation for our semi-parametric approach is mainly based on pragmatic arguments. In all the proposed approaches above (except the fixed effects model), the procedure can always be separated into two steps: first, estimate the production frontier (the locus of optimal production levels given the inputs), then exploit the panel structure of the data to estimate the (in)efficiencies. Therefore a procedure improving the estimation of the production frontier in the first step, as in the semi-parametric approach, is empirically attractive.

The bootstrap method proposed below gives some insights into the analysis of the sensitivity of the procedure. In particular, the bootstrap distributions of the estimators and of the efficiency measures may act at this stage, as an empirical proxy for theoretical results. This provides us a framework for future work.

5. Bootstrapping in Frontier Models

As pointed out above, the measures of efficiency are relative ones and provide means for ranking the different firms. It is therefore important to analyze the sensitivity of the estimated efficiencies to the sampling process.

In almost all cases, the sampling distributions are not available due to the non-linearity of the estimation procedures or to the lack of parametric distributional assumptions on the residuals. This is certainly a case where bootstrapping can help to get an insight on those issues.

The idea of the bootstrap in regression models is that resampling in the population of the obtained residuals provides a bootstrap version of the residuals and so a new (pseudo) sample of observations. On this pseudo sample, the estimation procedure is again performed, providing bootstrap estimators. Conditionally on the data, the sampling distribution of the new estimators does not depend on unknowns and mimics the (possibly unknown) sampling distribution of the estimators obtained in the first step. Technically, the sampling distribution of the bootstrap estimators is obtained by Monte Carlo replications of the procedure (see e.g., Efron [1983] for a general presentation and Freedman [1981] for the regression case).

Formally, the method can be briefly presented as follows in a regular linear model:

$$y_i = \beta_o + x_i'\beta + \epsilon_i \qquad i = 1, \ldots, n.$$

Let b_o, b and e_i be the estimated coefficients and residuals obtained by a particular method (OLS,...). Conditional on the data, let e_i^* $i = 1, \ldots, n^{12}$ denote a resample drawn with replacement from the e_i, $i = 1, \ldots, n$. Now define:

$$y_i^* = b_o + x_i' b + e_i^* \quad i = 1, \ldots, n.$$

Applying the same estimation procedure to the pseudo data (y_i^* x_i), we obtain the bootstrap estimators b_o^* and b^*. The result is that, as n becomes large, the distribution of $n^{1/2}(b - \beta)$ may be approximated by the (conditional to the data) distribution of $n^{1/2}(b^* - b)$. The latter is obtained by Monte Carlo replication of the procedure. This allows us, for instance, to approximate confidence intervals for the elements of β.

The following sections show how the bootstrap can be performed in the frontier models with a panel of data. In Boland [1990], these ideas have also been generalized in frontier models allowing for heteroskedasticity among firms.

Consistency of bootstrap distributions in frontier models is not addressed in this article. A first insight in that difficult problem may be found in Hall, Härdle, and Simar [1991] where the simplest model (fixed effects) is analyzed providing root-n consistency of the obtained distributions; a double bootstrap procedure is therefore proposed in order to obtain consistency of order n.

5.1. *The fixed effects model*

Here, the procedure is straightforward. The model is given by:

$$y_{it} = \beta_o + x_{it}' \beta - \alpha_i + \epsilon_{it} \begin{cases} i = 1, \ldots, p \\ t = 1, \ldots, T \end{cases}. \tag{15}$$

The OLS procedure provides the residuals e_{it} and the estimators b_o, b, a_i and eff_i. The bootstrap version of the e_{it} are e_{it}^*, then the pseudo observations y_{it}^* are computed by

$$y_{it}^* = b_o + x_{it}' b - a_i + e_{it}^* \begin{cases} i = 1, \ldots, p \\ t = 1, \ldots, T \end{cases}. \tag{16}$$

Applying the same estimation procedure with the data (y_{it}^*, x_{it}) we obtain the bootstrap versions b_o^*, b^*, a_i^* and eff_i^*. Repeating the procedure a large number of times (resampling with replacement e_{it}^* in the e_{it}, redefining at each step the pseudo sample (y_{it}^*, x_{it}) and computing the corresponding bootstrap versions of the estimators) we obtain what we need. In particular, this provides an approximation of the conditional distribution of eff_i^* and so of the sampling distribution of the eff_i.

5.2. The random effects model

The procedure is very similar, one must only be careful of bootstrapping the right residuals. The model to be estimated is the same as in equation (15). The GLS estimators b of β are described in Section 2.2.2 where the shifted version of b_O and the GLS residuals provide the firm effect estimators a_i.

The residuals to be resampled are thus simply given by

$$e_{it} = y_{it} - b_o - x_{it}' b + a_i \begin{cases} i = 1, \ldots, p \\ t = 1, \ldots, T \end{cases}. \tag{17}$$

Note by simple algebra, that those residuals can be directly obtained from the GLS residuals:

$$e_{it} = v_{it} - \bar{v}_{i\cdot}. \tag{18}$$

Then the procedure works as above: at each step, resampling with replacement in e_{it}, construction of the pseudo observation y_{it}^* by equation (16) and the estimation procedure of Section 2.2.2 (GLS) in order to obtain eff_i^*.

5.3. The non-parametric model

As shown in Section 3, the residuals e_{it} can be defined through the relation:

$$y_{it} = yd_{it} - a_i + e_{it}, \tag{19}$$

where yd_{it} denotes here the maximum level of output attained by units dominating the unit *it* and

$$a_i = \sum_{t=1}^{T} (y_{it} - yd_{it})$$

is the estimated firm effect. Here, the pseudo observations y_{it}^* are generated by

$$y_{it}^* = yd_{it} - a_i + e_{it}^*, \tag{20}$$

where e_{it}^* is the bootstrap version of the recentered residuals e_{it}. Then, as above, for each bootstrap sample, new estimations yd_{it}^* and a_i^* are obtained, yielding the estimations of the efficiencies eff_i^*.

5.4. The semi-parametric model

The estimation procedure proposed in Section 4 leads at the end (after FDH-filtering, OLS on efficient units, recomputation of all residuals, correction of b_O) to the estimators b_O, b, a_i and eff_i.

The residuals to be resampled are here again simply given by equation (17). After each pseudo sample is obtained by equation (16), the whole procedure is performed again providing the bootstrap versions b_O^*, b^*, a_i^* and eff_i^*.

Note that here, due to the FDH filter, the usual statistics on the OLS estimator b are not the correct ones. So the bootstrap method is also particularly useful in providing information on the sampling distribution of the estimators of β.

6. Application to railways

6.1. Introduction

Most of the methods presented above will be illustrated in the analysis of efficiency of 19 railway companies observed for a period of 14 years.[13] This data set has also been used in Deprins and Simar [1989a, b] for estimating efficiencies of the railways with a correction for exogeneous factors of environment. A careful analysis of the production activity of railways, using a more complete set of data, may be founded in Gathon and Perelman [1990] where input (labor) efficiency is analyzed. The aim of this section is rather to provide an illustration of the various approaches than an empirical study of the efficiency pattern of the various national railways.

The railways companies retained for the analysis are the following:

Network	Country	Network	Country
BR	Great Britain	NS	Netherlands
CFF	Switzerland	NSB	Norway
CFL	Luxembourg	OBB	Austria
CH	Greece	RENFE	Spain
CIE	Ireland	SJ	Sweden
CP	Portugal	SNCB	Belgium
DB	Germany	SNCF	France
DSB	Denmark	TCDD	Turkey
FS	Italy	VR	Finland
JNR	Japan		

The data are available for each network on an annual basis. In this study we used the period from 1970 to 1983. This provides 266 observations on the whole set of variables.

The production of a railway company is mainly characterized by two kinds of activity: the carriage of goods (freight) and the carriage of passengers. In the illustration proposed here, we concentrate the analysis on a characteristic of the production which aggregates the two activities: the output considered here is the total number of kilometers covered by the trains of a company during one year. This variable (noted PTTR in what follows), is certainly a crude measure of the production of a railway company in an efficiency framework (a railroad running many train-km cannot be very efficient if the trains are empty). Despite this fact, this crude measure will be used in this illustration since it offers a gross aggregate measure of its activity (passengers and freight).

We retain four input measures of capital, labor, energy and materials and two output attributes characterizing what we could call a degree of modernity of the network: the ratio of electrified lines in the network and the mean number of tracks by line. Deprins and Simar [1989a, b] have shown the importance of those attributes in the characterization of the output efficiencies. The following list presents the variables used in this application.

Output :
PTTR : Total distance covered by trains (in kms).

Inputs :
ETEF : Labor (total number of employees).
UMUL : Material (Number of coaches and wagons).
CMBF : Energy (consumption transformed in equivalent kwh).
LGTL : Total length of the network (in kms).

Output Attributes :
RLE : Ratio of electrified lines in the network (in %).
RVL : Mean number of track by line.

A brief statistical description of the data set is proposed in Table 6.

The functional form of the frontier model (in the parametric case) is a special case of the transcendental logarithmic function (Christensen, Jorgensen, and Lau [1973]), with a first order approximation in the logarithms of the input quantities (Cobb-Douglas technology) and second order terms in the logarithms of the output attributes.[14]

The production function is therefore:

$$\ln PTTR = \beta_O + \beta_1 \ln ETEF + \beta_2 \ln UMUL + \beta_3 \ln CMBF + \beta_4 \ln LGTL + \beta_5 \ln RLE + \beta_6 \ln RVL + \beta_7(\ln RLE)^2 + \beta_8(\ln RVL)^2 + \beta_9 \ln RLE \ln RVL.$$

6.2. The results

Table 1 presents the estimation of the production frontier using the different approaches described above. Table 2 shows the estimation of the firm effects in the fixed and in the random case. Finally, Table 3 gives the derived estimated efficiencies of each railway with its relative ranking.

From Table 1, we note in all the cases the goodness of fit (high R^2).

Table 1. Estimation of the Production Frontier.

Model:	Deterministic		Fixed Effect		Random Effect		Semi-parametric	
CONST	0.6541		12.8884		1.1732		1.0933	
ETEF	0.3563	8.12*	-0.1046	-1.85	0.2380	4.18	0.3917	7.01
UMUL	-0.5453	-15.0	-0.0910	-3.20	-0.1585	-4.97	-0.5369	-15.1
CMBF	0.1631	3.83	0.1001	3.98	0.2258	6.43	0.3242	5.88
LGTL	1.079	23.1	0.1961	1.18	0.7220	13.7	0.9001	17.0
RLE	0.0136	0.87	-0.0353	-1.12	0.0673	2.89	0.0296	1.88
RVL	4.428	14.4	-0.5822	-1.17	3.220	7.05	1.962	4.25
RLE^2	0.0512	11.9	0.0229	2.37	0.0404	6.32	0.0401	7.76
RVL^2	-1.365	-5.24	0.6028	1.50	-1.004	-2.68	0.2440	0.69
RLE*RVL	-0.1911	-3.71	-0.0103	-0.12	-0.2437	-3.14	-0.1502	-2.72
$e_{PTTR/RLE}$***	0.1656		0.0769		0.1326		0.1483	
$e_{PTTR/RVL}$	2.3287		0.1004		1.4096		1.8612	
R^2	0.987166		0.998696		0.944174**		0.994451	
deg. of free.	256		238****		256		123	

*The numbers printed in small symbols are the T-values.
**This is the R^2 of the OLS on the quasi-deviations.
***The estimated elasticities evaluated at the mean values of lnRLE and lnRVL.
****There are 18=19-1 additional parameters estimated.

Table 2. Estimation of the firm effects.

	Fixed Effects		Random Effects
Parameters	Estimates	Stand.dev. of γ_i	Estimates with $\sigma_{\alpha}^{\Delta} = 0.1105$
α_1	0.4074	1.56	0.3497
α_2	1.9166	1.27	0.2283
α_3	4.6304	0.91	0.7338
α_4	3.7321	1.27	0.5272
α_5	4.0759	1.23	0.4173
α_6	2.8541	1.30	0.2911
α_7	0.1397	1.62	0.5035
α_8	2.4461	1.25	0.3261
α_9	0.7846	1.54	0.4973
α_{10}	0.0000	1.58	0.2428
α_{11}	1.7966	1.27	0.0000
α_{12}	2.9810	1.34	0.4850
α_{13}	1.8337	1.38	0.5581
α_{14}	1.6262	1.50	0.5458
α_{15}	1.9504	1.47	0.6252
α_{16}	1.8899	1.34	0.5442
α_{17}	0.3326	1.65	0.5284
α_{18}	2.7970	1.42	0.7818
α_{19}	2.5522	1.37	0.4661

Table 3. Efficiency measures.

Network	Deterministic		Fixed Effect		Rand. Effect		Nonparam.			Semiparam.	
	Model (1)		Model (2)		Model (3)		Model (4)			Model (5)	
BR	0.699	5*	0.665	4	0.705	6	*8***	0.997	3	0.766	14
CFF	0.766	1	0.147	10	0.796	2	*0*	0.827	16	0.991	2
CFL	0.538	19	0.010	19	0.480	18	*12*	0.996	5	0.721	16
CH	0.616	11	0.024	17	0.590	12	*12*	0.996	4	0.798	9
CIE	0.656	7	0.017	18	0.659	7	*7*	0.948	14	0.802	7
CP	0.752	3	0.058	15	0.747	4	*9*	0.972	10	0.772	13
DB	0.603	13	0.870	2	0.604	11	*6*	0.952	12	0.727	15
DSB	0.649	8	0.087	12	0.722	5	*12*	0.999	2	0.813	5
FS	0.603	12	0.456	5	0.608	10	*12*	0.995	6	0.808	6
JNR	0.696	6	1.000	1	0.784	3	*13*	0.999	1	0.796	10
NS	0.756	2	0.166	7	1.000	1	*10*	0.984	8	1.000	1
NSB	0.640	9	0.051	16	0.616	9	*10*	0.992	7	0.798	8
OBB	0.600	14	0.160	8	0.572	16	*0*	0.822	17	0.788	12
RENFE	0.592	15	0.197	6	0.579	15	*10*	0.983	9	0.719	17
SJ	0.565	16	0.142	11	0.535	17	*0*	0.885	15	0.851	4
SNCB	0.538	18	0.151	9	0.580	14	*0*	0.796	18	0.627	18
SNCF	0.629	10	0.717	3	0.590	13	*6*	0.971	4	0.793	11
TCDD	0.538	17	0.061	14	0.458	19	*0*	0.347	19	0.401	19
VR	0.715	4	0.078	13	0.627	8	*6*	0.949	13	0.908	3

*The small numbers indicate the relative ranking of the different railways.

**The small italicized numbers in Model (4) indicates the number of times a railways was FDH-efficient.

Network	**Country**	**Network**	**Country**
BR	Great Britain	NS	Netherlands
CFF	Switzerland	NSB	Norway
CFL	Luxembourg	OBB	Austria
CH	Greece	RENFE	Spain
CIE	Ireland	SJ	Sweden
CP	Portugal	SNCB	Belgium
DB	Germany	SNCF	France
DSB	Denmark	TCDD	Turkey
FS	Italy	VR	Finland
JNR	Japan		

The analysis of the three tables confirms the inappropriateness of the *fixed effects* model in this framework. As pointed out in Section 2.2, in this model, each railway has its own production frontier with a different intercept and sharing only the slope with the others. This provides unexpected sign in Table 1 with smaller T-values than in the other cases; this is probably due to the relative time invariance of the regressors. The estimated values of α_i in Table 2 are quite different across the railways; since the difference between the intercepts are interpreted as (in)efficiencies, this provides the peculiar efficiency levels of Table 3 (ranging from 0.01 to 1.00): they are to be interpreted essentially as scale factors.

In all the other cases, we note also from Table 1, that we obtain the right signs for all the coefficients and for the elasticities (as in Deprins and Simar [1989]). It is indeed not surprising that if UMUL (the number of wagons and of coaches in good condition) is greater, the same number of passengers and the same amount of freight can be carried with less trains; and so with shorter distances covered by trains during the year.

The *deterministic* case requires some comments. Note that the maximum of the efficiency measures is 0.766, since these measures are obtained by averaging over the 14 years (the individual measures ranges from 0.45 (CFL-1983) to 1.00 (SNCF-1979 which may be viewed as a super efficient outliers?)).

In the *random effects* model, Table 2 gives the estimation of the firm effects and of the variance of this random effect. Note here, the difference across the railways is much more significant than in the fixed effects model. Further the estimation of the production frontier is much more reasonable giving sensible estimations of the efficiencies. This confirms again that in the framework of frontier models, the random effects model is much more appropriate than the fixed effects model.

In the *non-parametric* FDH-method, the estimation was performed with the output measure PTTR and only with the input factors ETEF, UMUL, CMBF and LGTL.[15] The efficiency measures are reproduced for each railway in Table 3 (Model (4)). We observe, as usual in this approach, the relatively high values of the efficiencies (except for TCDD (Turkey)).

The FDH-method provides 133 FDH-efficient observations (50%). Some railways never appeared in this group (CFF, OBB, SNCB and TCDD). The number of FDH-efficient units per railway is given in Table 3.

In the *semi-parametric* case, as expected, the estimation of the production frontier is fairly good: see the high R^2 and especially, very high T-values in Table 1. This is due to the fact that the data set has been filtered in order to eliminate the inefficient outliers; note, as pointed out above, these T-values are probably overestimated since they do not take into account the stochastic nature of the FDH filter (this will be confirmed by the bootstrap). The efficiency measures are then computed from the distances to the frontier for all the observations; they are reproduced in column (5) of Table 3. Note the very bad score of TCDD and SNCB; in contrast to NS, which is the most efficient railway. One can also observe the very good position of CFF which was, however, never FDH-efficient. The JNR railway, 13 years over the 14 detected as being FDH-efficient, obtains a relatively poor score with respect to the semi-parametric production frontier. Those differences are probably due to the fact that the production frontier takes into account some output attributes not present in the FDH method.

It is also worth mentioning that a two way ANOVA on the residuals recomputed for all observations in the semi-parametric case confirms that a firm effect is strongly present (p-value of the no-effect hypothesis is less than 10^{-7}) but that no time effect is detected (p-value of the no-effect hypothesis equal to 0.295).

It is interesting to note the relative coherence between the results of the semi-parametric approach and of the random effects model. However, the semi-parametric approach seems to be the most appealing since it provides the most precise estimation of the production frontier and the most sensible measures of efficiencies.

Finally, we briefly mention that in the semi-parametric case, we have also tried to estimate the production frontier from a larger subset of data, i.e., retaining from the sample more observations than only the 100 percent FDH-efficients. The results in the case of the 95 percent FDH-efficient units (167 observations) and in the case of the 90 percent FDH-efficient units (185 observations) may be compared with the preceding in Tables 4 and 5.

Note that, as expected (adding less efficient observations to the sample), the estimated returns to scale (with respect to the four input factors) are decreasing from 1.10, 1.08 and 1.07 respectively (in the random effects model, this is equal to 1.03 and in the fixed effects model we obtain the curious value of 0.10).

6.3. The sampling distributions of the efficiencies (using bootstrap)

The sampling distribution of the efficiencies were approximated using the method of bootstrap described in Section 5, by repeating 200 times the resampling with replacement of the residuals.

In order to save room we present in Figures 1 to 4 a summary of those distributions using multiple Boxplots provided by the software *Datadesk*. In these figures, the central box depicts the middle half of the distribution (between the 25th and 75th percentile), the horizontal line across the box is the median. The *whiskers* extend from the top and bottom and depict the extent of the *main body* of the distribution. Stars and circles stand for *outliers*. The shaded intervals represent 95 percent-confidence intervals for the medians.

A careful reading of the picture gives more insight for comparing the efficiencies of the railways. We only stress some interesting features.

The most important thing to point out is the fact that the rankings in Table 3 are certainly to be taken with care. Very often, a difference of 3 or 4 in the ranks is not statistically significant. The four pictures show certainly the difficulty of ranking the railways. In fact in most most cases, a ranking by groups would be more appropriate; this ranking by groups could for instance be based on the non-overlapping boxes.

Table 4. Estimation of the production frontier in the semi-parametric case.

Model:	100% FDH-eff		95% FDH-eff		90% FDH-eff	
CONST	1.0933		1.1908		1.3261	
ETEF	0.3917	7.01	0.3241	6.12	0.2843	5.67
UMUL	-0.5369	-15.1	-0.5101	-15.9	-0.5134	-15.6
CMBF	0.3242	5.88	0.3511	6.85	0.3852	7.57
LGTL	0.9001	17.0	0.9160	18.8	0.9170	18.9
RLE	0.0296	1.88	0.0231	1.61	0.0179	1.24
RVL	1.962	4.25	2.1315	5.28	2.19	5.62
RLE^2	0.0401	7.76	0.0375	8.04	0.0390	8.67
RVL^2	0.2440	0.69	-0.0085	-0.03	-0.1077	-0.37
RLE*RVL	-0.1502	-2.72	-0.1147	-2.25	-0.0945	-1.87
R^2	0.994451		0.993851		0.992996	
deg. of free.	123		157		175	

Table 5. Efficiency measures for semi-parametric methods.

Network	100% FDH-eff.		95% FDH-eff.		90% FDH-eff.	
BR	0.766	14*	0.766	14	0.800	13
CFF	0.991	2	0.988	2	0.987	2
CFL	0.721	16	0.725	15	0.726	16
CH	0.798	9	0.801	10	0.816	8
CIE	0.802	7	0.803	8	0.816	9
CP	0.772	13	0.782	12	0.810	11
DB	0.727	15	0.718	16	0.746	15
DSB	0.813	5	0.818	4	0.845	4
FS	0.808	6	0.810	5	0.844	5
JNR	0.796	10	0.803	9	0.830	7
NS	1.000	1	1.000	1	1.000	1
NSB	0.798	8	0.810	6	0.832	6
OBB	0.788	12	0.785	11	0.805	12
RENFE	0.719	17	0.701	17	0.715	17
SJ	0.851	4	0.809	7	0.815	10
SNCB	0.627	18	0.638	18	0.660	18
SNCF	0.793	11	0.768	13	0.798	14
TCDD	0.401	19	0.392	19	0.399	19
VR	0.908	3	0.866	3	0.889	3

*The small numbers indicate the relative rankings.

Network	**Country**	**Network**	**Country**
BR	Great Britain	NS	Netherlands
CFF	Switzerland	NSB	Norway
CFL	Luxembourg	OBB	Austria
CH	Greece	RENFE	Spain
CIE	Ireland	SJ	Sweden
CP	Portugal	SNCB	Belgium
DB	Germany	SNCF	France
DSB	Denmark	TCDD	Turkey
FS	Italy	VR	Finland
JNR	Japan		

Note, however, the JNR (Japan) in the fixed model and the NS (Netherlands) in the random effects model were always the most efficient in the 200 replications.

In the fixed effects model, the scale effects model, the scale effect mentioned above is confirmed, the 5 most efficient units are the largest one w.r.t. the output PTTR (see Table 6).

As is well known, the FDH approach (providing a minimal measure of inefficiency) yields high levels of efficiency but it is interesting to note that 5 railways (CFF, OBB, SJ, SNCB and TCDD) have in all cases a bad level of efficiency even for this measure.

Finally, it is worth mentioning that in almost all cases where parameters were estimated (α_i and β) the sampling distributions obtained by bootstrap were quite regular (bell-shaped) and very similar to what was expected (classical least squares results).

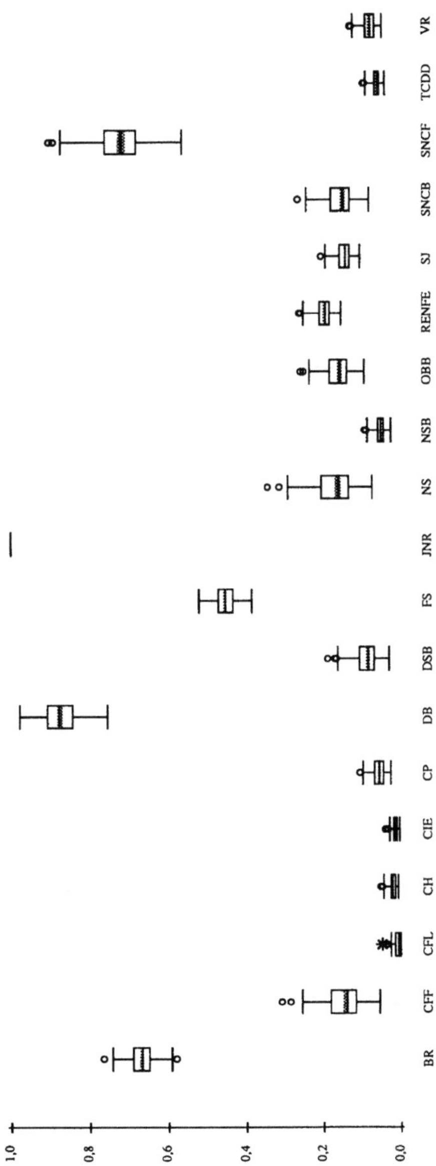

Figure 1. Box plot of efficiencies (fixed effect model).

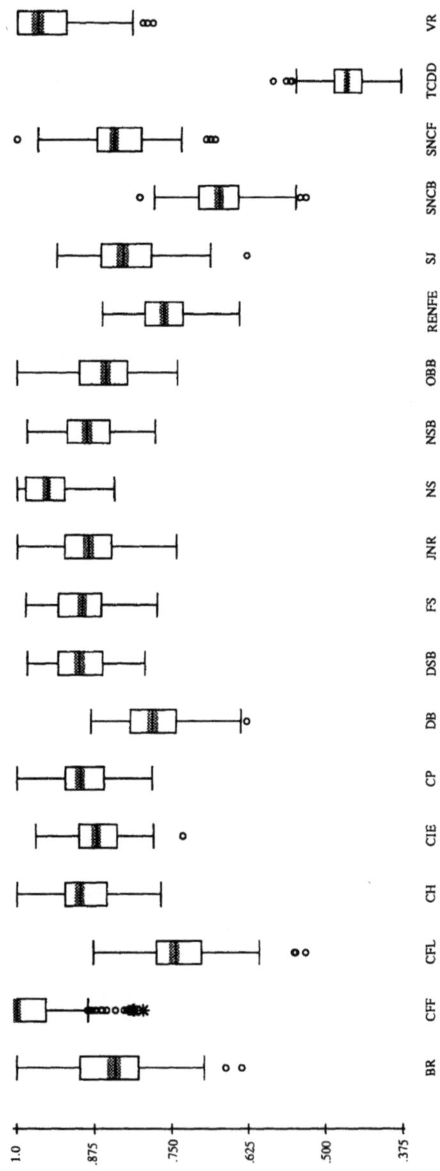

Figure 2. Box plot of efficiencies (random effect model).

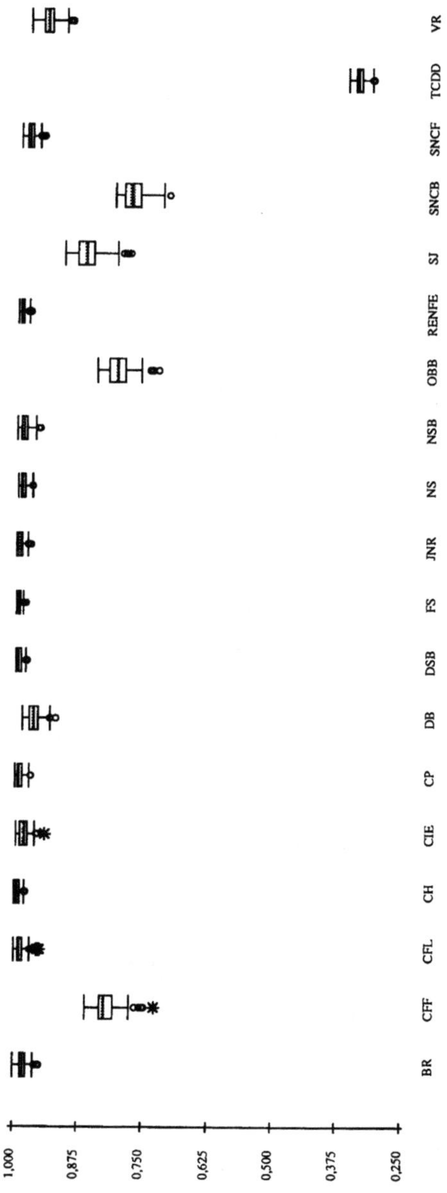

Figure 3. Box plot of efficiencies (FDH non-parametric method).

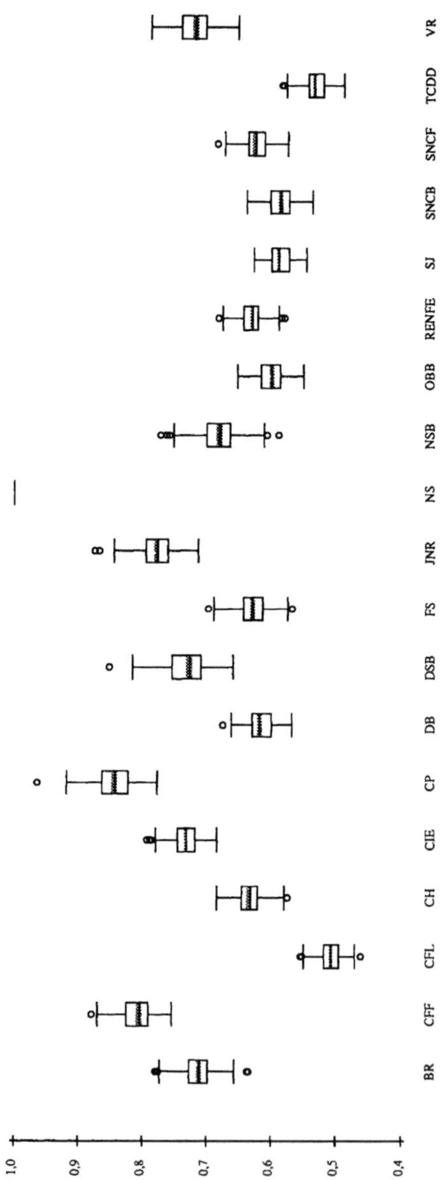

Figure 4. Box plot of efficiencies (semi-parametric approach).

Table 6. Some statistics on the data.

Total Units	PTTR kms	ETEF n	UMUL n	CMBF kwh	LGTL kms	RLE %	RVL n/m
Mean	176509	93310	71905	4574	9976	33,78	1,86
Stand. dev.	208628	118945	94214	5418	9661	26,01	0,48
Min	4028	3634	2942	117	270	0,04	1,21
Max	701517	429338	379648	26187	37571	99,49	2,66
Means by railways:							
BR	444808	204365	208492	11609	17979	19,99	2,54
CFF	94259	38223	35840	1575	2915	99,49	2,42
CFL	4356	3882	3662	145	271	52,59	2,39
CH	17393	12377	10080	686	2506	0,04	1,31
CIE	12134	8580	6317	418	2058	0,05	1,25
CP	32916	24729	7324	1022	3594	11,94	1,31
DB	600005	353947	325051	15707	28744	35,63	2,30
DSB	44939	18728	10224	1330	2085	5,37	2,26
FS	290270	213550	120056	5466	16407	50,82	1,82
JNR	676522	387695	138736	17001	21204	36,13	2,03
NS	107757	26901	15234	1372	2899	59,53	2,38
NSB	34149	16388	9758	542	4242	57,55	1,29
OBB	93708	70928	39834	2415	5865	47,16	1,77
RENFE	135492	70451	43849	3825	13411	33,58	1,49
SJ	100825	35193	49442	1710	11417	61,51	1,58
SNCB	90767	56718	45301	2405	4337	32,09	2,62
SNCF	489967	259974	257375	11088	35486	27,60	1,93
TCDD	39606	60793	19399	7239	8138	1,85	1,23
VR	43796	23469	22216	1346	5984	8,91	1,51

Network	**Country**	**Network**	**Country**
BR	Great Britain	NS	Netherlands
CFF	Switzerland	NSB	Norway
CFL	Luxembourg	OBB	Austria
CH	Greece	RENFE	Spain
CIE	Ireland	SJ	Sweden
CP	Portugal	SNCB	Belgium
DB	Germany	SNCF	France
DSB	Denmark	TCDD	Turkey
FS	Italy	VR	Finland
JNR	Japan		

In particular this is not true for the estimation of β in the semi-parametric model. The following table compares the means and standard deviations of the parameters obtained from OLS on FDH-efficient units (as pointed out above those statistics are incorrect) and the same statistics coming from the bootstrap distribution (expected to be more precise).

Comparison of OLS and Bootstrap statistics in the semi-parametric approach.

	Mean (OLS)	Std. Dev. (OLS)	Mean (BOOT)	Std. Dev. (BOOT)
CONST	1.0933		1.2764	0.2351
ETEF	0.3917	0.0552	0.2485	0.0740
UMUL	-0.5369	0.0355	-0.5690	0.0661
CMBF	0.3242	0.0551	0.3640	0.0567
LGTL	0.9001	0.0530	1.0245	0.0835
RLE	0.0296	0.0157	-0.0034	0.0156
RVL	1.962	0.4622	2.5023	0.7176
RLE^2	0.0401	0.00516	0.0410	0.00634
RVL^2	0.2440	0.3546	-0.3013	0.6117
RLE*RVL	-0.1502	0.0552	-0.0320	0.0659

The means are of the same order of magnitude but as expected, the standard deviations of the bootstrap distribution are slightly larger due to the stochastic nature of the FDH filter. This shows that inference with this method, using erroneously the OLS results may be misleading (overestimation of T-statistics). The bootstrap method proposed here provides thus a tool to improve inference.

As a conclusion, the bootstrap is certainly an appealing tool in the context of frontier estimation and efficiency analysis. It provides a means to analyze the sensitivity of the ranking of the different production units in terms of their inefficiency, with a measure of the statistical significance of the difference between the efficiencies; it can also provide proxy for the sampling distribution of estimators when analytical results are not yet obtained.

Appendix. Estimation of the random effects model

In matrix notation, stacking the T observations of each unit, the model can be written:

$$y = [i_{pT}\, X] \begin{pmatrix} \beta_o \\ \beta \end{pmatrix} + v \tag{A.1}$$

where,

$$v = \begin{pmatrix} v_1 \\ v_2 \\ \vdots \\ v_p \end{pmatrix}$$

with,

$$v_i = \alpha_i i_T + \epsilon_i \qquad i = 1, \ldots, p \tag{A.2}$$

and,

$$\epsilon_i = \begin{pmatrix} \epsilon_{I1} \\ \vdots \\ \epsilon_{iT} \end{pmatrix}$$

We have:

$$E(v) = a\ i_{pT}$$

But the covariance matrix of the random term v is no longer a scalar matrix (it has an intraclass covariance structure) and an OLS procedure is not statistically efficient. Indeed, we have

$$\Sigma_{v_i} = \sigma_\alpha^2\ i_T\ i_T' + \sigma_\epsilon^2 I_T = A = \begin{pmatrix} \sigma_\alpha^2 + \sigma_\epsilon^2 & \sigma_\alpha^2 & \dots & \sigma_\alpha^2 \\ \sigma_\alpha^2 & \sigma_\alpha^2 + \sigma_\epsilon^2 & \dots & \sigma_\alpha^2 \\ \vdots & \vdots & \dots & \vdots \\ \sigma_\alpha^2 & \sigma_\alpha^2 & \dots & \sigma_\alpha^2 + \sigma_\epsilon^2 \end{pmatrix}$$

and,

$$\Sigma_v = I_p \otimes A = \begin{pmatrix} A & O & \dots & O \\ O & A & \dots & O \\ \vdots & \vdots & \dots & \vdots \\ O & O & \dots & A \end{pmatrix} = \sigma_\alpha^2 (I_p \otimes\ i_T\ i_T') + \sigma_\epsilon^2\ I_{Tp}$$

Note that:

$$A^{-1} = \left(\frac{-\sigma_\alpha^2}{\sigma_\epsilon^2(\sigma_\epsilon^2 + T\sigma_\alpha^2)}\right) i_T i_T' + \frac{1}{\sigma_\epsilon^2} I_T$$

A feasible GLS estimator of β_O and β is obtained providing that a consistent estimator of σ_ϵ^2 and of σ_α^2 can be found. These can be obtained from the residuals of OLS on the equation (A.1).

Then, as it is well known in the panel literature, the usual decomposition of the variance of the OLS residuals leads to the following:

$$E\left[\sum_{i,t}(v_{it} - \bar{v}_{i\cdot})^2\right] = p(T - 1)\sigma_\epsilon^2 \tag{A.3a}$$

$$E\left[\sum_{i,t}(\bar{v}_{i\cdot} - \bar{v}_{\cdot\cdot})^2\right] = (p - 1)(\sigma_\epsilon^2 + T\,\sigma_\alpha^2) \tag{A.3b}$$

These expressions yield consistent estimators of σ_ϵ^2 and σ_α^2. It should be noted that the estimator of the latter variance could be negative.

The GLS estimators of (A.1) are thus given by:

$$\begin{pmatrix}\beta_O\\ \beta\end{pmatrix} = \left[[i_n \quad X]'\,\hat{\Sigma}_v^{-1}\,[i_n \quad X]\right]^{-1}[i_n \quad X]'\,\hat{\Sigma}_v^{-1}\,y$$

This calculation can be avoided, since (see Hausman and Taylor [1981]) the GLS estimator of β_O and β may be obtained by simple OLS on the following transformed data:

$$y_{it}^* = y_{it} - c\bar{y}_{i\cdot}$$
$$x_{it}^* = x_{it} - c\bar{x}_{i\cdot}$$

where the quasi-deviation parameter c is given by:

$$c = 1 - \sqrt{\frac{\sigma_\epsilon^2}{\sigma_\epsilon^2 + T\,\sigma_\alpha^2}}$$

This corresponds in fact to premultiplying equation (A.1) by the following matrix:

$$\Sigma_v^{-1/2} = I_{Tp} - c\left(I_p \otimes \frac{1}{T}\,i_T\,i_T'\right)$$

The parameter c is consistently estimated from the expressions (A.3) above. Now, the OLS on the quasi-deviations can be performed:

$$y_{it}^* = \beta_O(1 - c) + \beta' x_{it}^* + v_{it}^* \begin{cases} i = 1, \ldots, p \\ t = 1, \ldots, T \end{cases} \tag{A.4}$$

yielding the GLS estimators of β. The estimator of β_O will be shifted to insure the positiveness of the α_i.

In order to estimate (in)efficiencies, an estimation (prediction) of the α_i is needed. This comes from the residuals v_{it} which have to be recomputed from (A.1) with the more efficient estimates of β obtained by GLS.

In fact, the relation between the v_{it}'s and the v_{it}^*'s is given by:

$$v_{it} = v_{it}^* + \frac{c}{1-c} \bar{v}_{i\cdot}^*$$

Therefore,

$$\bar{v}_{i\cdot} = \bar{v}_{i\cdot}^* \left(\frac{1}{1-c}\right)$$

Since $E(\epsilon_{it}) = 0$ and $\alpha_i = \epsilon_{it} - v_{it}$, a natural estimate of α_i is simply given by:

$$\hat{\alpha}_i = \max_j \bar{v}_{j\cdot} - \bar{v}_{i\cdot}$$

where the maximum is introduced in order to provide positive values of the α_i's. The GLS estimator of β_O obtained above in (A.4) must also be shifted:

$$\tilde{\beta}_O = \hat{\beta}_O + \max_j \bar{v}_{j\cdot}$$

Notes

1. Note that in this article, only technical efficiencies are concerned, i.e., no cost or price elements are considered. Note also that the presentation is in term of *output* efficiencies.
2. The notation $z \approx D(\mu, \sigma^2)$ means that the random variable z is distributed according to the probability law D with mean μ and variance σ^2.
3. Cornwell, Schmidt, and Sickles [1988] propose a model where the effects may be time-varying too. This allows, for instance, to detect technical progress in the technology.
4. That means that different values of β_O, β and α_i may lead to the same conditional mean $E(y_i \mid x_i)$. This is due to the singularity of the matrix of the regressors.
5. Note that direct estimation of β and γ, giving the same results, can be obtained by simple OLS on equation (5).
6. Note that a descriptive analysis of the evolution of the efficiencies over the time could be obtained through $eff_{it} = \exp(v_{it} - \max v_{it})$. Averaging over the firms this would allow to detect eventual technical progress of the observed technology.
7. In order to obtain the variance of the efficiency measures, one has to take into account the exponential transformation from the α to the *eff*. For example, if α is distributed according to a Gamma distribution with mean a and variance σ_α^2, $\exp(-\alpha)$ has a mean and a variance given by:

$$E(\exp(-\alpha)) = \left(\frac{a}{a+\sigma_\alpha^2}\right)^{\frac{a^2}{\sigma_\alpha^2}}$$

$$Var(\exp(-\alpha)) = \left(\frac{a}{a+\sigma_\alpha^2}\right)^{\frac{a^2}{\sigma_\alpha^2}} \left(\frac{a}{a+\sigma_\alpha^2}\right)^{2\frac{a^2}{\sigma_\alpha^2}}$$

8. Note that an OLS procedure could also be performed on the quasi deviations as in (2.6), except that the quasi deviation parameter is here different for each group; it is given by

$$c_i = 1 - \sqrt{\frac{\sigma_\epsilon^2}{\sigma_\epsilon^2 + T_i\sigma_\alpha^2}},$$

but we would have problems for the estimation of the intercept.
9. One could of course retain from the first step more observations than only the efficient ones (e.g., those with efficiency levels greater than 95 percent, . . .). The statistician will have to balance the size of the retained sample with the introduction of inefficient units in the sample used to estimate the "efficient" frontier.
10. This idea came out from discussions with Rolf Färe and Shawna Grosskopf.
11. In order to clarify the presentation of the bootstrap, note the slight change of notation in this section: Greek letters for unobservables, corresponding Latin letters for the estimators and * for the bootstrap versions.
12. Note that, in order to avoid bias, the residual e_i have to be recenterd. Depending on the estimation procedure used, this may be unnecessary.
13. Data on the activity of the main international railway companies can be found in the annual reports of the *Union Internationale des Chemins de Fer* (U.I.C.). The data which are used in this application, were collected from these reports by the *Service d'Economie Publique de l'Université* de Liège (with the financial support of the Ministère Belge de la Politique Scientifique).
14. A lot of other specifications were also tested, but we retain this one since it provides a very good fit and all the coefficients have a good significant sign. Further, no technological progress was detected with our model: previous tests with linear trend or with dummy variables (one for each year) did not produce significant results. In order to save room in this illustration, these results are not reproduced here.
15. One would ask whether the variable UMUL has to appear in the FDH method, and if it appears why with a positive sign as we did. This is indeed questionable but OLS with Cobb Douglas production function produces the following result:

lnPTTR = 1.27 +	0.724 lnETEF +	0.297 lnUMUL +	(−0.094) lnCMBF +	0.109 lnLGTL
stan. deviations:	0.0898	0.0536	0.0675	0.0496

This provides a significant positive sign for UMUL and we used this variable as such in the FDH method.

References

Aigner, D.J. and S.F. Chu. (1968). "On estimating the industry production function." *American Economic Review* 58, pp. 826–839.

Aigner, D.J., C.A.K. Lovell, and P. Schmidt. (1977). "Formulation and estimation of stochastic frontier production function models." *Journal of Econometrics* 6, pp. 21–37.

Boland, I. (1990). "Méthode du Bootstrap dans des Modèles de Frontière." mémoire de maîtrise en sciences économiques, Université Catholique de Louvain, Louvain-la-Neuve, Belgium.

Christensen, L.R., D.W. Jorgensen and L.J. Lau. (1973). "The Translog function and the substitution of equipment, structures and labor in U.S. manufacturing 1929–68." *Journal of Econometrics*, 1, pp. 81–114.

Cornwell, C., P. Schmidt and R.C. Sickles. (1987). "Production Frontiers with Cross-Sectional and Time-series Variation in Efficiency Levels." mimeo.

Deprins, D. and L. Simar. (1989a). "Estimating Technical Inefficiencies with Correction for Environmental Conditions, with an application to railways companies." *Annals of Public and Cooperative Economics* 60(1), pp. 81–102.

Deprins, D. and L. Simar. (1989b). "Estimation de Frontières Déterministes avec Facteurs Exogènes d'Inefficacite." *Annales d'Economie et de Statistique* 14, pp. 117–150.

Deprins, D., L. Simar and H. Tulkens. (1984). "Measuring labor inefficiency in post offices." in M. Marchand, P. Pestieau and H. Tulkens (eds.) *The Performance of Public Enterprises: Concepts and measurements*, North-Holland, Amsterdam.

Efron, B. (1983). *The Jacknife, the Bootstrap and Other Resampling Plans*, SIAM, Philadelphia.

Farrell, M.J. (1957). "The measurement of productive efficiency." *Journal of the Royal Statistical Society A* 120, pp. 253–281.

Freedman, D.A. (1981). "Bootstrapping Regression Models." *The Annals of Statistics* 9(6), pp. 1218–1228.

Gathon, H.J. and S. Perelman. (1990). "Measuring Technical Efficiency in National Railways: A Panel Data Approach." mimeo, Université de Liège, Belgium.

Greene, W.H. (1980). "Maximum Likelihood Estimation of Econometric Frontier." *Journal of Econometrics* 13, pp. 27–56.

Hall, P. W. Härdle and L. Simar. (1991). "Iterated Bootstrap with Application to Frontier Models." CORE Discussion paper 9121, Université Catholique de Louvain, Louvain-la-Neuve, Belgium.

Hausman, J.A. and W.E. Taylor. (1981). "Panel Data and Unobservable Individual Effects." *Econometrica* 49, pp. 1377–1398.

Jondrow, J., C.A.K. Lovell, I.S. Materov and P. Schmidt. (1982). "On the estimation of technical inefficiency in stocahstic frontier production model." *Journal of Econometrics* 19, pp. 233–238.

Mundlak, Y. (1978). "On the Pooling of Time Series and Cross Section Data." *Econometrica* 46, pp. 69–86.

Schmidt, P. and R.E. Sickles. (1984). "Production Frontiers and Panel Data." *Journal of Business and Economic Statistics* 2, 367–374.

Thiry, B. and H. Tulkens. (1988). "Allowing for Technical Inefficiency in Parametric Estimates of Production Functions, with an application to urban transit firms." CORE discussion paper 8841, Université Catholique de Louvain, Louvain-la-Neuve.

U.I.C. (1970–1983). *Statistiques Internationales des Chemins de Fer.* Union Internationale des Chemins de Fer, Paris.

MIX
Papier aus verantwortungsvollen Quellen
Paper from responsible sources
FSC® C105338

If you have any concerns about our products,
you can contact us on
ProductSafety@springernature.com

In case Publisher is established outside the EU,
the EU authorized representative is:
Springer Nature Customer Service Center GmbH
Europaplatz 3, 69115 Heidelberg, Germany

Printed by Libri Plureos GmbH
in Hamburg, Germany